Tetsugaku Companions to Japanese Philosophy

Volume 2

This new Springer series collects and presents studies on many facets of Japanese philosophy. Its aim is threefold: to demonstrate the unique philosophical potential of Japanese philosophy; to provide systematic and critical texts for research as well as for teaching on Japanese philosophy; and to reinforce the academic status of Japanese philosophy as an academic discipline. The series focuses on representative Japanese philosophers and on various themes in Japanese philosophy. It explores pre-modern as well as modern philosophers and themes, and provides a platform for comparisons with Western and non-Western philosophical traditions. The series reflects a growing interest in non-Western philosophical movements as well as the undeniable influence of Japanese philosophy in Asia.

This new series:

- Demonstrates the rich potential of Japanese philosophy.
- Echoes recent developments in the field.
- Enhances the academic status of Japanese philosophy.

SERIES EDITORS
NOE Keiichi Tohoku University, Aoba-ku, Sendai, Japan CHEUNG Ching Yuen Chinese University of Hong Kong, Shatin, Hong Kong LAM Wing Keung Dokkyo University, Soka-shi, Saitama, Japan Email: springertetsugaku@gmail.com

More information about this series at http://www.springer.com/series/13638

W. J. Boot • Takayama Daiki

Editors

Tetsugaku Companion to Ogyū Sorai

 Springer

Editors
W. J. Boot
Leiden Institute of Area Studies (LIAS)
Faculty of Humanities
Leiden University
Leiden, The Netherlands

Takayama Daiki
Graduate School of Arts and Sciences
The University of Tokyo
Meguro-ku, Tokyo, Japan

ISSN 2662-2181   ISSN 2662-219X   (electronic)
Tetsugaku Companions to Japanese Philosophy
ISBN 978-3-030-15474-5   ISBN 978-3-030-15475-2   (eBook)
https://doi.org/10.1007/978-3-030-15475-2

This Springer imprint is published by the registered company Springer Nature Switzerland AG.
The registered company address is: Gewerbestrasse 11, 6330 Cham, Switzerland

Prefatory Notes

Japanese words and names are transcribed according to the Hepburn system, Chinese ones, according to *Pinyin*, and Korean ones, according to the McCune-Reischauer system.

In all essays and notes, we use the following abbreviations:

- *KGS* = Nagasawa Kikuya 長澤規矩也 & Nagasawa Kōzō 孝三, eds. 1979. *Kanbun gakusha sōran* 漢文学者総覧. Tokyo: Kyūko Shoin. (We refer to *KGS* in the case of those persons who have no lemma of their own in *Kōjien*.)
- "Legge's translation" refers to any of the many editions of James Legge's translations of the Chinese Classics. Nowadays, they are most easily consulted through the database <Chinese Text Project>.
- "Mor. + Latin numeral" refers to a volume in Morohashi Tetsuji 諸橋轍次, comp., *Dai Kan-Wa jiten* 大漢和辭典.
- *NKSM* refers to the *Nihon Kotenseki Sōgō Mokuroku* 日本古典籍総合目録, i.e., to the database of Kokuritsu Bungaku Kenkyū Shiryōkan (Kokubunken; NIJL)
- NST = Nihon Shisō Taikei

Contents

Part II   Essays

Contributors

AIHARA Kōsaku 相原耕作 (1970) is senior assistant professor at the School of Political Science of Meiji University (Tokyo). He studied at Tokyo Metropolitan University and received his Ph.D. at this university in 2005. His area of research is the History of Thought of the Edo Period. Within this field, he is especially interested in the interrelation between the discourse on language and political thought, which was the theme of his dissertation and also of the research grant (*Kaken*) he received in 2003–2005.

Olivier ANSART (1953) is senior lecturer in the Department of Japanese Studies in the University of Sydney (Australia). He holds a Ph.D. in Chinese studies from the University of Paris VII. He was director of the Nichi-Futsu Kaikan in Tokyo (1992–1996) and professor at Waseda University (until 2003) before moving to the University of Sydney. He studies the history of political thought in eighteenth-century Japan.

W. J. BOOT (1947) is emeritus professor of Japanese Language and Culture, Leiden University (the Netherlands). He studied Japanese, Chinese, Korean, and East-Asian History at the Universities of Leiden and Kyoto, received his Ph.D. in Leiden in 1983, and was appointed professor of Japanese and Korean Languages and Cultures at this university in 1985. He retired in 2012. His area of specialization is the History of Thought of the Edo Period.

KOJIMA Yasunori 小島康敬 (1949) studied at Gakushūin University (Tokyo) and presently is professor at International Christian University (ICU, Mitaka, Tokyo Metropolis). His areas of specialization are intellectual history, Japanese history, and philosophy. He has published widely in these fields. Recent publications include *"Knowledge" and Scholarship in the East-Asian World* (2014) and *Japan in Edo, Edo in Japan* (2017).

Lan Hung Yueh 藍弘岳 (1974) studied at Danjiang University (Taiwan) and Tokyo University. He received his Ph.D. at the latter university in 2008 with a dissertation on "Ogyū Sorai's theory of literature and Confucianism." Presently, he is associate professor at the Faculty of Social Research and Cultural Studies of National Chiao Tung University (Taiwan). His field of interest is the History of Thought and Culture of East Asia, with a special research interest in Japan. He recently published a book (in Japanese) about *Ogyū Sorai in the Chinese Literary Sphere: Medicine, Military Lore, and Confucianism* (2017).

Sawai Keiichi 澤井啓一 (1950) is emeritus professor of Keisen Women's University. He studied at Waseda University. After absolving his studies at this university, he taught at Keisen University from 1989 until his retirement in 2013. His area of specialization is the History of Thought of Early Modern East Asia. Recent publications are *World History as Seen from the Ryūkyū* (2011) and *Yamazaki Ansai* (2014).

Tajiri Yūichirō 田尻祐一郎 (1954) studied at the Tōhoku University (Sendai) and presently is professor at Tōkai University. His area of specialization is the History of Thought of Early Modern Japan, but he is also interested in the history of Confucianism in China and Korea. He published studies of Yamazaki Ansai (2006) and of Ogyū Sorai (2008) and is one of the editors of the *Pelican History of Japanese Thought* (2012–2015).

Takayama Daiki 高山大毅 (1981) studied at the University of Tokyo and received his Ph.D. at this university in 2013. In April 2019, he was appointed as an Associate Professor at the Graduate School of Arts and Sciences of the University of Tokyo. His research interests are Chinese literature by Japanese authors and the history of thought of the Edo period. Recently, he published his book *Rite and Rhetoric After Sorai: An intellectual History of Tokugawa Japan* (2016) and edited a special issue of the journal *Shisō* (Thought) about Ogyū Sorai (vol. 1112, 2016).

John A. Tucker (1955) is a professor of History at East Carolina University (Greenville, North Carolina, USA). He completed his Ph.D. at Columbia University through the Department of East-Asian Languages and Cultures in 1990. He has translated Itō Jinsai's *Go-Mō jigi* (Brill, 1998) and Ogyū Sorai's *Bendō* and *Benmei* (Hawaii, 2006). He edited a four-volume anthology, *Critical Readings in Japanese Confucianism* (Brill, 2012), and coedited, with Chun-chieh Huang, *Dao Companion to Japanese Confucian Philosophy* (Springer, 2013). He is the author of *The Forty-Seven Ronin: The Vendetta in History* (Cambridge, 2018).

Chapter 1
Introduction

W. J. Boot

This book is intended for interested academics – not only Japan specialists, but also those who are interested in Chinese and Korean thought, or in the comparative history of thought or philosophy. As editors, we decided to insert characters. Otherwise, the Japanese and Chinese catalogues and reference works would remain closed. We also include references to Japanese sources and secondary literature, because the overwhelming majority of the sources and studies of Sorai is only available in Japanese or Kanbun. Sorai's major works – *Bendō, Benmei, Seidan* – have been translated into English, but even then, if one can, it is advisable to look up things in the original. Translations, too, in the end are only a type of commentary, and even of basic terms various translations exist. One needs characters to know what one is talking about. Moreover, the linguistic differences between English and Japanese, and certainly the kind of Chinese and Japanese written in the eighteenth century, are such that maximum circumspection is needed.

Try to compile a list of books and articles about the intellectual history of early modern Japan, and you will discover that the bulk of the articles and books are about Ogyū Sorai (1666–1728).[1] The responsibility for this bias in modern research undoubtedly lies with Maruyama Masao 丸山真男 (1914–1996), or rather, with his book *Nihon seiji shisōshi kenkyū* ("A study of the history of political thought in Japan"; 1952). Thanks to this book, Sorai became the herald of universality and modernity in the history of Japanese thought, and the hero of Edo Confucianism.

---

[1] As I discovered, when I compiled my *Critical Readings in the Intellectual History of Early Modern Japan* (2012).

W. J. Boot (✉)
Leiden Institute of Area Studies (LIAS), Faculty of Humanities, Leiden University,
Leiden, The Netherlands
e-mail: w.j.boot@hum.leidenuniv.nl

© Springer Nature Switzerland AG 2019　　　　　　　　　　　　　　　　1
W. J. Boot, Takayama Daiki (eds.), *Tetsugaku Companion to Ogyū Sorai*,
Tetsugaku Companions to Japanese Philosophy 2,
https://doi.org/10.1007/978-3-030-15475-2_1

There are two aspects to this phenomenon. On the one hand, after the Second World War, Japanese intellectuals needed to free themselves from the spectre of Japan's uniqueness, so much emphasized in war-time propaganda. They longed for more universalistic, internationally valid approaches. In the history departments, Marxism became the standard, with Modernization Theory, after some American prodding, as a good second. In History of Thought, the Hegelian approach that Maruyama offered was more than welcome. This explains how it began.

The other aspect is that, once a discourse exists, it is easier to move inside that discourse, than to start something new. It helped that the large majority of specialists in the Intellectual History of Japan saw themselves as "thinkers," even as "philosophers," and not as philologists or historians. Rather than try and dig up new sources or study "new" thinkers, one was inclined to interpret the known texts and people within a new frame. But whether one chose Hegel, or Meinecke, or Modernization Theory, or Foucault, or Bourdieu, or Derrida as the frame, Sorai remained a pivotal figure in the construction of Early Modern Though in Japan. This explains, why Sorai lasted.

Yet, Sorai is a difficult case, especially for modern scholarship. How should he be classified? As a thinker? As a poet? As a philologist? As a calligrapher?[2] Of course, in his own time, there was no problem. Sorai was a Confucian, a *jusha* 儒者: he read Chinese and taught Chinese – the Chinese Classics everyone aspiring to the title of intellectual needed to know because they were the basis of the East-Asian general education, and the art of writing Chinese poetry, which was a favourite pastime of East-Asian intellectuals. In his advice to the shogun, known as *Seidan* 政談 ("Discourse on government"), Sorai even proposed to replace the lectures 講釈 (*kōshaku*) at the shogun's court by Chinese poetry competitions. His argument was, that writing poetry taught you how to handle the language, and once you knew the language, you would *ipso facto* be able to read the Classics and the histories.[3]

In modern academia, however, his activities spread over three departments: Chinese Studies, Japanese Literature, and Philosophy. In the Sinological departments, it was soon discovered that Sorai's writings and thought were hardly known in China and added little to what had already been done by the Chinese themselves. By avowing his debt to two *literati* of the Ming and by stating that his aim was the restoration of the ancient Chinese way, Sorai himself had done little to dispel this notion. In the 1970s a number of well-known Sinologists (Yoshikawa Kōjirō 吉川幸次郎, Shimada Kenji 島田虔次, Nishida Taichirō 西田太一朗, and others) were involved in an attempt to upgrade Sorai, which resulted, amongst other things, in the multi-volume, thoroughly edited *Ogyū Sorai zenshū* 荻生徂徠全集 ("Collected Works of OS"), published by Misuzu Shobō, but the project remained unfinished.[4]

---

[2] See the article by Bandō Yōsuke 板東洋介, "Ogyū Sorai to geidō shisō," pp. 30–50.

[3] *Seidan*, NST 36, p. 442. Also see the following translations: J.R. McEwan, *The Political Writings of Ogyū Sorai*, p. 140; Wm. Theodore de Bary, Carol Gluck, Arthur E. Tiedemann, eds, *Sources of Japanese Tradition* (second edn, vol. 2, pt. 1), p. 210; Olof G. Lidin, *Ogyū Sorai's Discourse on Government* (Seidan), pp. 319–320.

[4] It did not help, of course, that in the same year (1973) Imanaka Kanji 今中寛司 and Naramoto

The old habits of thought, dating from the Meiji Era, that China is "the East" (Tōyō 東洋) and Japan is not Asia, proved too strong. Sinologists study China.

The same pattern was at work in the Departments of Japanese Literature. There, one studies Japanese literature, defined as literature written in Japanese. There are a few exceptions (e.g. Matsushita Tadashi 松下忠, Hino Tatsuo 日野龍夫, Kai Takashi 揖斐高) but, as a rule, specialists of Japanese Literature are not interested in poetry or prose written in *Kanbun*. The situation is comparable to the study of Neo-Latin literature at European universities.

The departments of Philosophy were attuned to European, especially to German philosophy. An attempt was made, by Inoue Tetsujirō 井上哲次郎 (1856–1944), to create a history of Japanese *philosophy*, but that idea petered out in the early twentieth century. "Japanese philosophy" was replaced by "Japanese thought," and most philosophy departments washed their hands of it. The single Japanese university that invested in "Japanese thought" was Tōhoku University (Sendai). In 1923, a research unit (*kenkyūshitsu*) and chair for the study of the intellectual history of Japan[5] were instituted, to which Muraoka Tsunetsugu 村岡典嗣 (1884–1946) was appointed in 1924. It was, however, not from this department that Sorai's rise to fame began, but from the Faculty of Law of the University of Tokyo, where Maruyama Masao taught the History of Japanese Political Thought. Hence the title of his book, and hence the *cri du cœur* of a friend of mine at Kyoto University: "All Japanese thought is political thought." Of course, it is not, but especially in the context of Confucianism, it is the aspect that is most easily picked out.

It was all the more easily picked out in the case of Sorai, because one of his pretension was that the Way of the Ancient Kings was all about ruling the realm and governing the people, and not about the moral improvement of the individual. It also helped that he had written his *Seidan* in a Japanese that was considerably more approachable than the Chinese of his *Kanbun* texts. It certainly was the first element to be picked up in the west.[6]

In exposing his doctrine, Sorai made use of the universal hermeneutical gambit of "going back to the origin." It is a very effective move, especially when you are dealing with an authoritative textual canon that is supposed to contain all necessary truths. If you want to introduce new ideas of your own in such a context, the stance that "I got rid of crusty layers of ancient commentary and rediscovered the pristine truth," is a strong strategy. It conflicts, however, with the Neo-Confucian concept of *daotong* 道統 ("the genealogy of the Way"). This concept claims that there exists a genealogy of Confucian masters that goes back all the way to Confucius, and through him, to the early kings, and that only those teachers who are in the line of

---

Tatsuya 奈良本辰也 began publishing their own *Ogyū Sorai zenshū* with Kawade Shobō Shinsha. Eventually, five of its six planned volumes were published.

[5] The precise name of the chair was "the first chair for Culture and History" 文化史学第一講座. See < https://www2.sal.tohoku.ac.jp/shisoshi/intro.html >.

[6] The first one to address this topic in the west was J.R. McEwan in his *The Political Writings of Ogyū Sorai*.

succession, are legitimate.[7] It is comparable to the Buddhist genealogies connecting Buddhist masters to the Buddha himself.

If you were an aspiring Confucian scholar, but had no teacher of your own and, hence, did not fit into the genealogy of Confucian masters, you *had* to use this gambit, in which case we find arguments like the following: "Without the benefit of a teacher, I have rediscovered the truth that had lain dormant since the days of Confucius (or Yao and Shun, or Mencius), by assiduously reading the texts that have remained."[8] It is an attempt to turn the liability of not having had an accredited master into a strength.

If this gambit is to work, however, it is necessary to convince your colleagues. Sorai, in the end, did not succeed in doing that. He said too many things that proved unacceptable to his fellow Confucians.[9] Especially his denial of the necessity of moral self-cultivation and of the possibility of "becoming a Sage through study" met with a negative response. It did not help, either, that he derided his colleagues' command of Chinese; after all, teaching Chinese was their livelihood. Evidently, he did not feel the need to adapt and to maintain a measure of consensus and an outward show of professional unity.

There are explanations. When very young, Sorai had studied for some time at the academy of the Hayashi family in Edo, but then he followed his father into exile and studied on his own, with a limited library, in the countryside. When he came back to Edo, he immediately set up his own school and began teaching. As an autodidact, he did not have a teacher or belong to a school to which he had to feel some sort of loyalty or obligation. Moreover, he was a samurai – "born to rule." These factors are at least a partial explanantion of his vehemence and lack of consideration for other people's feelings and social positions.

We can make a short list of particularities of Sorai's thought that influenced his popularity and reception:

1) In methodology, he preached "empathetic reading" – read and re-read, immerse yourself into the texts, until you understand.
2) As a thinker, he denied, as I said already, the importance of moral self-cultivation as one of the two aspects of the Confucian Way and stressed political practice and practical utility.
3) As a Japanese, he lacked a chauvinistic instinct. For him, the teachings of the ancient Sages as contained in the classical Chinese corpus were of universal validity, hence, applicable in Japan, too, as a matter of course. (He did, however, make a distinction between "China" as an ideal – the China of the Sages, the classical China from before the Qin – and present-day China. With the Qin, the feudal system had disappeared, and after the Han, barbarians had overrun large

---

[7] Cf. *Sources of Japanese Tradition* vol. 2, Pt 1, p. 189.

[8] This was, for instance, the way in which Hayashi Razan 林羅山 (1583–1657) presented Fujiwara Seika 藤原惺窩 (1561–1619), who also did not have a teacher of his own. For details and an analysis, see Boot, W.J., *Adoption and Adaptation*, pp. 24–26 (book), or pp. 29–31 (digital edition).

[9] For a succinct overview of Sorai's outrageous ideas, see Tucker, *Sources of Japanese Tradition* vol. 2, pt. 1, pp. 188–195.

parts of China, which had changed the language.[10] Modern China was not the example Japan would need to emulate.)

4) He combined an interest in Confucian thought not only with a liking for Chinese literature, but also with an interest in military lore, in practical politics, and even in Chinese law. He was, after all, a samurai, so to him it must have seemed obvious that he had public responsibilities. This distinguished him from the ordinary Confucian scholars.

A priori, one could say that the particularity mentioned under 1) is both too hard on the pupils ("read on, my lad, until you understand," will not work with most of them) and lacks scholarly rigour ("who judges / how do you prove, that you have understood correctly?"). On the other hand, the discipline this method imposed *did* greatly improve the quality of the Chinese verse produced by Japanese intellectuals.

The particularities mentioned under 2) and 3) are unlikely to have endeared him to his contemporaries and to later generations. Especially the denial of self-cultivation became an issue. It not only went against the procedure outlined in *Daxue* ("The Great Learning"), the denial also had practical implications. If self-cultivation was no longer an option, then the sole task that remained for a Confucian scholar was to participate in the government of the realm. In Japan, however, governing was the prerogative of the warrior class, and even for a warrior much depended on the status of his family. Followers of Sorai who were not warriors, could do little but vent their frustrations by writing poetry and engage in "delinquent and amoral behaviour."[11] At least, that became the general consensus about his intellectual offspring.

Sorai was one of the more controversial Confucian scholars of the Edo Period, but also one of the most important. His case against the orthodox Neo-Confucianism of the Song ("the teachings of the Cheng and Zhu Xi") was backed up by thorough philological scholarship, and his conclusions touched on what was, at the time, the central issue in the intellectual debate, not only in Japan, but also in China. There were many who doubted the truth and relevance of the orthodox teachings. In China, this shows in the teachings of Wang Yangming 王陽明 (1472–1528) *and* in the rise of Evidential Research (*Kaozhengxue* 考証学) from the late Ming onward. In seventeenth-century Japan, we find followers of Wang Yangming, though not many, and we find critical philologists like Yamaga Sokō 山鹿素行 (1622–1685) and Itō Jinsai (1627–1705). Sorai fits into this second group; he was not the first, but he was vociferous, and managed to become, for some time, the centre of the debate.

In essence, the debate was about moral cultivation *versus* verifiable knowledge. Originally, orthodox Neo-Confucianism had spanned both. In line with the Eight

---

[10] See Sorai's second letter to Mizuashi Hakusen 水足博泉 (1707–1732; *KGS* 4269), quoted (with some annotation) in *Ogyū Sorai*, NST 36, p. 512a.

[11] These are words of Ōta Kinjō 大田錦城 (1765–1825; *KGS* 979), quoted from Watanabe Hiroshi, *A History of Japanese political Thought, 1600–1901* (2012), p. 185. The quotation is from Chap. 10 of this book, which has the ominous title "Amorality and Rebellion: The Collapse of the Sorai School."

Wires of *Daxue*, it had declared that the aim of Confucian self-cultivation was to become a morally perfect man, to whom the rule of the empire could be entrusted. Self-cultivation began with "going to the things and extending one's knowledge" 格物致知 (*gewu zhizhi*), which in practice meant reading the Classics, trying to understand them and to incorporate them into one's behaviour and person, and thus, gradually, "to reveal one's inborn human nature" (*honzen no sei*). There are various formulations describing this final goal, but "illuminating one's luminous virtue" and "becoming a Sage yourself through study" mean more or less the same. "Knowledge," in this context, rather resembled the stage one reached in Buddhism after sufficient practice. It was not so much positive knowledge of definite things, but rather "wisdom," understood as inner quiet, and the ability to react immediately and adequately to all external stimuli.

Opposition came from two sides. At one side, we have Wang Yangming, who subscribed to the goal, but not to the method. He pointed out that, if the aim was to "become a Sage", there were more efficient methods than reading all these books and exploring all principles (*li* 理) one by one. On the other side, we find people like Sorai, who denied that it was possible at all to become a Sage.

Sorai also was the one who, most forcefully, redefined the Sages, or rather: the Classics, as sources of knowledge of concrete things – knowledge, he claimed, that was needed in order to govern a country. Of course, reading the Classics ("correctly") involved a lot of philological work, and Sorai was not averse to doing that, but differently from the general run of philologists, he managed not to become preoccupied with the texts themselves. If some of his colleagues had eyes only for the intellectual challenge of reconstructing the texts and their context, and forgot about governing the state, Sorai never forgot that, in terms of *Daxue*, service to the state was the final goal of the extension of knowledge. The downside was that, according to later critics, he had not been as critical in his critical philology as he should have been, and had too often read in the texts what he wanted to read, instead of what was written.

These discussions were confined to the intellectual elite. Officially, Neo-Confucian orthodoxy remained the norm and Zhu Xi's interpretation of the Classics had to be memorized for the Chinese state examinations until 1911. In private, though, many held different, "heterodox" views. In Japan, it was easier to express these than in China, because the Japanese state (the Tokugawa *bakufu*) had little interest in Confucianism. The one exception is the *Kansei igaku no kin* of 1790, when orthodox Neo-Confucianism was prescribed as the basis of warrior education, or at least of the education of those warriors who were vassals of the *bakufu*. In the proclamation of the ban, reference was made to immoral and debauched students. The head of the newly nationalised Confucian academy, the *Shoheizaka gakumonjo* 昌平坂学問所, was ordered to maintain orthodoxy in Edo, and to propagate it as much as possible in the various domains. Sorai was not mentioned in the edict, but it is clear whose students were intended.[12]

---

[12] Actually, as Tucker argues (*Sources of Japanese Tradition* vol. 2, pt. 1, p. 195) the *bakufu* had little to fear from Sorai. For the Kansei Prohibition, see Backus, Robert L., "The Relationship of

Apart from this introductory chapter, the present book consists of eight chapters in which Sorai's more important works are introduced – *kaidai* 解題 in the Japanese manner. These are followed by seven longer, essay-like chapters. Together, the first eight chapters treat a good part of Sorai's major writings – at least, that part that is relevant to the study of his thought and of his exercises in philology.

The first four essays discuss various aspects of Sorai's personality and thought. The first is an intellectual biography of Sorai, written by Sawai Keiichi, which is heavily based on a new reading of Sorai's letters. It is followed by an essay by Kojima Yasunori about Sorai's theory of learning, which attached great importance to learning things by doing, and which privileged practice. They are followed by an essay by Olivier Ansart about Sorai's ideas about the gods and spirits (*kijin* 鬼神) and heaven (*ten* 天), which he analyses under two perspectives – the internal perspective of ordinary humans, and the external one of the Sages – which analysis he also presents as "the key to a coherent reading of Sorai's writings." Next follows an essay by John Tucker, in which he treats Sorai's opinion regarding the famous incident of the forty-seven *rōnin* (*Akō gishi* 赤穂義士), that shook Edo in the last month of Genroku 15 (February 1703). The final three essays are about the reception of Sorai. The first, by W.J. Boot, deals with the reception of Sorai in Japan in the second half of the Edo Period, both among his disciples and among his critics. In order to let the reader form his own opinion of the nature of the debate, a number of examples of the polemics are included. Lan Hung Yueh's essay discusses the spread and reception of Sorai's books in China and Korea, and concludes that, yes, Sorai was known, but, no, his influence was not as great as is sometimes assumed. In the final chapter, the co-editor of this volume, Takayama Daiki, deals with the reception of Sorai in modern Japan, beginning with Maruyama Masao and ending with an analysis of the two modes of contemporary research on Sorai.

All contributions by our Japanese collaborators have been translated into English by W.J. Boot.

Leiden, 10-11-2018

Bibliography

Bandō Yōsuke 板東洋介. 2016. "Ogyū Sorai to geidō shisō" 荻生徂徠と芸道思想. *Shisō* 1112: 30–50.

Boot, W.J. 1983. *The Adoption and Adaptation of Neo-Confucianism in Japan: The Role of Fujiwara Seika and Hayashi Razan*, PhD dissertation, Leiden. (See also the homepage of the Netherlands Association for Japanese Studies <ngjs.nl/specialist>).

Boot, W.J. 2012. *Critical Readings in the Intellectual History of Early Modern Japan*. Leiden: Brill.

Confucianism to The Tokugawa Bakufu as Revealed in The Kansei Educational Reform," *HJAS* 34 (1974), pp. 97–162, and "The Kansei Prohibition of Heterodoxy and Its Effects on Education," *HJAS* 39, 1 (1979), pp. 55–106.

de Bary, Wm. Theodore, Carol Gluck, Arthur E. Tiedemann, eds. 2006. *Sources of Japanese Tradition*. Second edn. New York: Columbia University Press.

Imanaka Kanji 今中寛司, Naramoto Tatsuya 奈良本辰也, eds. 1973–1978. *Ogyū Sorai zenshū* 全集, 5 vols. Tokyo: Kawade Shobō Shinsha.

Lidin, Olof G. 1999. *Ogyū Sorai's Discourse on Government* (Seidan). *An annotated Translation*. Izumi vol. 5. Wiesbaden: Harrassowitz Verlag.

McEwan, J.R. 1962. *The Political Writings of Ogyū Sorai*, London: Cambridge University Press.

Yoshikawa Kōjirō 吉川幸次郎 et al., comp. 1973. *Ogyū Sorai*. Nihon Shisō Taikei vol. 36. Tokyo: Iwanami Shoten.

Part I
Kaidai / Introductions

Chapter 2
Yakubun sentei 訳文筌蹄

Aihara Kōsaku

Yakubun sentei is the result of the linguistic studies to which Ogyū Sorai devoted himself in his younger days. The book is best known because in it Sorai expressed his objections against the traditional way in which Chinese characters and Chinese texts were read in Japan, and proposed a new method of reading.

In the traditional Japanese way of reading characters, a distinction is made between *on'yomi*, in which characters are pronounced according to their Chinese pronunciation, and *kun'yomi*, in which characters are pronounced as the Japanese word that corresponds to the meaning of the Chinese character; in the latter case, it happens that different characters are given the same reading. Sorai tackled the study of characters that share the same *kun'yomi* but have a different meaning or different nuances. And, because he felt that one should translate into an ordinary, simple kind of Japanese, he explained the differences in meaning between these characters in such a way that they were easily understood.

The traditional Japanese way of reading Chinese texts is called *Kanbun kundoku* 漢文訓読 ("interpretative reading of Chinese texts"), in which one reads the characters in the order of the Japanese sentence, going up and down the original Chinese one.[1] Sorai was of the opinion that, because you read the Chinese as if it were Japanese, this method did not allow one to arrive at a full understanding of the original Chinese. Therefore, he insisted that one read the Chinese directly, in the Chinese word order.

---

[1] Major differences between the two languages are that Japanese is a SOV language, while Chinese, like English, is an SVO language, and that, consequently, Japanese has postpositions, while Chinese has prepositions. Hence, the necessity of going up and down the Chinese sentence. (WJB)

Aihara Kōsaku (✉)
School of Political Science and Economics, Meiji University, Tokyo, Japan
e-mail: moto45ai@ybb.ne.jp

© Springer Nature Switzerland AG 2019
W. J. Boot, Takayama Daiki (eds.), *Tetsugaku Companion to Ogyū Sorai*,
Tetsugaku Companions to Japanese Philosophy 2,
https://doi.org/10.1007/978-3-030-15475-2_2

Sorai's *yakubun* ("sentence translation") was conceived as *a method* to understand Chinese texts according to the original Chinese; it was not an end in itself. This was implied in the words *sen-tei* in the title, for both *sen* and *tei* are names of traps, used respectively for catching fishes and rabbits; once they have served their purpose, they can be thrown away.

This was how the youthful Sorai organised his teaching. When in later years his notes were published as *Yakubun sentei*, they met with a favourable response and were published repeatedly, even in the Meiji Period (1868–1912). *Yakubun sentei*, however, is a work that dates from the days before Sorai, through criticizing Zhu Xi 朱熹 (1130–1200), had defined his own, original kind of Confucianism called "Sorai-*gaku*" ("Sorai's teachings"). Hence, his own attitude versus reprinting the book changed, and the reprints follow a rather complicated trajectory.[2]

It is assumed that Sorai began writing *Yakubun sentei* in Genroku 4 (1691), at the age of twenty-six. In Shōtoku 4 or 5 (1714 or 1715), he revised the text and published part of it as *Yakubun sentei shohen* 初編 ("The first set of *YS*"). Initially, the plan was to publish also a "Second set," but Sorai changed his mind and publication was abandoned. In Genbun 3 (1738), however, after Sorai's death, part of *Yakubun sentei* was plagiarized and published under the title of *Kun'yaku jimō* 訓訳示蒙 ("Instructions for translating"). Later on, in Kansei 8 (1796), a *Yakubun sentei kōhen* 後編 ("Second set of *YS*") was published; this edition was considerably enlarged and corrected by its editor.

In each edition, the "general outline" with which the book begins, is followed by a chapter in which the phenomenon of characters with identical readings is explained. The main text, which is a straightforward, helpful character dictionary of such characters, was highly appreciated.

The "general outline" gives a good impression of Sorai's approach to language.[3] Contrary to the order in which the books were published, the *Daigen jissoku* 題言 十則 ("Ten prefatory remarks") of *Yakubun sentei shohen*, written around Shōtoku 1 (1711), constitute Sorai's final words on the subject. The "general outline" in *Kun'yaku jimō* is supposed to be an earlier version, while in the section "Bunri sanmai" 文理三昧 ("Meditation on grammar") of *Yakubun sentei kōhen* we find Sorai's preface of 1691, which is regarded as a study of his earliest period.

When we compare these three introductions, we see a change in Sorai's approach to language between *Kun'yaku jimō* and *Yakubun sentei kōhen* on the one hand, and *Yakubun sentei shohen*, on the other. In the first two, Sorai proposes a method of translation that emphasizes an analytical reading of the Chinese text, based on the meaning of the individual characters 字義 (*jigi*) and the grammar 文理 (*bunri*). Special attention was paid to the so-called auxiliaries 助字 (*joji*), which fulfil an important grammatical function. In *Daigen jissoku*, however, the relative impor-

---

[2] For details, see Togawa Yoshio 戸川芳郎 and Kanda Nobuo 神田信夫, "Introduction. Prefatory notes," *Ogyū Sorai zenshū* vol. 2: *Gengo-hen*; Nagasawa Kikuya 長澤規矩也, "Introduction" 1, *Kango bunten sōsho* vol. 1; Togawa Yoshio, "Introduction", *Kango bunten sōsho* vol. 3; Kurozumi Makoto 黒住真, "*Yakubun sentei* wo megutte."

[3] For details, see Aihara Kōsaku 相原耕作, "Joji to kobunjigaku: Ogyū Sorai seijiron josetsu."

tance of "grammar" has receded. Instead, all kinds of methods of reading directly, without analysis, are presented, and the emphasis falls on imitation and practice.

At the back of this change lies the introduction of *kobunjigaku* 古文辞学 ("the study of ancient words and phrases"). From the beginning, Sorai had emphasized the differences between Japanese and Chinese. *Kobunjigaku*, however, emphasized the changes over time within the Chinese language itself and encouraged the imitation and practice of "the ancient words and phrases" (*kobunji*), i.e., the superior poetry and prose of ancient China. The method of *kobunjigaku*, which consisted in composing your own poems and prose as a patchwork of ancient words and phrases, was diametrically opposed to an analytical understanding of the Chinese language. In *Daigen jissoku* are juxtaposed *yakugaku* 訳学 ("translation studies"), intended as a means to overcome the spatial gap between Japan and China, and *kobunjigaku*, intended as a means to overcome the chronological gap between antiquity and modern times. One wonders, though, whether the two really were in harmony.

Some scholars suggest that the reason why Sorai revised his publishing plans was that the first *Yakubun sentei* smelled too much of Zhu Xi. Others entertain the theory that the part about auxiliaries had become redundant, because in the ancient words and phrases auxiliaries are few. It is also possible, however, that the distance between *yakugaku* and *kobunjigaku* had gradually increased, and that it had become difficult to practise both at the same time.

As if deliberately ignoring Sorai's intentions, *Yakubun sentei* continued to be used. The reason why *Yakubun sentei* did not become obsolete, even though the study of ancient words and phrases and of Sorai's teachings went out of fashion, may well have been that the main text of *Yakubun sentei* had nothing to do either with *kobunjigaku* or with Sorai's teachings.

Bibliography

Aihara Kōsaku 相原耕作. 2004. "Joji to kobunjigaku: Ogyū Sorai seijiron josetsu" 助字と古文辞学: 荻生徂徠政治論序説. *Tōkyō Toritsu Daigaku Hōgakkai zasshi* 44: 2.

Kango bunten sōsho 漢語文典叢書, 7 vols. 1979–1981. Yoshikawa Kōjirō 吉川幸次郎 et al., comp. & ed. Tōkyō: Kyūko Shoin.

Kurozumi Makoto 黒住真. 2003. "*Yakubun sentei* o megutte" 『訳文筌蹄』をめぐって. Kurozumi Makoto. *Kinsei Nihon shakai to Jukyō* 近世日本社会と儒教. Tokyo: Perikansha.

Nagasawa Kikuya 長澤規矩也. 1979. "Introduction" 1. *Kango bunten sōsho* vol. 1. Tokyo: Kyūko Shoin.

Togawa Yoshio 戸川芳郎 and Kanda Nobuo 神田信夫, eds & intr. 1974. *Ogyū Sorai zenshū* vol. 2: *Gengo-hen* 言語編. Tokyo: Misuzu Shobō.

Chapter 3
Sorai's Military Studies

Kojima Yasunori

From his youth until his final days, Ogyū Sorai held an uncommon interest in military lore. Opinions differ on the question whether he had this interest *although* he was a Confucian, or *because* he was a Confucian. The answer depends on which aspect of Confucianism one wants to emphasize. If one regards Confucianism as a teaching that gives priority to the cultivation of the self, then any interest in military lore will automatically diminish. If, on the other hand, one sees Confucianism as "pacifying the empire," i.e., as a teaching that stresses governing the realm and the state, then it will of course be necessary to study military lore as one of the techniques necessary for governing.

Sorai was a Confucian who self-consciously espoused the second standpoint. He taught that the first "duty" of the lord was "to bring peace to the people." Hence, from an awareness that "battles, too, were fought for bringing peace to the people" (*Sonshi kokujikai* 孫子国字解 10), he occupied himself with the annotation of military books. There is room to argue whether this interest of Sorai's in military lore should be regarded as decisive and as the "original form" of Sorai's teachings, which he perfected in his later years, or whether it functioned as a catalyst as he was elaborating his own system of thought, but there is no doubt that military lore occupied a position of major importance within Sorai's teachings.

Underneath, I will introduce, in the order in which they were written, the following works on military lore: *Sosho kokujikai* 素書国字解 ("The *Sushu* explained in Japanese"), *Sonshi kokujikai* 孫子国字解 ("*Sunzi* explained in Japanese"), *Goshi kokujikai* 呉子国字解 ("*Wuzi* explained in Japanese"), *Kenroku* 鈐録 ("Record of military lore"), and *Kenroku gaisho* 鈐録外書 ("Record of military lore – external writings").

Kojima Yasunori (✉)
International Christian University, Mitaka, Tokyo, Japan
e-mail: kojima@icu.ac.jp

© Springer Nature Switzerland AG 2019
W. J. Boot, Takayama Daiki (eds.), *Tetsugaku Companion to Ogyū Sorai*,
Tetsugaku Companions to Japanese Philosophy 2,
https://doi.org/10.1007/978-3-030-15475-2_3

***Sosho kokujikai* (6 fasc.)** Tradition claims that the book *Sushu* (J. *Sosho*) was composed by the recluse Huangshigong 黄石公 ("Lord Yellow Stone") who lived at the end of the Qin Dynasty and is looked up to, together with Taigong Wang 太公望, as the ancestor of military lore; this, however, is a later attribution. *Sosho kokujikai* consists of the original Chinese text of *Sushu*, with reading notes and an annotation added by Sorai. It was revised by his disciple Usami Shinsui 宇佐美灊水 (1710–1776), who had it printed in Meiwa 6 (1769). Its original preface, by Sorai, is dated Hōei 1 (1704).

Shinsui records that Sorai wrote the book at the behest of his lord Yanagisawa Yoshiyasu 柳沢吉保 (1658–1714). He also writes that he (Shinsui) "revised and augmented the book, leaving out the theories of the Song Confucians." There exists an older, manuscript copy of the text in 6 fascicles, which is entitled *Sosho kokujikai* and is kept at the Kadō Bunko 稼堂文庫 in the Municipal Library of Kanazawa. This so-called Yanagisawa Bunko-bon gives the text as it was before Shinsui's revisions. This manuscript copy is ascribed to Yanagisawa Yoshiyasu, but we may assume that in fact it is Sorai's work. In Yoshiyasu's chronicle *Rakushidō nenroku* 楽只堂年録, which was compiled by Sorai, there is an entry under Hōei 3/11/12 (1706) recording the presentation of this text to the later shogun Tokugawa Ienobu 徳川家宣 (1662-1709-1712).

As the words "Peace and peril of the state ultimately depend on getting men or loosing men. This is a famous remark of Lord [Yellow] Stone, and the considerations of the Sages and wise men, too, did not go beyond these [two]" (fasc. 6) indicate, the theme that runs through the book is the recruitment of men of talent, who are fit to fulfil the "public offices" that have as their main function "giving peace to the people." The idea that men of talent are of crucial importance to governing is prominently taken up and discussed by Sorai in his later writings such as *Sorai-sensei tōmonsho* 徂徠先生答問書 ("Master Sorai's responses") and *Seidan* 政談 ("Discourse on government"), but here we see the origin of this idea.

***Sonshi kokujikai* (13 fasc.)** This is the military handbook that is regarded as the work of the military thinker Sun Wu 孫武 of the Chinese Period of the Warring States (403-221 B.C.), to which Sorai added reading notes and commentary. The manuscript was finished in Hōei 4 (1707), and the book was printed in Kan'en 3 (1750). Based on the awareness that "the material force (Ch. *qi*; J. *ki*) of heaven and earth is alive, active, and productive day and night, and never ends, and that man, too, is an active, living being," the book explores how to react to the "inexhaustible changes" occurring in actual warfare. Perhaps it was this realistic awareness that battle situations could not be foreseen and went beyond principle (Ch. *li*; J. *ri*), that gave rise to Sorai's doubts of Zhu Xi's teachings, which try to explain all things by "principle."

The first characteristic of this work I should mention is, that it emphasizes the necessity of instituting "regulations" (regarding the composition of the army, the division of functions and responsibilities, and command signals) as the way to command in a systematic way the many varieties of human nature that one finds in an army. The second characteristic is, that Sorai adopts a strategic way of thinking that he learned from Sunzi, namely, that one conspires not only against one's enemies, but also against one's allies. The third one, related to the preceding point, is that he does not eliminate the belief in oracles or deities as superstition, but regards it as something that will raise the fighting spirit of the men in the harsh and unforeseeable conditions of actual warfare, which shows a deep insight into the human psyche.

The book is deeply imbued with militaristic ideas and insights. Perhaps for this reason, Bitō Jishū 尾藤二洲 (1747–1813) criticized it as follows: "He (= Sorai) is not an orthodox scholar. The only thing he is interested in is utility. The fact that he liked *Sunzi* and has composed a commentary of this book in Japanese shows where his real interest lay."[1]

Goshi kokujikai **(5 fasc.)** *Wuzi* is a military classic that since ancient times has been praised equally with *Sunzi*. Sorai has added reading marks and notes the text, but the book was never completed, and never printed. It is unclear when the text was composed but, judging by the contents, it seems likely that this was done after *Sonshi kokujikai* had been written. Compared to *Sonshi kokujikai* with its dense military thought, in *Goshi kokujikai* we discern an intention to subsume military lore into Confucianism, e.g., where he says: "The way of the military, too, is one aspect of the Confucians' effort of bringing order to the state and peace to the empire" (fasc. 1).

Again, his remark that "the teachings of the lord of men in the end all come down to custom," shows that he has noted the concept of "customs" and is paying attention to "Rites" as the important factor that produces these "customs." This can be seen an intimation of the theory of "Rites and Music," which he will develop in his later years. Although he still leaves intact an intellectual framework that resembles the orthodox Neo-Confucianism of the Song, we can discern a development towards the special form of thought that will be characteristic of Sorai's later years. The fact that book was never finished may also have to do with this.

Kenroku **(12 fasc.)** Sorai's own preface is dated Kyōhō 12 (1727). An attempt to print the book in the fief Yamato Kōriyama in Ansei 2 (1855) met with disaster; it was finally reprinted in Ansei 4 (1857). It was a work of Sorai's very last year, which he wrote out of concern that Japan had "military stratagems" (conspiracies), but did not possess "military laws," i.e., a systematically organized military structure. That is why he poured out all his accumulated knowledge of military lore on such various topics as "systematic taxation," "the military system," "hierarchy," "formations," "district governors," "marching," "camping," "rules of the camp," etc. In many places the book overlaps with arguments made in *Seidan*, in which he proposed to the *bakufu* to send the warriors back to the agricultural villages and attach them to the soil, but in *Seidan* he hardly took up reforms of the military system; that aspect was developed here.

---

[1] See Bitō Jishū, *Seigaku shishō*, NST 37, p. 346.

It goes without saying that Sorai's purpose in writing *Kenroku* was to promote the thesis that "military campaigning is of great importance in ruling the state." At various places in his narrative he harshly criticizes the military studies of "the present-day military specialists of the feudal houses" as nothing but "swimming lessons on *tatami*." This is a typical flourish of Sorai the empiricist. From his youth, Sorai had revered the Seven Military Classics, but in his final years, he came to regard them as "empty speculation." Instead, he showed much interest in the arms and in the battle tactics of the Ming Period. That explains the conspicuous references to, and accounts of the military methods of Yu Dayou 俞大猷 (1503–1579) and Qi Jiguang 戚繼光(1528–1588), whose only interest was practical utility.

***Kenroku gaisho* (6 fasc.)** It is unclear when this text was written. It circulated as a manuscript, but there also exists a version printed in moveable wooden type, without a colophon. The text takes the form of an exchange of letters between Okada Hikozaemon Gihan[2] 岡田彦左衛門宜汎 and Sorai, treating ten instances of "doubts about military methods." The themes include changing times and military studies, the composition of units, battle formations, command and orders, logistics, cavalry, military arts, etc. In the same way as *Kenroku*, the text criticizes as useless in practice the "lectures on *tatami*," in which modern "military specialists" trot out their theories. Instead, it preaches that one must learn from the experiences of skilful men ("stories told by specialists"), who had lots of experience of actual battle. Next, the text emphasizes the necessity to use this empirical knowledge to develop fighting skills in response to the times, and not to become captive of rules and formalities. In fascicle 6, the authors follow the careers of generations of ancestors and relations by marriage who possessed detailed knowledge of military matters. This fascicle is also valuable for the biographical information it contains.

Bibliography

Bitō Jishū 尾藤二洲. 1972. "*Seigaku shishō* 正学指掌". In Rai Tsutomu 頼惟勤, ed. *Sorai gakuha* 徂徠学派, NST 37, 318–354. Tokyo: Iwanami Shoten.

---

[2] Dates unknown. Gihan was a senior retainer (*karō*) of the fief Moriyama.

Chapter 4
Ken'en zuihitsu 蘐園随筆 ("Jottings from the Miscanthus Garden"), Ken'en jippitsu 蘐園十筆 ("Ten Writings from the Miscanthus Garden")

Takayama Daiki

Sorai wrote *Ken'en zuihitsu* in the days when he still was a follower of Zhu Xi. It was printed in Shōtoku 4 (1714). The issues taken up in this book are many and various, but a great many of its pages are devoted to criticism of Itō Jinsai 伊藤仁斎 (1627–1705). Therefore, it drew the attention of such followers of Zhu Xi as Takeda Shun'an 竹田春庵 (1661–1745; *KGS* 2692) and Yabu Shin'an 藪慎庵 (1688–1744; *KGS* 4555), who regarded it as a book that refuted Jinsai's teachings. In his later years, Sorai regretted as immature that he wrote a polemical book that was inspired by feelings of enmity against Jinsai.

In the second fascicle of *Ken'en zuihitsu*, Sorai describes what caused him to become suspicious of Jinsai. Among Sorai's colleagues serving the Yanagisawa was a disciple of Jinsai's, who pointed out to Sorai the similarities between his theories and those of Jinsai. So, Sorai sent a letter to Jinsai in order to establish contact, but Jinsai failed to respond. Moreover, after Jinsai's death his disciples appended Sorai's letter to Jinsai's biography *Kogaku-sensei ketsumei gyōjō* 古学先生碣銘行状 ("Stele inscription and biography of Master Ancient Studies") and printed it, without having obtained his assent. This attitude of Jinsai and of the people surrounding him seems to have registered with Sorai as narrow-mindedness towards scholars of other schools, and as eagerness to propagate their own. When, in *Ken'en zuihitsu*, Sorai time and again criticizes Jinsai as someone who persisted in trying to found his own, original school, this incident is at the back of this criticism.

The argument of Sorai's criticism of Jinsai is as follows: the theories of Confucius and the other Sages and the theories of such later scholars as the Cheng brothers 程 and Zhu Xi all have the same essential content, but there are differences in wording. The discrepancies stem from the fact that, whereas the words of Confucius, a man of the ancient period, were simple and rich in implications, the Cheng brothers and

Takayama Daiki (✉)
Graduate School of Arts and Sciences, The University of Tokyo,
Meguro-ku, Tokyo, Japan

© Springer Nature Switzerland AG 2019
W. J. Boot, Takayama Daiki (eds.), *Tetsugaku Companion to Ogyū Sorai*,
Tetsugaku Companions to Japanese Philosophy 2,
https://doi.org/10.1007/978-3-030-15475-2_4

of Zhu Xi in their discussions gave detailed explanations of the contents of Confucius' words. Jinsai clung to this superficial difference, and on the strength of it maintained that the Cheng brothers and Zhu Xi in their discussions deviated from the Way of the Sages. A person, however, who did not stick to the details of the wording and who had the intellect that allowed him to take an inclusive look at the whole of their thought, would be able to understand the theories of the ancient Sages and those of the Cheng brothers and Zhu Xi as mutually consistent.

Sometimes, Jinsai, too, would show superior insights, but these had all already been expressed by the Cheng brothers and Zhu Xi. Jinsai failed to notice that, because he could not accurately read classical Chinese. His insufficient linguistic abilities were the reason that his criticisms of Zhu Xi's teachings were beside the point.

With arguments like these, Sorai severely criticized Jinsai. We must, however, also pay attention to the fact that he has his own, peculiar understanding of Zhu Xi's teachings. Generally speaking, in Zhu Xi's teachings, man is considered to be invested from birth with a perfect moral nature, called *honzen no sei* 本然之性 ("original nature"). Sorai, on the other hand, thought that man had the *capacity* to grow into a perfect moral nature; that was *his* definition of "original nature." Jinsai, too, thought that man was not endowed with an inborn perfect moral nature; he preached that one should make the buds of the moral nature with which one was equipped by birth grow and develop. In this respect, the ideas of Sorai in his early period and of Jinsai were close.

In connection with the ideas Sorai developed later on, when his own thought had matured, it is interesting to see a discussion emerge about "customs" (*fūzoku*). In *Taiheisaku* 太平策 ("A plan for the great peace"), a text he wrote in his later years, Sorai declared that "customs are practice; the way of scholarship, too, is a matter of practice," and also said that "in the Way of the Sages practice is of first importance, and in the rule of the Sages customs are of first importance." Evidently, Sorai regarded habits and conventions as extremely important. Already in *Ken'en zuihitsu* 4, Sorai explains that the rule of the "Sages" worked through influencing "practice" and "custom."

In the appendix of *Ken'en zuihitsu*, *Bunkai* 文戒 ("Warning against [mistakes in] writing"), Sorai criticizes the mistakes such scholars as Itō Jinsai and Yamazaki Ansai 山崎闇斎 (1618–1682) made in classical Chinese. Just as he did in *Yakubun sentei*, in *Bunkai*, too, Sorai maintains that one should not rely on *kundoku*, which was a complicated way of reading Chinese as Japanese, but that one should understand classical Chinese as Chinese. Sorai's routine of pointing out mistakes in Chinese usage when criticizing other scholars was taken over by a scholar of a later generation, Yamamoto Hokuzan 山本北山 (1752–1812; KGS 4702), who otherwise was critical or Sorai.

A source that gives access to Sorai's thought of the period between *Ken'en zuihitsu* and such works as *Bendō* and *Benmei*, is *Ken'en jippitsu*. It consists basically of Sorai's reading notes. It is supposed to have counted ten fascicles originally, but nowadays only nine survive. *Ken'en jippitsu* also contains entries regarding the interpretation of the *Lunyu* and other classical books. By comparing these with *Rongo-chō* etc., it is possible to follow the changes in Sorai's thought.

Bibliography

Tajiri Yūichirō 田尻祐一郎. 2008. *Ogyū Sorai*. Tokyo: Meitoku Shuppansha.
Wakamizu Suguru 若水俊. 1993. *Sorai to sono monjin no kenkyū* 徂徠とその門人の研究. Tokyo: San'ichi Shobō.

Chapter 5
Gakusoku 学則 ("School Rules"), *Sorai-sensei tōmonsho* 徂徠先生答問書 ("Master Sorai's Responsals")

Takayama Daiki

Gakusoku was published in Kyōhō 12 (1727) as a separate volume under the title *Sorai-sensei gakusoku. Sorai-sensei tōmonsho*, too, was published in the same year. After Ogyū Sorai had constructed his own, original system of learning, which is known as "Sorai's teachings" (*Sorai-gaku*), these two are the only books by his hand that were published before his death. Both are works that tell the main points of Sorai's teachings, but the language in which they do so is greatly different.

Gakusoku is patterned after the style of Li Panlong 李攀龍 (1514–1570). It is written in archaic, obscurantist prose; if one does not have a rich knowledge of ancient Chinese sources, one will be unable to read it. Therefore, various commentaries were compiled, e.g. Usami Shinsui's *Gakusoku-kō* 考 (no date of publication known) and *Sorai-sensei Gakusoku narabi ni furoku hyōchū* 徂徠先生学則并附録標注 ("*GS* with appendices and notes") by Itō Randen 伊東藍田 (1734–1809; *KGS* 329).

On the other hand, *Tōmonsho* is written in *sōrōbun*, which was at the time the language used in letters and official documents. It was easy to understand.[1] *Tōmonsho* takes the form of a collection of letters, in which Sorai gives answers to all kinds of questions. Some of the sections may be based on a real exchange of letters. It is generally assumed that the book that at the time was read most widely as an introduction to Sorai's teachings was not the difficult *Gakusoku*, but the plain and simple *Tōmonsho*.

"Responsals" (an unusual word in English) as the translation of *Tōmonsho* is taken over from the title of Samuel Yamashita's translation of the same. (WJB)

---

[1] Characteristic of *sōrōbun* is that all sentences end with the auxiliary *sōrō* (a verb of politeness, literally meaning "to serve"), hence the name. (WJB)

Takayama Daiki (✉)
Graduate School of Arts and Sciences, The University of Tokyo,
Meguro-ku, Tokyo, Japan

© Springer Nature Switzerland AG 2019
W. J. Boot, Takayama Daiki (eds.), *Tetsugaku Companion to Ogyū Sorai*,
Tetsugaku Companions to Japanese Philosophy 2,
https://doi.org/10.1007/978-3-030-15475-2_5

There is a controversy about the time when *Gakusoku* was composed. According to *Bunkai zakki* 文会雑記 ("Desultory notes from literary meetings"),[2] the first of the "rules" of *Gakusoku* was completed in the year when Dazai Shundai entered Sorai's school (Shōtoku 1: 1711), more than fifteen years before the publication of the book. Again, in a letter he sent to Yabu Shin'an 藪慎庵 (1688–1744; *KGS* 4555) in Kyōhō 4 (1719), Sorai speaks of "the booklet *Gakusoku*, which I wrote a long time ago." Although, on the basis of these records, the possibility exists that Sorai had been revising the text until his very last year, it seems more likely that the completion of *Gakusoku* was early as compared to *Bendō* and *Benmei*. For our understanding of Sorai's thought, it is necessary to keep in mind the possibility that there are discrepancies between *Gakusoku* and the insights of Sorai's final years.

As *Gakusoku* is a short work, I will introduce the contents underneath, section by section. Rules One and Two are arguments about language. Sorai explains that it is important to be aware of the difference between the ancient and the modern languages. When one reads classical Chinese, it should not be read *kundoku*-style, i.e., as if it were a Japanese text with characters in the wrong order and without the particles and auxiliaries, which the reader had to supply himself; classical Chinese should be understood with "the heart" and with "the eyes," through silent reading. The gap between "ancient language" and "modern language," so Sorai argues, can be overcome through careful reading of the ancient sources and through imitation of the expressions you find there. In Rules Three and Four, it is explained that it is impossible to expound "the Way" in the abstract, separately from a concrete system, and that the basis of scholarship is to know the nature of the ancient Chinese system of government and the changes that followed in later ages. In Rules Five and Six, Sorai declares that the government of the "Sages" was tolerant; they were never as morally strict as Confucians of later generations, nor did they severely reproach others with their faults. Rule Seven says that each man has received different the talents and abilities from "Heaven," and that he should develop his strong points and help the ruler to establish his rule.

It is impossible to introduce the complete content of *Tōmonsho*, so I shall make a few observations about its characteristics. As I said already, *Tōmonsho* is written in easily understood *sōrōbun*, using familiar comparisons. Its contents are such that they can be understood by warriors and feudal lords who do not have any specialised knowledge of Confucianism. (In those days, many members of the warrior class did not know anything about Confucianism.) Hiraishi Naoaki argues that Sorai's intention in printing the book was to spread his own view of politics among the feudal lords and warriors.[3] Sorai's earlier writings *Yakubun sentei* and *Ken'en zuihitsu*, too, were printed with the express purpose of expanding the influence of his own faction within the world of scholarship. As Sorai was aware of the strategic use of printing, I think that Hiraishi's view is correct.

---

[2] *Bunkai zakki* is a commonplace book (*zuihitsu*), written by Yuasa Jōzan 湯浅常山 (1708–1781). The date of completion is not known. The book was not printed during the Edo Period, but to judge by the number of surviving manuscripts, it was hugely popular.

[3] See Hiraishi, "*Sorai-sensei tōmonsho kō.*"

Tōmonsho was written on the premise that it would circulate widely. It is, therefore, different from *Seidan* and *Taiheisaku*, which gave top-secret advice to the Tokugawa government. It does not develop the argument that one should change "customs" through establishing a "system of rites and music." Its main emphasis lies on the mental preparation of the ruler and the appointment of talented men, and there are also sections that warn against light-hearted reforms of the system.

In connection with military preparedness, he advocates that the warriors should be returned to the soil (i.e., the policy that warriors who are living in the cities, separated from their fiefs, should return to their fiefs and settle there), but otherwise remarks about the system of government are few. *Tōmonsho* can best be seen as a work that tells how the rulers should behave within the framework of the existing political system.

Another characteristic of *Tōmonsho* is that it tells in detail how one should study. In *Tōmonsho*, Sorai concretely lists titles of books, rejects books that are influenced by the Neo-Confucianism of the Song, and urges his correspondents eagerly to read books from before the Song and to become proficient in composing poetry and prose. The reason is that in Sorai's opinion familiarity with the language of antiquity is a necessary condition for a correct understanding of the "Way." Furthermore, *kaidoku* 会読 (reading a book together in a group, seminar-style) and the reading of Chinese texts that have not been provided with the customary *kundoku* reading marks are recommended as effective methods of study.

The discussions in *Tōmonsho* must have been a suitable guide for readers who were trying to study Sorai's teachings on their own. It is quite likely that Sorai entered sections with contents such as these into *Tōmonsho* with an eye to popularizing his own teachings. *Tōmonsho* ends with references to *Bendō* and *Benmei*, which can be seen as a kind of announcement of forthcoming publications. *Tōmonsho* was strategically composed as an introduction to Sorai's teachings.

Bibliography

Hiraishi Naoaki 平石直昭. 1993. "*Sorai-sensei tōmonsho* kō: keiten chūshaku to seisaku teigen no aida." 『徂徠先生答問書』考—経典注釈と政策提言の間, *Shakaikagaku kenkyū* 45.

Minear, Richard H. 1976. "Ogyū Sorai's Instructions for Students: A Translation and Commentary." *Harvard Journal of Asiatic Studies* 36: 5–81.

Yamashita, Samuel Hideo. 1994. *Master Sorai's Responsals: An Annotated Translation of* Sorai Sensei Tōmonsho. Honolulu: University of Hawai'i Press.

Chapter 6
Bendō and *Benmei*

John A. Tucker

Written as companion texts, the *Bendō* 弁道 ("Distinguishing the Way") and the *Benmei* 弁名 ("Distinguishing Names") present Ogyū Sorai's most mature and comprehensive expression of his philosophical thought. Sorai modestly spoke of the texts in a letter to a student, Uno Shirō 宇野士朗 (1701–1732), calling them "my humble achievements" (*funei no waza* 不侫の業なり).[1] In another letter to a student, Yamagata Shūnan 山県周南 (1687–1752), Sorai related that after a prolonged bout with ill-health, he feared passing like the morning dew. Therefore, he took up his writing brush and completed the two works. Sorai added that while more than a millennium had passed since Confucius' death, the Way had only been clarified in recent times. Yet rather than boast of this, Sorai suggested that his hand in the process had been by heaven's decree. With the two works, he added that even if he passed away soon, his life would not have been wasted.[2]

Sorai thus viewed the *Bendō* and *Benmei* as central to his heaven-ordained mission of clarifying the way, one that linked him closely to Confucius. A post-war scholar of Sorai's thought, Kanaya Osamu 金谷治 (1920–2006), suggests that the *Bendō* and *Benmei* were Sorai's "lifework," into which he had poured his mind and blood.[3] Kanaya added that a deep reading of the *Bendō* and *Benmei* would provide students with a thorough understanding of Sorai's "theoretical system." Kanaya also noted that the "philosophical thought" evident in the two *Ben* facilitates apprecia-

---

[1] Ogyū Sorai, "Reply to Uno Shirō" 復于士茹, *Sorai-shū* 徂徠集 22, p. 24b.

[2] Ogyū Sorai, "Letter to Yamagata Shūnan" 與縣次公, *Sorai-shū shūi* 徂徠集拾遺 (*Sorai's Works, Gleanings*). Cited from Kanaya Osamu 金谷治, "*Bendō* 弁道," *Ogyū Sorai shū* 荻生徂徠集, Nihon no Shisō vol. 12, p. 48.

[3] Kanaya, "*Bendō*," *Ogyū Sorai shū*, p. 48.

J. A. TUCKER (✉)
Department of History, East Carolina University, Greenville, NC, USA
e-mail: tuckerjo@ecu.edu

© Springer Nature Switzerland AG 2019
W. J. BOOT, TAKAYAMA Daiki (eds.), *Tetsugaku Companion to Ogyū Sorai*,
Tetsugaku Companions to Japanese Philosophy 2,
https://doi.org/10.1007/978-3-030-15475-2_6

tion for Sorai's "practical" works, *Seidan* and *Taiheisaku*.[4] Unlike most Confucian works by Tokugawa scholars, Sorai's two *Ben* were published in Qing dynasty China in 1836 (Daoguang 16), by the scholar Qian Yong 銭泳 (1759–1844), giving them an international broadcast that has continued in contemporary times with successive English translations by Olof Lidin (1926–2018), Tetsuo Najita (b. 1936), and John A. Tucker (b. 1955).[5]

The *Bendō* is the briefer, more summary volume, serving as a prolegomenon to the more rigorous and detailed *Benmei*. At a glance, it might appear that the *Bendō* does little more than offer an in-depth explanation of the meaning of "the Way." However, the text itself branches off in a variety of directions, succinctly addressing the meanings of several dozen related philosophical terms. In far greater detail, the *Benmei* opens its conceptual analyses with a discussion of "the Way," and then proceeds, with sustained textual analyses, to discuss, critique, and define the meanings of literally dozens of key notions. In short, the *Bendō* offers a comprehensive overview of Sorai's thinking, one helpful for beginners but equally valuable for the well-versed, while the *Benmei* provides Sorai's most extensive and systematic analyses of philosophical terms. Together, they comprise his philosophical masterworks. They have been republished in more modern Japanese editions than any other texts Sorai authored.

Nishida Taichirō 西田太一郎 has called attention to errors regarding when the two *Ben* were published.[6] As Nishida observes, the *Bendō* includes an end-note stating that it was completed on the fifteenth day of the seventh lunar month of Kyōhō 2 (1717). Many Sorai scholars have taken this date not simply as an indication of when the first draft of the manuscript was completed, but, mistakenly, as the date for the text's completion, and in some cases, for its publication. Moreover, many have assumed that the *Benmei* was completed and published about the same time. However, in a letter to Honda Tadamune 本多忠統 (1691–1757), a Confucian scholar and *daimyō* of Nishidai in Kawachi Province, dated Kyōhō 4 (1719), Sorai noted that the *Bendō* was largely finished, but had been revised a couple of times.[7] Apparently, minor revisions continued until just before Sorai's passing in 1728. According to *Ken'en zatsuwa* 蘐園雑話 ("Random discussions from the Miscanthus Garden"), Sorai first drafted the *Bendō* and *Benmei* from memory. To ensure that errors were corrected prior to publication, Sorai relied on his former student, Yamanoi Konron 山井崑崙 (1681–1728), to check references. However, Konron passed away shortly after Sorai, leaving final preparation of the texts to Hattori Nankaku 服部南郭 (1683–1759), Dazai Shundai 太宰春台 (1680–1747), and other disciples. Commenting on the texts, Shundai stated that "the two *Ben* were our teacher's greatest achievements. Therefore, the two *Ben* must be transmitted. His

[4] Kanaya, "*Benmei* 弁名," *Ogyū Sorai shū*, p. 108.

[5] Olof G. Lidin, trans., *Distinguishing the Way (Bendō)*. Tetsuo Najita, trans., *Tokugawa Political Writings*. John A. Tucker, trans., *Ogyū Sorai's Philosophical Masterworks: The Bendō and Benmei*.

[6] Nishida Taichirō, "Kaidai: *Bendō, Benmei, Gakusoku, Sorai-shū*", *Ogyū Sorai*, NST vol. 36, pp. 619–621.

[7] Ogyū Sorai, "Letter to Lord [Honda] Iran" 與猗蘭侯, no. 17, *Sorai-shū*, vol. 20, p. 9b.

other such writings amounted to nothing more than dirt and husks."[8] Shundai's words convey, in part, his determination to ensure that his late master's philosophical masterworks were not lost to posterity.

Nearly a decade after Sorai's death, in Genbun 2 (1737), the texts were first published. It should be noted that the modern edition of the *Bendō* and *Benmei* found in the Nihon Shisō Taikei is based on the edition of Kansei 1 (1789), a revised and corrected version based on the earlier editions of 1737 and 1740. Most later editions of the *Bendō* and *Benmei* are also based on the 1789 edition.[9] One of Sorai's later disciples, Usami Shinsui 宇佐美瀗水 (1710–1776), authored detailed commentaries entitled *Bendō kōchū* 弁道考注 and *Benmei kōchū* 弁名考注, that informed the modern edition of those texts prepared by Nishida Taichirō in the Nihon Shisō Taikei volume.[10] Also extant is a transcription of a ten-volume commentary on the *Benmei*, apparently unpublished, authored by Saitō Shizan 齋藤芝山 (1743–1808; *KGS* 2072), entitled *Benmei hogi* 辨名補義.

The *Bendō* and *Benmei* well display Sorai's philosophical semantics, conceptual analysis, and linguistic sensitivity as methods of addressing problems related to governing the world and bringing peace and stability to humanity. The *Bendō* and *Benmei* are Confucian texts because the terms they define are deeply rooted in Confucian writings such as the *Analects* 論語 (*Lunyu* / *Rongo*), *Mencius* 孟子 (*Mengzi* / *Mōshi*), and *Xunzi* 荀子 (*Xunzi* / *Junshi*), as well as the Six Classics 六經 (*Liujing* / *Rikukei*) – the *Shujing* / *Shokyō* 書經 ("Classic of History"), the *Shijing* / *Shikyō* 詩經 ("Classic of Poetry"), the *Yijing* / *Ekikyō* 易經 ("Classic of Changes "), the *Liji* / *Raiki* 礼記 ("Records of Rites"), the *Chunqiu* / *Shunjū* 春秋 ("Spring and Autumn Annals"), and the lost *Book of Music*. However, one of Sorai's most striking claims is that Confucius was not a Sage (*shengren* 聖人 *seijin*), but instead only a transmitter of culture. In the *Benmei*, Sorai allows that Confucius might be considered a Sage, but he does this with evident reluctance. Therefore, if Sorai's pronouncements are taken as decisive indications of his lineage as a philosopher, it is problematic to see him, without qualification, as a Confucian scholar. As noted above, Sorai even suggests that he and Confucius share a mission, that of transmitting the way of the early kings. Unequivocally, Sorai praises the early kings (*xian*

---

[8] Dazai Shundai, *Shundai-sensei bunshū* 春台先生文集. Cited from Kanaya, "*Benmei*," *Ogyū Sorai shū*, p. 108. "Dirt and husks" (*tu ju* 土苴 *dosho*) alludes to the ancient Daoist text, *Zhuangzi* 莊子, chapter 28, "Doing Without Royal Power" (*Rang wang* 讓王).

[9] Nishida, "Kaidai," p. 620. Nishida did not compare the 1740 (Genbun 元文 5) edition of the *Bendō* and *Benmei* with either the 1737 or the 1789 edition. A line-by-line comparison of the 1740 edition with the edition of 1789 establishes that the latter was a reprint of the former. The 1740 edition, in turn, was a revised and emended version of the edition of 1737. Thus, the 1740 edition was the forerunner of the edition of 1789, on which the modern editions of the *Bendō* and *Benmei* have been based.

[10] Usami's *Bendō kōchū* was published in Edo in Kansei 12 (1800), in one volume. The manuscript for his two-volume *Benmei kōchū*, however, remains unpublished. The modern edition of the *Bendō* and *Benmei* published in *Ogyū Sorai shū*, edited by Kanaya Osamu, also relies on Usami's texts. The *Bendō sho* 弁道書, published in Kyōhō 20 (1735) by Dazai Shundai, is less an account of Sorai's ideas than an exposition of Shundai's thought.

wang 先王 *sennō*) as Sages because of their innovative work in founding the essentials of culture and civilization, thus providing the grounds for the possibility of social and political peace and prosperity. It is to the early kings' words, as recorded in the Six Classics, that Sorai claims to return. Over and again, he criticizes other thinkers for their reliance on the words of Confucius and, most pointedly, Mencius, insisting that they alone are insufficient and erroneous grounds for formulating philosophical truth. In this respect, Sorai distanced himself considerably from the Confucian mainstream. His philosophical writings, if identified with a rubric, were arguably expressions of his so-called *kobunjigaku* 古文辞学 ("study of ancient words and phrases").

Alternatively, if Sorai's *Bendō* and *Benmei* are interpreted in terms of their philosophical genre and the larger discourse from which they emerged, they appear most convincingly as works extending the philosophical project of Song Confucians, often referred to as Neo-Confucians, especially the Zhu Xi lineage. Ironically, Sorai disagrees with Zhu Xi and his philosophical representatives in Tokugawa Japan, primarily the followers of Yamazaki Ansai's, and their views about Zhu's thought. However, Zhu Xi also disagreed with many of the earlier Song masters that he, on many counts, otherwise followed. Zhu also recognized the value of doubt and questioning as integral to progress in learning. Sorai's many doubts about Zhu Xi's thinking should not, then, set him apart from the larger tradition of Neo-Confucianism that Zhu's philosophy spawned. Similarly, Sorai's call for a return to antiquity can be viewed as a reformulation of Zhu Xi's earlier call for a return to the study of ancient Confucian texts. With Zhu Xi, this return to antiquity was a means of bypassing the pernicious influence of Buddhist thought and practice. Most specifically, Zhu wanted to revive the study of the *Analects* of Confucius and the *Mencius*. To that end, he wrote commentaries on them, explaining their ideas in detail. He also elevated two other texts, the *Great Learning* 大学 (*Daxue* / *Daigaku*) and *Doctrine of the Mean* 中庸 (*Zhongyong* / *Chūyō*), as crucial works for Confucian learning. Yet Zhu also simplified the Confucian curriculum, deemphasizing the relative importance of the Six Classics. Sorai's call for a return to antiquity reemphasized the Six Classics as the first priority of Confucian learning, and deemphasized later works, especially the *Mencius*, as misguided statements, corrupted by the rhetoric of debate with heterodoxies. Even while taking issue with Zhu Xi, Sorai was thus continuing Zhu's project of returning to antiquity. Like Zhu, Sorai wrote commentaries on the *Analects* (*Rongo-chō* 論語徵), the *Great Learning* and *Doctrine of the Mean*. Sorai typically disagreed with Zhu's claims, but his engagement with these texts furthered the practice of textual exposition that Zhu earlier advanced.

Methodologically, the two *Ben* are sustained exercises in philosophical lexicography, or the systematic analysis of the philosophical meanings of terms. Viewed historically, Sorai's two *Ben* furthered this methodology and its genre, also referred to as philosophical lexicography, which had been pioneered by one of Zhu Xi's last disciples, Chen Beixi 陳北溪 (1159–1223) in *Xingli ziyi* / *Seiri jigi* 性理字義

("The Meanings of Philosophical Terms").[11] Rather than authoring commentaries, Beixi advanced a new approach to Confucian philosophical exposition by systematically explaining the meanings of some three dozen terms including "the decree [of heaven]" 命 (*ming / mei*), "human nature" 性 (*xing / sei*), "the mind" 心 (*xin / shin*), "feelings" 情 (*qing / jō*), "abilities" 才 (*cai / sai*), "purpose" 志 (*zhi / kokorozashi*), "thought" 意 (*yi / i*), "humaneness" 仁 (*ren / jin*), "righteousness" 義 (*yi / gi*), "propriety" 礼 (*li / rei*), "wisdom" 智 (*zhi / chi*), "faithfulness" 信 (*xin / shin*), "Confucians teach people to seek humaneness" 孔門教人求仁 (*Kongmen jiao ren qiu ren / Kōmon hito ni jin o motomuru koto o oshiyu*), "Master Cheng's Discussion of Humaneness" 程子論仁 (*Chengzi lun ren / Teishi jin o ronzu*), "loyalty and faithfulness" 忠信 (*zhong xin / chū shin*), "loyalty and empathy" 忠恕 (*zhong shu / chū jo*), "sincerity" 誠 (*cheng / makoto*), "reverence" 敬 (*jing / kei*), "respect and reverence" 恭敬 (*gong jing / kyō kei*), "the way" 道 (*dao / michi*), "principle" 理 (*li / ri*), "virtue" 徳 (*de / toku*), "the great ultimate" 太極 (*taiji / taikyoku*), "the august ultimate" 皇極 (*huangji / kōkyoku*), "centrality and harmony" 中和 (*zhong he / chū wa*), "the mean and ordinary" 中庸 (*zhong yong / chū yō*), "rites and music" 礼楽 (*li yue / rei gaku*), "the standard and the expedient" 経権 (*jing quan / kei ken*), and "ghosts and spirits" 鬼神 (*guishen / kijin*). While the contents vary from edition to edition, the above listing corresponds to the 1553 Korean edition of Beixi's text.[12] That edition first entered Japan in the 1590s, following Toyotomi Hideyoshi's Korean expeditions, and came to have a profound impact on the genre and methodology of a number of works by Tokugawa Confucians.

Hayashi Razan 林羅山 (1583–1657) punctuated the 1553 edition for reading as Sino-Japanese (*Kanbun*) in what became the first major Japanese edition, published in 1632. Razan later wrote a colloquial explication of Beixi's text entitled *Seiri jigi genkai* 性理字義諺解 ("The Meanings of Philosophical Terms Explained in Japanese"), published posthumously in 1659. Razan's Japanese rendition, based on the 1632 edition, was widely read among Tokugawa Confucians. It was followed by a number of methodologically similar works which, while continuing the project of conceptual explication of Confucian terms, typically took issue with the philosophical semantics of Chen Beixi and Hayashi Razan. It should be mentioned that while Beixi's accounts were somewhat loyal to the ideas of Zhu Xi, Zhu never wrote a text of this sort, and in many cases Beixi simply expounded his own interpretations of Zhu's thought, typically paraphrasing Zhu, without citation, rather than quoting him. Subsequent expressions of the genre in Tokugawa Japan, including Razan's own Japanese rendition of Beixi's work, followed this trend toward conceptual

---

[11] Kanaya, "*Benmei*," *Ogyū Sorai shū*, p. 108. Kanaya notes that Sorai's text, and Itō Jinsai's *Go-Mō jigi*, continued the approach to philosophical exposition that Beixi's text had pioneered. He does not discuss Beixi's text in detail. Nor are Hayashi Razan's and Yamaga Sokō's contributions broached.

[12] For an English translation, see Wing-tsit Chan, trans., *Neo-Confucian Terms Explained*. Chan's translation is of the 1840 edition, which differs in content and arrangement from the 1553 Korean edition and most Tokugawa editions.

reinterpretation, albeit in the name of, at least ostensibly, a faithful return to the original meanings of the notions discussed.

Yamaga Sokō's 山鹿素行 (1622–1685) *Seikyō yōroku* 聖教要録 ("Essentials of the Sagely Confucian Teachings") further developed the genre and methodology. Although Sokō opposed Zhu Xi's glosses, in the second and third volumes of his *Seikyō yōroku*[13] he organized his account of Confucian teachings via conceptual analyses of terms similar to those in Beixi's text, often in the same order. In doing so, Sokō continued the project in philosophical lexicography pioneered by Beixi in late-Song China and furthered by Razan in Japan. Not surprisingly, Sokō had studied with Razan as a youth, around the time that the first Japanese edition of Beixi's text was published. Sokō's *Seikyō yōroku*, published three decades later in 1665, offended the philosophical sensibilities of a key powerbroker in the Tokugawa shogunate, Hoshina Masayuki 保科正之 (1611–1673), resulting in his exile from Edo in 1666, for nearly a decade. While many later works of philosophical lexicography appeared in Tokugawa Japan challenging the ideas of Zhu Xi, they were typically published posthumously, presumably in an effort to avoid the fate visited upon Sokō due to publication of his *Seikyō yōroku*.

Itō Jinsai's *Go-Mō jigi* 語孟字義 ("The Meanings of Philosophical Terms in the Analects and Mencius") further advanced the genre of philosophical lexicography by, again, calling for a return to the ancient meanings of terms, this time as found in the *Analects* and *Mencius*. The ties between the *Go-Mō jigi* and Beixi's *Ziyi* are unmistakable: the Japanese reading of two key words in Beixi's title, *Ziyi* 字義, is *jigi*, a key notion in Jinsai's title and a code for his methodology. Throughout the *Go-Mō jigi*, Jinsai mentions Beixi and his *Ziyi*, critiquing them at every turn. Yet the conceptual repertoire explored in the *Go-Mō jigi* echoes that of the *Ziyi*, often following its arrangement and content.[14] Jinsai's diary even relates that when he drafted

---

[13] The *Seikyō yōroku*, volume two, discusses "the mean" 中 (*chū*), "the way" 道 (*michi*), "principle" 理 (*ri*), "virtue" 德 (*toku*), "humaneness" 仁 (*jin*), "propriety" 礼 (*rei*), "sincerity" 誠 (*makoto*), "loyalty and empathy" 忠・恕 (*chū, jo*), "reverence and respectfulness" 敬・恭 (*ke, kyō*), "ghosts and spirits" 鬼・神 (*ki, shin*), "yin and yang" 陰陽 (*inyō*), "the five processes" 五行 (*gogyō*), "heaven and earth" 天地 (*tenchi*). In volume three, he discusses "human nature" 性 (*sei*), "the mind" 心 (*kokoro*), "thought and feelings" 意・情 (*i, jō*), "intentions, generative force, and thinking" 志・気・思慮 (*kokorozashi, ki, shiryo*), "the production of humanity and the world" 人物之生 (*jinbutsu no sei*), "the *Book of Changes'* notion of the great ultimate" 易有太極 (*Eki ni taikyoku ari*), and "the origin of the way" 道元 (*dōgen*).

[14] Jinsai's *Go-Mō jigi* discusses: "the way of heaven" 天道 (*tendō*), "the decree of heaven" 天命 (*tenmei*), "the way" 道 (*michi*), "principle" 理 (*ri*), "virtue" 德 (*toku*), "humaneness, righteousness, propriety, and wisdom" 仁・義・礼・智 (*jin, gi, rei, chi*), "the mind" 心 (*kokoro*), "human nature" 性 (*sei*), "the mind of the four beginnings" 四端之心 (*shitan no kokoro*), "human feelings" 情 (*jō*), "abilities" 才 (*sai*), "intention" 志 (*kokorozashi*), "ideas" 意 (*i*), "moral intuition and moral abilities" 良知・良能 (*ryōchi, ryōnō*), "loyalty and trustworthiness" 忠信 (*chūshin*), "loyalty and empathy" 忠恕 (*chūjo*), "sincerity" 誠 (*makoto*), "reverence" 敬 (*kei*), "harmony and honesty" 和・直 (*wa, choku*), "learning" 学 (*gaku*), "expediency" 権 (*ken*), "Sages and worthies" 聖賢 (*seiken*), "princes and commoners" 君子小人 (*kunshi shōjin*), "true kings and hegemons" 王覇 (*ōha*), "ghosts and spirits" 鬼・神 (*ki, shin*), "the *Book of Poetry*" 詩 (*Shi*), "the *Book of History*" 書 (*Sho*), "the *Book of Changes*" 易 (*Eki*), "the *Spring and Autumn Annals*" 春秋 (*Shunjū*), "On the Four Classics" 総論四経 (*sōron shikei*).

the *Go-Mō jigi*, he was giving lectures on Beixi's *Ziyi* at his school in Kyoto. Despite Jinsai's many disagreements with Beixi and Zhu Xi, the *Go-Mō jigi* furthered the genre, method, and discourse Beixi, as a student of Zhu Xi, pioneered.

Jinsai's text, published posthumously in 1705, had earlier circulated in an unofficial form as a pirated manuscript, and as such brought Jinsai considerable note throughout the realm. As a young scholar, Sorai wrote to Jinsai expressing his admiration for Jinsai's teachings. For whatever reason, Jinsai never responded, prompting Sorai's resentment, which possibly resulted in the harshness of Sorai's later attacks on Jinsai's philosophical lexicography. Generally speaking, Jinsai's thought, issuing from his hometown, Kyoto, conveyed, under the guise of a return to ancient Confucian texts, a philosophical sensibility more in keeping with the interests of the emerging "townspeople" (*chōnin* 町人) and aristocracy of Kyoto, Osaka, and other urban areas than that of the samurai elite ruling the realm from Edo and castle towns throughout the realm. Yamaga Sokō's philosophical lexicography had, it should be emphasized, unabashedly styled itself as a teaching meant for the samurai population as the leading elite. In this respect, Jinsai's thought was revolutionary, in a quiet way, insofar as it suggested the empowerment of people generally, samurai or not. Jinsai's thought later influenced the philosophical outlook of the Kaitokudō 懐徳堂, a merchant academy based in Osaka.

Sorai's philosophical lexicography is often described as an outgrowth of his opposition to Jinsai's *Go-Mō jigi*. At another level, it was also taking issue with the philosophical lexicography of Beixi's *Ziyi*, especially as recast in Japanese terms by Hayashi Razan through the latter's *Seiri jigi genkai*. Not only did Sorai call for a return to the Six Classics, he emphasized, as part of his proclaimed "study of ancient words and phrases" (*kobunjigaku*), the importance of reading ancient Chinese texts as ancient Chinese texts, rather than relying on modern translations that recast notions in ways closer to contemporary usages than those current in antiquity. As noted, Sorai addressed his philosophical lexicography to the ruling elite, not the townspeople of urban Japan. Sorai's long service to Yanagisawa Yoshiyasu, the favourite of the fifth shogun, Tsunayoshi 綱吉 (1646–1709), influenced his decision to address those in power, and not the samurai population as a whole. After all, even among samurai, there were problematic elements. Rather than address them wholesale, Sorai made his philosophical lexicography relevant specifically to the "princes" (*kunshi* 君子) of the realm, i.e., those wielding actual power, not the common lot of would-be leaders. In short, Sorai's lexicography emphasized the authority of the ruling elite, expressing a kind of ideology of shogunal absolutism rather than a more liberal, people-centred philosophy as with Jinsai or even the samurai-centred thought of Sokō.

In the *Benmei*, Sorai discusses "the way" 道 (*michi*), "virtue" 徳 (*toku*), "humaneness" 仁 (*jin*), "wisdom" 智 (*chi*), "Sagehood" 聖 (*sei*), "rites" 礼 (*rei*), "ritual principles" 義 (*gi*), "filial piety and brotherly deference" 孝悌 (*kōtei*), "loyalty and trustworthiness" 忠信 (*chūshin*), "empathy" 恕 (*jo*), "sincerity" 誠 (*makoto*), "respectfulness, reverence, caution" 恭・敬・荘・慎独 (*kyō, kei, sō, shindoku*), "humility deference, obedience, and not boasting" 謙・譲・遜不伐 (*ken, jō, son, fubatsu*), "courage, martial arts, strength, and firmness" 勇・武・剛・毅 (*yū, bu, kō, ki*), "purity, scrupulousness, and having no desires" 清・廉・不欲 (*sei, ren, fuyoku*), "frugality" 節倹 (*sekken*), "impartiality, correctness, and straightforwardness" 公・正・直 (*kō, sei, choku*), "the mean, the ordinary, harmony, and rectitude" 中庸・和衷 (*chūyō, wachū*), "goodness" 善良 (*zenryō*), "originating, flourishing, advantageous, and firm" 元・亨・利・貞 (*gen, kō, ri, tei*), "heaven, fate, Lord-on-high, and ghosts and spirits" 天・命・帝・鬼・神 (*ten, mei, tei, ki, shin*), "human nature, human feelings, and abilities" 性・情・才 (*sei, jō, sai*), "mind, purpose, and ideas" 心・志・意 (*shin, shi, i*), "thoughts, plans, calculations" 思・謀・慮 (*shi, bō, ryo*), "rational principle, generative force, and human desires" 理・気・人欲 (*ri, ki, jin'yoku*), "yin, yang, and the five processes" 陰陽・五行 (*inyō, gogyō*), "the five constants" 五常 (*gojō*), "ultimate standards" 極 (*kyoku*), "learning" 学 (*gaku*), "culture and refinement, substance and function, roots and branches" 文質・体用・本末 (*bunshitsu, taiyō, honmatsu*), "the standard and expediency" 経・権 (*kei, ken*), "things" 物 (*butsu*), "princes and commoners" 君子・小人 (*kunshi, shōjin*), and "true kings and hegemons" 王覇 (*ōha*).

Philosophical lexicons such as Sorai's *Benmei* were not simply primers meant for beginning students. Intrinsic to their systematic and methodological concern with the right meanings of words is a decidedly political nuance, one firmly grounded in the *Analects* 13.3. There, a disciple asks Confucius what he would do first if given charge of ruling a state. Confucius replied that he would make sure that "names" (*ming* 名 *mei*) were used correctly. Realizing that his disciple did not understand the connection between establishing the right meanings and usage of words and governance, Confucius explains that when words are not used in accordance with their right meanings, social and political chaos ensues. For that reason, Confucius emphasized the primary importance of being careful in using language. Viewed in this context, Beixi's *Ziyi*, Razan's *Seiri jigi genkai*, Yamaga Sokō's *Seikyō yōroku*, Itō Jinsai's *Go-Mō jigi*, and Sorai's *Benmei* are works of Confucian political philosophy, defining what each author understood as the semantic grounds for the possibility of good government. Not surprisingly, in the preface to the *Benmei*, Sorai affirms his understanding of this dimension of philosophical lexicography by quoting a portion of the *Analects* 13.3, emphasizing that the prince is cautious in using language.

Most comprehensively, Sorai's philosophical vision asserts that philosophical concepts (literally "names," *mei* 名) were coined by the Sages, whom he identifies as the early kings of ancient China (not Confucius). Sorai claims that there have been no Sages since the early kings, and that their achievement, establishing the foundations of culture and civilization, had been completed, making it a virtual impossibility that there would ever be later Sages. Rather than seek to invent, innovate, or create, the proper task for humanity in Sorai's view is to follow the way of the Sages, which in essence consists of the rites and music. The task of the ruler is to ensure that his people follow this way. By doing so, he guarantees that they will realize most fully their individual natures, and thereby contribute to the peace and prosperity of the realm. Promoting the latter amounts to humaneness (*jin* 仁),

a virtue that, in Sorai's view, belongs to rulers. This virtue is not something that each and every person should seek to realize for themselves.

Unlike Zhu Xi and many earlier Confucians, Sorai did not hold that commoners should set their ethical sights high in terms of individual development. Zhu Xi and others suggested that people might become Sages through rigorous study and learning, but Sorai rejected that notion as foolishly misguided and based on a misunderstanding of the words of the Sages. Rather than broad learning and extensive reading, discussion, and debate as Zhu Xi and many other Confucians advocated, Sorai insisted that people focus exclusively on following the way. Rather than affirming the original goodness of human nature, Sorai claimed that human nature differs from one person to the next and has no ethical homogeneity whatsoever. The goal for people is realization of their unique natures by following the rites and music established by the early kings, not by seeking moral perfection or breadth in learning.

Contrary to Zhu Xi and other Confucians who suggested that heaven is to some degree knowable, and its decrees, comprehensible, Sorai claimed that heaven is beyond human knowledge, and any attempt at comprehending it reflects ignorance on the part of those doing so. Rather than a naturalistic understanding of spiritual phenomena like ghosts and spirits or discussions regarding the nature of their existence, Sorai affirmed plain and simple that they exist, and that their existence should not be questioned. The Sages had spoken of them, as well as of divination as a means of communicating with them, and so their existence and the validity of divination should be taken as articles of faith, without question. By extolling the authority of the early kings as Sages, and then identifying the ruling elite of the day, princes, as their representatives, Sorai fashioned an ideology of shogunal absolutism, vesting comprehensive cognitive authority in the rulers, and leaving the governed with little other than following the way set before them.

Sorai's teachings attracted a significant number of followers, but they were also attacked vigorously by a number of eighteenth-century scholars, especially those associated with the Kaitokudō merchant academy based in Osaka. Goi Ranshū 五井蘭洲 (1697–1762; *KGS* 1909), author of *Hi Butsu* 非物 ("Refuting Sorai"), emerged as the first such critic of Sorai. Ranshū argued that Sorai privileged the ruling elite and neglected, relatively speaking, the people. Ranshū's student, Nakai Chikuzan 中井竹山 (1730–1804), was another critic. Other critics also emerged from the ranks of nativist scholars who found Sorai's elevation of Chinese Sages and ancient Chinese philosophy irreverent. Instead, nativists extolled ancient Japanese deities and ancient Japanese writings as the only ones of abiding value. With the Tokugawa shogunate's 1790 *Kansei igaku no kin* 寛政異学の禁 ("Kansei prohibition of heterodox learning"), Sorai's philosophical teachings, especially those in the *Bendō* and *Benmei*, were banned as heterodoxies, officially forbidden from academies controlled by the shogunate. By the end of the Tokugawa, Sorai's learning was challenged from all sides. During the Meiji (1868–1912) period, Sorai's thinking suffered further because it had extolled the shogunate and shown virtually no respect for the imperial throne. Only with the writings of Maruyama Masao 丸山眞男

(1914–1996) in the 1940s, has Sorai's thought experienced a significant revival, one informing the continuing post-war boom in Sorai studies in Japan and internationally.

Bibliography

Chan, Wing-tsit, trans. 1986. *Neo-Confucian Terms Explained: The Pei-hsi tzu-i by Ch'en Ch'un, 1159–1223*. New York: Columbia University Press.

Kanaya Osamu 金谷治, ed. 1970. *Ogyū Sorai shū* 荻生徂徠集. Nihon no Shisō vol. 12. Tokyo: Chikuma Shobō.

Lidin, Olof G., trans. 1970. *Distinguishing the Way (Bendō)*. Tokyo: Sophia University.

Najita, Tetsuo, trans. 1998. *Tokugawa Political Writings*. Cambridge: Cambridge University Press.

Nishida Taichirō 西田太一郎. 1987. "Kaidai: *Bendō, Benmei, Gakusoku, Sorai-shū*" 解題：弁道・弁名・学則・徂徠集. In Yoshikawa Kōjirō 吉川幸次郎 et al., eds. 1987. *Ogyū Sorai* 荻生徂徠. NST vol. 36. Tokyo: Iwanami Shoten.

Ogyū Sorai 荻生徂徠. 1791. *Sorai-shū* 徂徠集. Ōsaka: Bunkindō.

Tucker, John A., trans. 2006. *Ogyū Sorai's Philosophical Masterworks: The Bendō and Benmei*. Honolulu: University of Hawaii Press.

Yoshikawa Kōjirō 吉川幸次郎 et al. eds. 1987. *Ogyū Sorai* 荻生徂徠. NST vol. 36. Tokyo: Iwanami Shoten.

Chapter 7
Rongo-chō 論語徴 ("Proof of the Analects"), *Daigaku-kai* 大学解 ("Explanation of the Great Learning"), *Chūyō-kai* 中庸解 ("Explanation of the Mean")

Sᴀᴡᴀɪ Keiichi

Ogyū Sorai formulated an original view of the history of the Classics. In his understanding, Confucius was the turning point: with him, the character of the Classics underwent a fundamental change. This view had enough destructive power to deconstruct the orthodox Neo-Confucian view of the Classics, which made use of the genealogical concept of the genealogy of the Way (道統 *dōtō*).

In the period before Confucius, stretching from Yao and Shun to the founding of the Zhou kingdom, i.e., the idealized past called by Sorai the "world of the early kings," the only texts that were written down were the *Shijing* ("Classic of Poetry") and the *Shujing* ("Classic of History"). The rest was performed, in the way of ceremonies and rites, as systematised routines. The aggregate of these routinized practices was defined by Sorai as the "Way of the early kings," which only the Sages, i.e., the kings-and-creators, had been able to conceptualize in its entirety. When we come to the times of Confucius, however, "the world of the early kings" was degenerating. Confucius, feeling the crisis, travelled all over China together with his disciples, searching for the traces of the "Way of the early kings" just as it was beginning to fall apart. The traces he found he turned into words, and thus he compiled the "Six Classics."

In Sorai's opinion, Confucius also re-edited the *Shijing* and the *Shujing*, though they had already been written down. In other words, the Confucian Classics, which are nowadays transmitted as the *Five Classics*, the *Yuejing* 楽経 ("Classic of Music") having been lost early on, were "created" by Confucius as a necessary measure, taken to ensure the transmission of the "Way of the early kings" to later generations. The Classics all internalized this stress. Hence, the main premise of Sorai's view of

---

Sᴀᴡᴀɪ Keiichi (✉)
Keisen University, Tama, Tokyo, Japan
e-mail: ksawai@keisen.ac.jp

© Springer Nature Switzerland AG 2019
W. J. Bᴏᴏᴛ, Tᴀᴋᴀʏᴀᴍᴀ Daiki (eds.), *Tetsugaku Companion to Ogyū Sorai*,
Tetsugaku Companions to Japanese Philosophy 2,
https://doi.org/10.1007/978-3-030-15475-2_7

the Classics was that as one deciphered the phrases of the texts, one should take this situation into account as an extra-textual code.

Sorai's historicising view of the Classics was supported by a kind of "history of civilisation" – a "narrative" of the growth and ruin of the "Way of the early kings" over a period of several thousands of years. It is important to note that into this narrative Sorai inserted a "linguistic theory," in which language was understood as the correspondence between "things" (物 *mono*) and "words" (名 *na*). He maintained that Confucius had been able to turn the ancient routinized practices into words, precisely because the "ancient words and phrases" still existed and they still preserved the correspondence of "things" and "names." With the passing of time, however, the two had become separated; nowadays, the only language in circulation was a barren, conceptual language that had lost its correspondence with "things."

The ground of Sorai's criticism of both Zhu Xi's interpretation of the texts and of the interpretation by Itō Jinsai, who was himself a critic of Zhu Xi, was that they were based on the language of the present day and that, therefore, they could not decipher correctly the "ancient words and phrases" of the texts. *In concreto*, when he himself interpreted these texts, Sorai deciphered the wording and the context with help of his extra-textual code. His aim was to explore ways that would allow him to get at the "ancient words and phrases," and while he was doing so, he corrected the mistakes Zhu Xi and Jinsai had made because they relied on "modern speech."

I have first given this outline of Sorai's view of the Classics, because it is directly related to our understanding of the commentaries he wrote, namely *Rongo-chō*, *Daigaku-kai*, and *Chūyō-kai*. As I stated earlier, Sorai thought that Confucius and his disciples had undertaken the work of turning into words the "routines of the early kings." The *Analects* and the *Liji* he characterizes as records compiled by Confucius' disciples in connection with this work. Unlike Zhu Xi and Jinsai, he did not recognize the *Analects* as the text in which the essence of Confucianism was revealed; in Sorai's view, the *Analects* should be seen as a fragmentary record of matters that lay outside the text. Although, of course, it was possible with help of the *Analects* to decipher indirectly what Confucius' school had regarded as important, that was neither systematically arranged, nor directly expressed.

Sorai conjectured that the existing *Analects* was based on materials that the disciples had each recorded separately, and that next, on the basis of these materials, Qin Zhang 琴張 (Qin Lao 琴牢) compiled the first half (*jōron* 上論) and Yuan Si 原思 (Yuan Xian 原憲) the second half (*karon* 下論) of the *Analects*. In other words, the text of the *Analects* as such was the work of the disciples. Hence, Sorai's explanation of the *Analects* is based on the premise that, both in regard to the Master's actions and to his pronouncements, there existed discrepancies between Confucius' intentions and the way in which these were understood by his disciples.

In *Rongo-chō*, therefore, while pointing out the mistakes Zhu Xi and Jinsai made because they did not understand the ancient words and phrases, he also introduced a variety of interpretations that were based on his own judgement of the extra-textual situation and the internal coherence of the text. Sorai claimed that he was only including *chō* 徵, that is to say, things for which reliable proof existed (hence, the title of his commentary), but it is difficult to discover any kind of system in what he writes. Rather than to think of *Rongo-chō* in the traditional way, as "scholarly" philology, one had better see it as a text that allows us to enjoy the richness of Sorai's thought and ideas.

Daxue ("The great learning"[1]) and *Zhongyong* ("The mean") originally were part of the *Liji*, so Sorai understood them as records that each were made for their own, separate purposes. *Daxue* he regarded as a record of discussions about the *yōrō no rei* 養老の礼 ("Rites for Nurturing the Elderly") that were held in the educational establishments in the "world of the early kings." He followed the standard theory that the text had been transmitted in the school of Zengzi 曾子, but he demonstrated his originality by interpreting all phrases that begin with the words *suo wei* 所謂 ("so-called") as questions, and the phrases that follow, as answers. Again, such words as *mingde* 明德 ("illustrious virtue"), *qinmin* 親民 ("loving the people"), and *gewu* 格物 ("the investigation of things"), which in the orthodox Neo-Confucianism of Song and Ming were regarded as important terms, Sorai interpreted, not as terms that represented specific concepts, but as mere words that fulfilled a metaphorical function – an interpretation that suited a proponent of the school of ancient words and phrases.

Sorai also follows the traditional understanding of *Zhongyong* as a work of Zisi 子思, but in his interpretation of Zisi's problematics he deploys an argument that is extremely idiosyncratic. According to Sorai, in Zisi's times there arose a heretical sect, "the followers of Mr Lao," who had adopted a line of reasoning in which terms relating to "natural spontaneity" (*ziranxing* 自然性) such as "heaven" 天 and "nature" 性 were used. They came to criticize Confucius' teachings as "fake," i.e., as based on human artifice. Zisi had countered by saying that Confucius' teachings, too, were based on "natural spontaneity," but this meant that heretical claims were now included inside Confucianism. This in turn triggered the changes that occurred in Confucianism from Mencius until Zhu Xi and Jinsai.

With this historical setting in mind, Sorai proceeded to annotate *Zhongyong*. There, too, he experimented with an interpretation that was in line with the ancient words and phrases, in which words like "the mean" (*zhongyong*) and "sincerity" 誠 (*zheng*) were regarded as metaphorical expressions. Note, that underneath this argument of Sorai lies an interpretation that was inspired by an argument Wang Shizhen 王世貞 (1526–1590) made in his *Du shu hou* 讀書後 ("After reading books"), namely, that by differences in the style one could tell the period in which a text was composed, and whether it was true or false.[2] Of course, during the Ming, but also in the case of Sorai, who had been deeply influenced by Ming literati, literature and thought were not two separate domains.

---

[1] "Great Learning" is the standard translation of *Daxue*. As Legge explains in the first footnote to his translation, it is a literal translation of the two characters, which he chose in order to sidestep Chinese discussions about the interpretation of the title. Sorai was one of those who subscribed to the interpretation of "school where the scions of the royal and aristocratic families studied after finishing primary school" 小学. Hence, in Sorai's case, "National Academy" would be a suitable translation.

[2] See *Ken'en nihitsu* 蘐園二筆 ("Second fascicle of *Ken'en jippitsu*"), items 56, 57, 125 (*Ogyū Sorai zenshū* vol. 17, p. 344, 354). See also Sawai Keiichi, "Ogyū Sorai no *Daigaku* kaishaku," pp. 151–166.

Rongo-chō, Daigaku-kai, and *Chūyō-kai* were more or less completed around Kyōhō 3 (1718), immediately after *Bendō* and *Benmei* had been written, but it is told that also afterwards, until right before his death, Sorai was making corrections. *Rongo-chō* was first printed in Genbun 2 (1737) and reprinted many times thereafter. *Daigaku-kai* and *Chūyō-kai* were both printed in Hōreki 3 (1753). Although *Daigaku-kai* and *Chūyō-kai* have their own, original division in chapters, they follow the style of traditional annotations in the sense that explanations are given of the words and the meaning of the individual sections. *Rongo-chō*, on the other hand, only rarely discusses the meaning of individual sections as a whole. It mostly picks on parts of phrases within a section, and the discussion develops around criticism of Zhu Xi and Jinsai, which makes it a difficult text to read.

Presumably for this reason, one of Sorai's disciples, Matsudaira Yorihiro 松平頼寛 (1703–1763), *daimyō* of Moriyama (Mutsu), compiled the *Rongo-chō shūran* 集覧 ("Collected Views of Proof of the Analects"), in which he collected all annotations from the pre-Song period, and those by Zhu Xi and Itō Jinsai, put these in front of each section of *Rongo-chō*, and also gave the *loci* for a number of the words and phrases Sorai used. This book was printed in Hōreki 10 (1760).

Rongo kokun 古訓 ("Old commentaries of the *Analects*"; printed in Genbun 4, = 1739) by Dazai Shundai, too, was written with the difficulties of *Rongo-chō* in mind. Shundai added the text of *Lunyu* and excerpts of the ancient commentaries and of those by Zhu Xi, and at the same time also inserted his own theories. In this way, Sorai's disciples published annotations of his works and continued his arguments. At the same time, however, many critical works, too, were published by scholars of the Kaitokudō 懐徳堂 and others. All this greatly contributed to the study of the Classics in the later part of the Tokugawa Period. *Rongo-chō*'s influence on the *Kaozhengxue* ("Evidential Research") of the Qing and on Confucianism in Korea has also been pointed out. The appearance of *Rongo-chō* thus was of great importance within the development of Confucian hermeneutics in early modern East-Asia.

Bibliography

Ogyū Sorai 荻生徂徠. 1976. *Ken'en nihitsu* 蘐園二筆. *Ogyū Sorai zenshū*, vol. 17. Tokyo: Misuzu Shobō.

Sawai Keiichi 澤井啓一. 1982. "Ogyū Sorai no *Daigaku* kaishaku" 荻生徂徠の『大学』解釈, *Firosofia* フィロソフィア 70: 151–166.

Chapter 8
Seidan 政談 ("Discourse on Government") and *Taiheisaku* 太平策 ("A Plan for the Great Peace")

Tᴀᴊɪʀɪ Yūichirō

Seidan (4 fasc.) contains Ogyū Sorai's ideas about institutional reform; it was written in answer to a request for advice by the reigning Shogun Tokugawa Yoshimune 徳川吉宗 (1684–1716–1745–1751). It seems to have been presented to the shogun in Kyōhō 11 (1726). On the last page, Sorai had written that he wanted the book to be burnt after reading, but gradually its contents spread, and in the final years of the *bakufu* it was printed.

Seidan begins its *exposé* with the growth of the number of robbers and the worsening security of Edo. Then the argument continues with such questions as "Why does the number of robbers increase?", and "Why do measures to contain them show no results?" Sorai points out that the root of the problem is that Edo is flooded by people who come as they like; that the growth of Edo as a city has been a chaotic process; and that, on the other hand, farming villages in the countryside are suffering from a population drain. At the same time, both in the cities and in the villages, great changes are occurring in the people's mentality. The close interpersonal relations of the communities, that lasted for many generations, are being destroyed, and people have come to prefer short-term, bland ways of associating with each other through the medium of money.

Confronted with these realities, Sorai advocated that the *bakufu* should return to the basics of governing, which meant, concretely, that family registers should be properly kept; that in cases when someone had left his place of residence, passports should be supervised strictly and no one should be allowed to tarry in another province for longer than three years; that the samurai should live on their fiefs; that the weakened military ethos should be restored; and that the samurai should carry the responsibility for the maintenance of order within their fiefs.

Tᴀᴊɪʀɪ Yūichirō (✉)
Department of Civilization, Tōkai University, Tokyo, Japan
e-mail: ytajiri@tokai-u.jp

© Springer Nature Switzerland AG 2019
W. J. Bᴏᴏᴛ, Tᴀᴋᴀʏᴀᴍᴀ Daiki (eds.), *Tetsugaku Companion to Ogyū Sorai*,
Tetsugaku Companions to Japanese Philosophy 2,
https://doi.org/10.1007/978-3-030-15475-2_8

Moreover, Sorai argued that it was desirable to make everyone stick to the soil, and that from above a system of rites and music should be established. The rites and music that Sorai preached differed from the contemporary system, which in his view consisted of nothing but conventions that had emerged from a haphazard development of manners and customs. A system of rites and music should be determined by the authority of cultured politicians, who had a deep insight into the trends of human feelings and into the changes in customs, and who were well aware of the systems of ancient times. This system should cover everything, from the ceremonies of state all the way down to the daily life the people – how they clothed themselves, ate, and dwelled. It had to express in an aesthetically pleasing way the class structure of a society at the apex of which presided the shogun.

In Sorai's diagnosis, it would have been preferable if rites and music had been determined by Tokugawa Ieyasu 家康 (1542–1616) himself, at the time of the founding of the *bakufu*. In the absence of such a system, the *bakufu* had coped up till now by trying to awe the people with its military might. The people, however, had noticed the incompetence and lack of policy of the *bakufu*, and the rapid development of the commercial economy since the Genroku Era (1688–1704) had strengthened a spirit of luxury. The people's desires had been aroused, and this in turn had led to the poverty of all classes. Sorai mentioned the possibility that through an increase of the rice price riots might occur in Edo and in other cities, and alluded to the danger that at a time of political crisis a movement might develop that would see the imperial court as the true ruler of the country. The present reign might very well be the last chance to undertake a bold reform of the system.

Apart from reforming the governmental system, Sorai also maintained that it was an urgent task of the government to educate and employ men of talent. Contrary to the common-sense argument, that deplored the scarcity of talent, Sorai argued that, if one opened one's eyes to society as a whole, it would certainly be possible to discover men of talent. Of course, one should not look for men of talent who would be satisfactory in all respects. One should appreciate the other's strong points and see how he did when you left it to him to act on his own. Sorai strongly felt that such offices as that of the land stewards (*daikan* 代官), who were in contact with the ordinary people, were of great importance. Men of talent should be posted to places where they were far removed from bureaucratic risk avoidance; could closely associate with the populace; and could help the ordinary people to recover their original, collective nature.

Taiheisaku (1 fasc.), too, was written in response to a request for advice from Yoshimune and was probably presented to him before *Seidan*. In *Taiheisaku*, Sorai first makes a sharp distinction between the teachings of Zhu Xi, in which primary importance is given to the investigation, experience, and comprehension of the "real" human heart, and the "Way of the Sages," which is a means to bring order to the empire and ensure a peaceful life for the people. What one must study as a ruler is, of course, the latter. According to Sorai, the nature of the "Way of the Sages," i.e., the rule by rites and music of ancient China, is universally applicable, and any institutional reform of the Tokugawa state, too, should take it as its guiding principle. Sorai flatly rejects the argument that "the Way of the Sages" is restricted by the national conditions in China, and that Japanese politics must be based on the Way of the Gods (*shintō* 神道) and the Way of the Warrior (*bushidō* 武士道). Sorai *did* acknowledge, however, that the style of governing seen in ancient Japan, with its unity of religion and politics, in some respects coincided with the ancient form of "the Way of the Sages."

Sorai compares governing of the empire with the work of a physician. A physician should not be led astray by random symptoms of the patient; he should determine where the root of the illness is located. To a patient who has basic strength he can give a bold treatment that reaches the root of the illness, but for another patient a treatment commensurate with his bodily strength is indicated. In some cases, one will also be satisfied with measures that temporize the progress of the illness. In this way, Sorai argues that one should be careful not to rush through the reform of the Tokugawa state; that especially the one at the top should understand that the aim of "the Way of the Sages" is to ensure a peaceful life of the ordinary people; that he should make it his business to employ men of talent; and that he should achieve political results that are ever so much closer to "the Way of the Sages."

Chapter 9
Ogyū Sorai's *Collected Works* (*Sorai-shū*)

Sawai Keiichi

Ogyū Sorai's *Collected Works* is a collection of Sorai's poetry and prose in Chinese (Kanbun), compiled and published after his death by his disciples Hattori Nankaku and Dazai Shundai. It counts seven fascicles of poetry, twelve fascicles of prose, and eleven fascicles of letters – thirty fascicles in all. It contains works that Sorai wrote between Hōei 1 (1704), when he was thirty-nine years of age, and Kyōhō 12 (1727), when he had turned sixty-two. He died in the following year.

The best-known printed edition is the so-called Tanimura printing 谷村版 (Tanimura-*ban*) of the Genbun Era. It was printed in three stages: first, the poems in seven fascicles (three volumes) in Kyōhō 20 (1735); next, the collected prose in twelve fascicles (six volumes) in Genbun 2 (1737); and finally, the letters in eleven fascicles (eight volumes) in Genbun 5 (1740). Thereafter, all kinds of different reprints were published by other bookshops, but until Meiji 2 (1869) all kept the same colophon of Genbun 5. Because the poetry, prose, and letters were sold separately, it is difficult to determine which copies are of the first edition. There is a good chance that the copies that are at present kept in libraries all over Japan are combinations of volumes that stem from different periods.

The compositions in Sorai's *Collected Works* go from the period when he served Yanagisawa Yasuaki 保明 (who later changed his name to Yoshiyasu), studied "spoken Chinese" (*Tō-wa* 唐話), and advocated a new methodology which he called "translation studies" (*yakugaku*) or "Learning from Nagasaki" (*Kiyō no gaku* 崎陽 之学), up to the time when he discovered the ancient words and phrases as studied in Ming China by Li Panlong and Wang Shizhen, established his own, original theory of ancient words and phrases (*kobunjigaku*), and students gathered to study at his school, not only from Edo, but from all over Japan. Thus, through the medium of the *Collected Works*, it is possible to know Sorai's activities during the last one-third of his life.

Sawai Keiichi (✉)
Keisen University, Tama, Tokyo, Japan
e-mail: ksawai@keisen.ac.jp

© Springer Nature Switzerland AG 2019
W. J. Boot, Takayama Daiki (eds.), *Tetsugaku Companion to Ogyū Sorai*,
Tetsugaku Companions to Japanese Philosophy 2,
https://doi.org/10.1007/978-3-030-15475-2_9

In order to get an all-round picture of Sorai, it is important to read not only his well-known writings about the Classics (e.g. *Rongo-chō*), or about present-day politics (e.g. *Seidan*), but also his works about literature such as his *Zekku-kai* 絶句解 ("Explanation of four-line poems") and *Shika-shun* 四家雋 ("The best of the four poets"). More than anything else, however, it is necessary to scrutinize his prose compositions and letters. If one should also want to explore Sorai's psyche, one must also analyse the poems that are collected in the Poetry Section of his *Collected Works*. This applies even if one regards these writings as mere imitations of thoughts and sentiments that had already been formulated previously, by others, according to the method of "ancient words and phrases."

The order in which the individual pieces are presented in the *Sorai-shū* follows the traditional classification of Collected Works. The poems are placed under such headings as "five-syllable *jueju*" an "seven-syllable *lüshi*,"[1] and prose pieces under such headings as "prefaces" (*jo* 序), "records" (*ki* 記), etc., while the letters are classified according to such criteria as the rank and status of the persons to whom the letters are addressed, and the nature of their relation with Sorai. Broadly speaking, they are in chronological order, but in order to determine correctly when they were written, careful study is necessary.

When one has rearranged all the compositions in *Sorai-shū* in chronological order, one will not just be able to appreciate them as literary products, but one will also get to know Sorai's social network and his emotional changes. Most importantly, however, it becomes possible to understand how deep Sorai's method of writing with "ancient words and phrases" went – a topic that up till now has hardly been studied. Because Sorai himself loudly proclaimed that he had transferred the method of "ancient words and phrases" from the writing of poetry and prose to the study of the Classics, it has come to be discussed in terms of a hermeneutical approach of the Classics. The most fundamental methodology in Sorai's thinking was, however, that through mastering the writings that took the "ancient words and phrases" as their ideal models, one would be able to capture the feelings and perceptions they contained, and that from there one would be able to regain the ancient world. It stands to reason that he could not just propose this theoretically but would also have to show it in his personal practice. Conceivably, the poems and prose compositions included in his *Collected Works* are concrete examples that will bear this out. It is difficult, however, to discern whether, as time went by, Sorai's thought and feelings really got closer to those of the ancient Chinese.

There is, however, an evident change in the technical skill with which he applied his "ancient words and phrases." In compositions of the early period, he employed a relatively simple method, i.e., he began by defining a scene that fitted the poem or piece of prose; then he collected words and phrases from classical works that were closely related to that scene, and then he composed his phrases. In his later works, on the contrary, a variety of scenes would be prepared; then he devised ways to rotate these scenes or put them together as Russian dolls. With help of dictionaries

---

[1] *Jueju* 絶句 are poems of four lines, counting five or seven characters per line; *lüshi* 律詩 have eight lines, and again either five or seven characters per line. (WJB)

and commentaries, he also changed characters in the phrases he used, thus taking care that the readers would not immediately recognise them. Thus, in terms of technique, he evidently made great progress.

At the back of *Sorai's Collected Works* stood an inner circle whom Sorai called "my party." This group, untrammelled by matters of status, enjoyed a kind of intellectual playfulness. Writer and reader were not fixed, but stood in an interactive relationship. A space had emerged in which they enjoyed the exchange of poetry and prose, trying to guess each other's carefully thought-out literary effects. Others, who did not belong to "my party," studied and enjoyed their creations, having understood that these writings had emerged from such a relationship. This characteristic was, of course, common to the whole of East-Asian literature, modelled as it was on China. When we reflect, however, how it took hold in early modern Japan, it will be necessary to consider it in connection with the *honkadori* 本歌取り ("intertextuality") in the *waka* of ancient Japan, and the creation of "worlds" in the puppet and *kabuki* theatres. Sorai's "ancient words and phrases" and *Sorai's Collected Works* were born from a mixture of the "newest" methods that were taken over from China and Japan's own native methods.

Part II
Essays

Chapter 10
An "Intellectual-Historical" Biography of Ogyū Sorai

Sawai Keiichi

1 From Childhood to Boyhood

Ogyū Sorai was born in the second month of Kanbun 6 (1666) in Niban-chō in Edo as the second son of the physician Ogyū Hōan 方庵 (1626–1706). Hōan's father, Genpo 元甫 (d. 1633), was a private doctor who had studied with Manase (Imaōji) Genkan 曲直瀬 (今大路) 元鑑 (1577–1626), also known as Dōsan III. Sorai's father, in his turn, may have studied with Manase Gen'en 元淵 (1636–1686), also known as Dōsan V.[1] When Sorai was five years old, in 1671 (Kanbun 11), his father Hōan became the physician in ordinary (*sobai* 側医) of Shogun Tokugawa Tsunayoshi 綱吉 (1646–1680–1709), who at that time still was *daimyō* of Tatebayashi; before that, in 1669, he had studied for some time in Kyoto, possibly with Gen'en, possibly with other physicians of his school. No doubt, the network of the Manase (Imaōji) helped him to improve his medical skills and knowledge, and to find employment.

This means that the members of the Ogyū family did not belong to the "Method of Ancient Medicine" (*koihō* 古医方), which just at that time had begun to flourish in Kyoto, but that they stood on the side of the established, authoritative "School of the Latter Days" (*Kōseiha* 後世派) or "Zhu's Medical Method" (*Shuihō* 朱医方).

---

[1] The founder of the Manase family of doctors was Manase Dōsan 曲直瀬道三 (1507–1594), who studied a new kind of Chinese medicine, called *Li Zhu yixue* 李朱医学 ("Medicine of Messrs. Li and Zhu."), and established himself as a physician and teacher of medicine in Kyoto. In 1592 (Tenshō 20) he received the clan name Tachibana and the family name Imaōji from Emperor Go-Yōzei. His successors as heads of the family customarily called themselves "umpteenth-generation Dōsan." Genkan and Gen'en moved between Kyoto, where they served the court, and Edo, where they served the *bakufu*. In 1658, Gen'en was assigned a residence in Edo.

Sawai Keiichi (✉)
Keisen University, Tama, Tokyo, Japan
e-mail: ksawai@keisen.ac.jp

© Springer Nature Switzerland AG 2019
W. J. Boot, Takayama Daiki (eds.), *Tetsugaku Companion to Ogyū Sorai*,
Tetsugaku Companions to Japanese Philosophy 2,
https://doi.org/10.1007/978-3-030-15475-2_10

This has important implications when we consider the origin of Sorai's later intellectual standpoints.

In Enpō 5 (1677), at the age of eleven, Sorai entered the school of Hayashi Gahō 林鵞峰 (1619–1680) and attended the lectures given by Hayashi Hōkō 林鳳岡 (1644–1732). Perhaps, *if* his father had not been banished from Edo, he might have spent his life as an important disciple of the Hayashi, or as a physician in the service of the *bakufu* or a powerful *daimyō*. However, in Enpō 7 (1679), when Sorai was thirteen, Hōan was banished from Edo for some misdeed; it is unclear, what his offence had been. He moved to the village Honnō in the province of Kazusa, where he had relatives.

After the move to Honnō, Sorai, who had just begun his study of Confucianism under the Hayashi, borrowed and read the *Sishu daquan* 四書大全 ("Great Compendium of the Four Books"); reportedly, he virtually taught himself. In later years, Sorai reminisced that at the age of sixteen or seventeen, as a result of his solitary studies, he had come to understand a number of things. Looking back, he said, rather ironically, that his period in Kazusa had been of greater benefit to him than the "benefits" he received from Tokugawa Tsunayoshi later on, when he served Yanagisawa Yoshiyasu 柳沢吉保 (1658–1714). What he appreciated most was that he had lived in the rough but simple countryside, where he was not swayed by the fashions of the city. This had taught him to look at reality from the outside, and that became the basis of his scholarship and thought. Not only in his *Seidan*, but also in compositions included in *Sorai-shū*, Sorai repeatedly said that, if he had been born and raised in the big city called Edo, it would have been impossible for him to understand the actual situation of the society of Tokugawa Japan, and also the "facts" of ancient China as recorded in the Classics and histories, for he would not have acquired the sensibility needed to imagine other worlds.[2]

What Sorai argued here, was, that one should not just stare at the phenomena, but that one should nurture a perceptive, conceptual capacity within oneself to understand those phenomena correctly. This was the beginning of the argument he later made in *Ken'en zuihitsu* 蘐園随筆, that it was important to grasp "the great things," or again the stress he put in *Benmei* on the ability of the Sages[3] to understand the whole and to look ahead, which ability was what made them Sages.

It is assumed that in those days Sorai's studies consisted in the repeated, careful reading of a small number of texts for beginner's such as *Daigaku genkai* 大学諺解 ("The Great Learning explained in the vernacular"), which he had had been at great pains to acquire. He did, however, add some tricks of his own, for instance that he

---

[2] See e.g. his *Kō Chūseki no Jō ni utsuru o okuru no jo* 送岡仲錫徙常序 ("Preface for the sending-off of Oka Chūseki, who is moving to Hitachi"), *Sorai-shū* 11:11b-14a (pp. 113–114); Tōyō Bunko vol. 880, pp. 301–318. N.B. Kō Chūseki is his student Okai Kenshū 岡井嶔洲 (1702–1765). *Jo*, here translated as "preface," is a set genre in *Kanbun* literature. Typically, it is used to introduce a person and to explain your relation with him when he is departing on a journey and similar occasions.

[3] "Sages" is translation of *shengren* 聖人 (J. *seijin*), i.e. the ancient Chinese, and hence Confucian creators of human culture. They range from Fu Xi to the Duke of Zhou, or, according to some, to Confucius. (WJB)

did not swallow whole the traditional readings, but paid attention to the way in which words were used, and followed the patterns and connections within the text. I mention this, because, unlike the conceptual power mentioned above, this technique for interpreting texts is related to the methods he developed later, such as "translation studies" (*yakugaku*) and "the study of ancient words and phrases" (*kobunjigaku*). The chapter *Bunrirei* 文理例 ("Examples of grammar") of his post-humously published *Kun'yaku jimō*[4] ("Instructions for translating") shows through concrete examples how the meaning and content of phrases taken from *Daxue* ("Great Learning") change, depending on differences in the punctuation. It shows clearly in which direction Sorai's efforts and interests were moving in those days. His technique for following the connections within the text was to concentrate on the functions fulfilled in *Kanbun* by parts of speech like empty words and auxiliaries, but this blossomed into a methodology only after he had returned to Edo and gained access to new knowledge.

Another thing that deserves attention in the case of the young Sorai is the exchange Sorai's father Hōan kept up, during his period of study in Kyoto and during his exile from Edo, with such persons as his wife's foster father Kojima Masatomo 児島正朝 (dates unknown) and her real father Torii Tadashige 鳥居忠重 (dates unknown), who lived according to a warrior "tradition" that went back to the beginning of the Edo Period or even earlier.[5] Sorai also reminisces that his grandfather from his father's side had not been a mere physician, but had maintained his pride "as a warrior" and therefore had never entered into the service of a *daimyō*.[6] This means that he was strongly influenced by people who did not heed the great changes the warrior class had gone through during the hundred years that had passed since the founding to the *bakufu*, but turned their backs to the currents of the times.

Sorai displays this intellectual bias, which we would call "conservative," without reservations in his analysis of the contemporary situation, which he gives in later works such as *Seidan*. We must keep in mind, however, that in Sorai's case this never simply was a matter of "nostalgia" or "conservatism." Take, for instance, his "military studies" (*heigaku*) – a subject that was closely involved with the nature of the warrior class. Sorai criticized as obsolete the formations of cavalry and infantry that existed since the Sengoku Period (1467–1580) and were an outstanding aspect of popular schools like the *Kōshū-ryū* 甲州流 ("The School from Kai"). Having absorbed military knowhow from handbooks of the Ming, he showed a considerable interest in technical innovation and even designed formations that centred around cannon and other firearms.[7] His military knowledge also shows in the board game, played on a *go* board and called *kōshōgi* 広象棋 ("broad *shōgi*"), which he is thought to have devised on his own. We also get glimpses of it in his *Kenroku*, which

---

[4] *Bunrirei* is the second fascicle of *Kun'yaku jimō*. The text was printed in 1738 and reprinted in 1766.

[5] It seems that, when Hōan was in Kyoto, his family lived in the Kojima mansion in Edo, and that, when he was banished, he moved to the village where his wife's other father, Torii, was living.

[6] Sorai mentions this in *Kenroku gaisho* 鈐録外書 6.

[7] See his *Gunji kagi no jo* 郡司火技叙, *Sorai-shū* 9:7a-8b (p. 87); *Tōyō Bunko* vol. 880, pp. 94–111.

he probably wrote in his final year.[8] Sorai's greatest strength was that, on the one hand, he had a strong interest in, and a positive attitude towards new, fashionable knowledge, while, on the other hand, he maintained a fundamental position on the "conservative" side.

Sorai was probably allowed to return in 1690 (Genroku 3), at the age of twenty four. It is well known that, back in Edo, he was at first "ploughing with his tongue" (*zekkō* 舌耕; i.e., working as a lecturer) in front of the Zōjōji in Shiba. It must have been during that period that he dictated to his students the first draft of his *Yakubun sentei*, even though its first tome was only published much later, in Shōtoku 5 (1715).[9] *Yakubun sentei* addresses the Japanese "readings" of the Chinese "empty words" (verbs) and "half-empty words" (adjectives) and explains the different nuances.[10] It was a problem that had interested him already during his days in Kazusa, and the book shows that Sorai had acquired considerable proficiency in Chinese usage.

In the eighth month of Genroku 9 (1696), when he turned thirty, he entered into the service of Yanagisawa Yoshiyasu (at that time still known as Yasuaki) as mounted guard (*umamawari* 馬廻) with a stipend of fifteen rations.[11] In the ninth month he had an audience with Shogun Tsunayoshi in the Yanagisawa residence, and was assigned the task of asking difficult questions about the lecture given by Hayashi Hōkō. Of course, other people, too, were appointed to ask difficult questions, such as Shimura Teikan 志村禎幹 (dates unknown), who later on would do the editing of the Five Histories that printed by the Yanagisawa,[12] and Hosoi Kōtaku 細井広沢 (1658–1735; *KGS* 3922), Sorai's senior, who was well-known for his many talents and accomplishments. Although it was not the case that only Sorai had especially been appointed, the event shows that Sorai was one of the acknowledged specialists serving the Yanagisawa in matters related to Confucianism.

Thereafter, as a "Confucian vassal" (*jushin* 儒臣) of the Yanagisawa, he not only listened to lectures given by Tsunayoshi in Edo Castle, and gave lectures when Tsunayoshi "deigned to visit" the Yanagisawa residence, but he also sorted out the records of the fief and stated his opinion on its administration, thus steadily consolidating his position. When his stipend was raised in Genroku 10 (1697) with ten rations, his status, too, was changed to "Confucian scholar" (*jusha*). Sorai had a

---

[8] For details, see above, the Introduction by Kojima.

[9] For details, see the Introduction by Aihara.

[10] As a rule, a Chinese character has various possible readings in Japanese, and the same Japanese word can be written with different characters. Sorai relates these readings to the meaning and function of the character in the original Chinese context.

[11] One "ration" 扶持 (*fuchi*) was supposed to be sufficient to feed, clothe, and house one person.

[12] The Five Histories are the histories of the Six Dynasties that ruled the north of China between 220 (end of the Han Dynasty) and 589 (beginning of the Sui Dynasty). Of these, *Song Shu* 宋書 ("History of the Song") and *Chen Shu* 陳書 ("History of the Chen") were punctuated by Teikan; *Nan-Qi Shu* 南斉書 ("History of the Southern Qi") and *Liang Shu* 梁書 ("History of the Liang") were punctuated by Sorai; and *Jin Shu* 晋書 ("History of the Jin") was punctuated by Teikan and Sorai together. The books were published between 1701 and 1706.

successful career. In Genroku 13 (1700) he received a personal fief of 200 *koku*.[13] Afterwards, Sorai's stipend was raised at appropriate occasions; eventually, in Shōtoku 4 (1714), under the new *daimyō* Yanagisawa Yoshisato 吉里 (1687–1745), it was increased to 500 *koku* because of his successful completion of *Kenbyō jit-suroku*.[14] This remained the maximum; Sorai's salary was comparable to that of other middle-ranking vassals of the Yanagisawa house.

In the meantime, Sorai's father, Hōan, too, had been pardoned. He returned to Edo, and in the same year in which Sorai was taken into service by the Yanagisawa, Hōan became resident physician (*goban ishi* 御番医師) of the *bakufu*. In Genroku 10 (1697), he was promoted to personal physician (*o-soba ishi* 御側医師) of Tsunayoshi, and at the end of that year he was given the rank of *hōgen* ("Eye of the Law").[15] At the same time, he also worked as "teacher of healing" (*chiryō shinan* 治療指南) under Manase Genki 元耆 (Dōsan VI; 1675–1737); in this capacity, he was responsible for the coaching Genki's students. His father's connections were one reason why Sorai, too, had many contacts with physicians.

Sorai's younger brother Ogyū Hokkei 北渓 (1673–1754) had his audience with the shogun in Genroku 12 (1699). In Hōei 1 (1704), when his father Hōan retired, he succeeded him in the service of the *bakufu*, but as a Confucian scholar, not as a physician. In *Sorai-shū* it is explained that Hokkei became a Confucian scholar because Sorai had told him that, if you want to succeed as doctor, you had to be socially adept, and if you did not have that in you, you would either have to concentrate exclusively on improving your skills, or choose another profession.[16] I do not know whether this anecdote is true or not, but Hokkei achieved great results in his philological work within the Sorai School, e.g., *Minritsu kokujikai* 明律国字解 ("Explanation of the Laws of the Ming in Japanese Script"), *Toryōkō-kō* 度量衡考 ("Essay on Lengths, Measures, and Weights"), and *Shichi-Kei Mōshi kōbun hoi* 七経孟子考文補遺 ("Addenda to Edited Texts of the Seven Classics and Mencius"). The period stretching from the end of the Genroku to the Hōei Era was the highpoint in the careers of Hōan and the other members of the Ogyū family.

Hōan died in Hōei 3 (1706), at the age of eighty. The year before, Sorai had lost his wife of the Miyake family; it seems that at that occasion he conducted the funeral

---

[13] The difference between a stipend expressed in rations (*fuchi*) and a fief (*ryōchi*) is that stipends were paid out in rice, while a fief was a designated piece of land, part of the yield of which one could consider one's own. Rations were expressed in "so many men," while fiefs were expressed in *koku*, i.e. the amount of rice needed to feed an adult man during one year. The stated income of *koku* indicated an average, putative yield, and of course, the farmer and his family, too, had to eat, so the 200 *koku* was not all Sorai's to consume. (WJB)

[14] *Kenbyō jitsuroku* 憲廟実録 ("The chronological history of the reign of Tsunayoshi") in 31 fasc. was composed by Yanagisawa Yoshiyasu, Ogyū Sorai, and Dazai Shundai. It only exists in manuscript form; no printed editions ever appeared.

[15] *Hōgen* 法眼 is a Buddhist title. It was given to physicians, because they were officially categorized as Buddhist monks, and were also supposed to shave and dress like monks. (WJB)

[16] See *Chō-han'i Nakamura Gen'yo o okuru no jo* 送長藩医仲邨玄与序 ("Preface for Seeing off the Physician Nakamura Gen'yo of the fief Chōshū"), *Sorai-shū* 10:3a-7a (pp. 97–99); Tōyō Bunko vol. 877, pp. 249–272.

rites according to the *Zhuzi jiali* 朱子家礼 ("House Rituals of Master Zhu").[17] As regards the funeral rites for his father, we only know that, according to the rules of the *bakufu*, a mourning period of 50 days was observed; no further details are known. Apparently, however, he expressed the feeling that he was not satisfied with a mourning period of fifty days. This experience may have been a reason for Sorai to interest himself in funeral and sacrificial rites later on.

2   From "Translation Studies" to the "Study of Ancient Words and Phrases"

It is not clear at what time Sorai began the study of spoken Chinese 唐話 (*Tō-wa*), but a Yanagisawa house record relates that at the occasion of a visit by Tsunayoshi in Genroku 16 (1703), when Kuraoka Sozan 鞍岡蘇山 (1679–1750; *KGS* 1750) gave a lecture on *Daxue* ("Great Learning") in spoken Chinese, Sorai acted as interpreter, so by that time his study of spoken Chinese must have advanced considerably. There is also a record that says that, at a visit by Tsunayoshi in Hōei 2 (1705), the vassals of the Yanagisawa held discussions and conversations in Chinese. Because, at that occasion, Sorai held a discussion with Sosan, Sosan will have been his closest partner among the many Confucian vassals of the Yanagisawa who were studying *Tō-wa*.

In one of the prefaces in *Sorai-shū*[18] Sorai mentions Nakano Kiken 中野撝謙 (1667–1720) – he served Makino Narisada 牧野成貞 (1634–1712), who stood equally high in Tsunayoshi's favour as Yanagisawa Yoshiyasu – and his student Andō Tōya 安藤東野 (1683–1719) as his comrades in the study of spoken Chinese. Before long, through Tōya's introduction, Dazai Shundai 太宰春台 (1680–1747), who had also been learning spoken Chinese, entered Sorai's school. Around this nucleus, not only the study of spoken Chinese, but also the new field of scholarship that Sorai called "learning from Nagasaki" 崎陽之学 (*Kiyō no gaku*) or "translation studies" 訳学 (*yakugaku*) took off. In the winter of Shōtoku 1 (1711), Sorai, in consultation with his comrades, wrote the *Yakusha-yaku* 訳社約 ("Covenant of the Translation Society")[19] for a group of translators that began its activities in his house in Ushigome.

"Nagasaki Learning" refers to the city of Nagasaki, and "translation studies" implies a method of translating that requires reading the text in Chinese, *as Chinese*,

---

[17] See his *Hin Miyake-shi boshi* 嬪三宅氏墓誌 ("Grave Inscription for my Wife Miyake"), *Sorai-shū shūi*, pp. 344–345. N.B. The ordinary funeral rites in Japan were Buddhist. That Sorai followed the Confucian rites as reformulated by Zhu Xi (1130–1200) was exceptional, though not unknown.

[18] This is *Ya-sei no Raku e yuku o okuru no jo* 送野生之洛序 ("Preface for Sending-off Student [Naka]no to the Capital"), *Sorai-shū* 10:11a-13b (pp. 101–102); Tōyō Bunko vol. 877, pp. 36–56.

[19] See *Sorai-shū* 18:8a-9b (pp. 186–187).

and then translating it into Japanese, instead of the traditional *kundoku*-way of reading *Kanbun*. Sorai gave a summary of his methodology in the introduction (*Daigen* 題言) of *Yakubun sentei*, which he finished around Shōtoku 1 (1711); the first set of *Yakubun sentei* was printed in Shōtoku 5 (1715). It shows that for Sorai the study of spoken Chinese meant more than merely following a fashion; he clearly intended to develop it into the methodology of his own personal scholarship and thought. Of course, it will also have been an important factor that the main books one read to study spoken Chinese were such vernacular novels as *Shuihuzhuan* 水滸伝 ("Water Margin"), *Xiyouji* 西遊記 ("Journey to the West," a.k.a. *Monkey*), *Xixiangji* 西廂記 ("The Story of the Western Wing"),[20] etc.

The new methodology was needed because one could not tackle these vernacular novels, which represented the apogee of "popularization" in the field of Ming literature, with the contemporary *kundoku* technique, which had developed from the tradition of the medieval court erudites.[21] Through the *goroku* 語録 (Ch. *yulei*; "collected sayings") of Zen priests, and of Zhu Xi and other Neo-Confucians, educated Japanese had gotten used to reading texts interspersed with expressions from the spoken language of the Song Dynasty. However, in order to capture accurately the nuances of a spoken language that was rooted in the daily life of the common people, as was the case with the vernacular novels of the Ming, the technical expertise of the Chinese interpreters in Nagasaki was definitely needed. As it happened, at that time there were men who had fallen out of the system of official interpreters in Nagasaki, where in principle only one child could inherit the position of interpreter. They were willing to commercialise part of their knowledge, making it known to the outside world. The knowledge of "Dutch Studies," too, spread and circulated along a similar trajectory.

The next problem, how to find the "correct" counterparts in Japanese, required knowledge not only of Chinese, but also of the Japanese language. This problem was addressed by Dazai Shundai and his school and, before long, also by the scholars of National Learning (*Kokugaku* 国学), who had their "theory of particles and auxiliaries" (*te-ni-wo-ha ron*). In that sense, too, Sorai's interest in language may well have caused a major change in early modern linguistic theory.

---

[20] These texts were composed in a spoken variety of contemporary Chinese (vernacular Chinese or *baihua* 白話). *Shuihuzhuan* and *Xiyouji* are prose works ("novels") and were composed under the Ming, while *Xixiangji* is a *zaju* 雑劇, i.e. a theatre play, dating from the Yuan. All texts have been translated into English. (WJB)

[21] In the Middle Ages, the "court erudites" were the families of Kiyohara and Nakahara. They had their own variety of *kundoku*, but there were others. *Kundoku* is basically the reading-off of the characters of a Chinese sentence in the Japanese order, while adding Japanese readings (*on-yomi* or *kun-yomi*) to the characters and inserting particles, verb endings, and auxiliaries as needed. It was a kind of translation, but it only worked for the standard kind of classical Chinese; the *baihua* texts contained characters, particles, and idiom for which there simply existed no conventions. (WJB)

Why "translation studies" became problematic shows clearly in the preparation of the Japanese translation of *Liuyu yanyi* 六諭衍義 (J. *Rikuyu engi*),[22] which raised Sorai's fame in his later years; his preface of the official printed edition is dated Kyōhō 6 (1721).[23] The problem was that the information reaching Japan through Nagasaki from the middle of the Ming until the beginning of the Qing – not only such cultural pursuits as calligraphy and painting, poetry and prose, or knowledge of the Classics, but also knowledge of geography and history, or of military and commercial techniques – contained vernacular expressions that could no longer be tackled through *kundoku* techniques that took the poetry and prose of the Tang and Song as their standard.

The fact that Muro Kyūsō 室鳩巣 (1658–1734) abandoned the preparation of a Japanese version of *Liuyu yanyi* tellingly illustrates, how difficult it was to understand texts interspersed with vernacular expressions, even when you were, as Kyūsō was, supported by the school of Kinoshita Jun'an 木下順庵 (1621–1698), which had succeeded the Hayashi family as the main stream of Japanese Confucianism and just in those days had begun its spectacular rise.

So popular was the quickly developing mass culture of the Ming becoming in Nagasaki and in the rest of Japan that scholars were willing to take the trouble. Not only the study of spoken Chinese and translation studies, but also the popularity of "ancient words and phrases" are phenomena occasioned by the reception of the mass culture of the Ming. I will come back to that later; first, I will have to explain how this "popularization" of thought and culture during the Ming came about.

Some scholars interpret the appearance of a group variously called "Yangming Learning," "Left-Wing Wang Learning," or the "Faction that held that Innate Knowledge Will be Realized in Practice" as an intellectual trend towards the popularization of the "Teaching of the Way" (*Daoxue*).[24] This argument takes cognizance of the fact that, while under the Song the supporters of Confucianism mainly came from the middle and small landowning families (*shitaifu* 士大夫), who produced most of the bureaucrats, under the Ming support had widened to the layer of local gentlemen (*xiangshen* 郷紳), who were graded below the *shitaifu*, and even to ordinary people like merchants and such. This meant that the intellectuals, who were the

---

[22] The title could be translated as "Augmented Commentary on the Six Admonishments." The Six Admonishments stemmed from the first emperor of the Ming Dynasty. They were "Be filial to your parents, respect elders and superiors, live in harmony with your neighbours, instruct and discipline your children and grandchildren, be content with your occupation, commit no wrongful acts." The emperor wanted these admonishments to be proclaimed six times per month in the villages; they were supposed to morally improve the people. For details, see Kornicki, "From *Liuyu yanyi* to *Rikuyu engi taii*." (WJB)

[23] *Kankoku Rikuyu engi jo* 官刻六諭衍義叙 ("Preface to the Official Edition of the Extended Commentary on the Six Admonishments"), *Sorai-shū* 9:1a-2a (p. 84); Tōyō Bunko 880, pp. 70–80.

[24] *Daoxue* 道学 ("The Teaching of the Way") is the general name of Confucian studies, learning, practice, and indoctrination. *Yangming xue* 陽明学 ("Yangming Learning") is so called after its originator, Wang Yangming (1472–1528). *Wang xue zuopai* 王学左派 ("Left-wing Wang Learning") and *Liangzhi xiancheng pai* 良知現成派 ("Innate Knowledge Will be Realized in Practice Wing") are later derivations, associated with the name of Wang's disciple Wang Gen 王艮 (1483–1541).

supporters of Confucianism, expanded downward through the social classes. This development, however, was certainly not restricted to Confucianism. General education, which had been the monopoly of the *shitaifu* class, too, expanded downward at this time and changed its shape in ways that fitted the people in the lower strata of society.

This author regards these developments as one form of "nativization," but the phenomenon was not restricted to China; similar phenomena also occurred in Korea and Japan. In Korea and Japan, however, one needs to keep in mind that, parallel with this development, there occurred still another kind of nativization, which is frequently discussed within the study of intellectual history, generally under the heading of "the problem of Japanization." Now, the products of the popularization-as-nativization that occurred in Ming China were imported into Korea and Japan, and there, in both societies and at approximately the same time, they were "nativized" a second time. If we lose sight of the twofold nature of the event, we cannot claim to have a sufficient understanding of the phenomena that occurred at that time. Sorai's "ancient philology" is a suitable object for appreciating this twofold nativization.

The culture of the Ming that Sorai had received was not restricted only to the field of literature, be it the *baihua* novels, which were the object of his "translation studies," or, better still, the "ancient words and phrases," which were regarded as a higher kind of literature; this culture was a "fashion" that spread over a variety of fields, from art (calligraphy and painting, seal cutting) to medicine and astronomy, and even to military technology. It is, for instance, well known that Sorai was the representative figure of the style of calligraphy called "Chinese style" (*karayō* 唐様), but he also showed a strong interest in the closely related area of seal cutting.

Seal cutting supposedly began with the famous calligrapher of the Song, Mi Fu 米芾 (1051–1107), but during the Ming it developed rapidly. Seals originally had served mainly as marks to indicate the calligrapher or painter, but they had brought forth "artists" who specialised in their cutting. Next, people appeared who collected and appraised these seals; in this way, eventually, seal cutting established itself as separate, independent field. It was brought to Japan by monks of the Ōbaku Sect[25]; once there, it developed in new, original ways. During Sorai's life the "Early Edo School" appeared. Sorai associated with its leading lights, e.g., Ikenaga Dōun 池永道雲 (d. 1737) and Hosoi Kōtaku, as is shown by prose pieces and letters in the *Sorai-shū*.[26] I will not go into detail, but it is important to note that these popular arts of the Ming were not introduced into Japan as they were, but that they were "nativized" and spread in a form that fitted the personal taste of the Japanese involved.

---

[25] The Ōbaku Sect 黄檗宗 is a Zen sect that was brought to Japan in the course of the seventeenth century, through Nagasaki, by Chinese monks seeking refuge from the Manchu occupation. Its main temple eventually became the Manpukuji 万福寺 in Uji. (WJB)

[26] See *Ittō banshō no jo* 一刀万象序 ("Preface of *One sword, ten thousand forms*"), *Sorai-shū* 8:5a-6b (p. 77); Tōyō Bunko 877, pp. 125–143、*Shibi jiyō jo* 紫薇字様叙 ("Preface of *The imperial style of writing*"), *Sorai-shū* 9:2b-3b (pp. 84–85); Tōyō Bunko 877, pp. 332–343.

Let us, however, return to Sorai. Together with his increased interest in languages, centred around "translation studies," his understanding of the Classics, too, seems to have progressed during this period. After all, it was in Hōei 1 (1704) that he sent a letter to Itō Jinsai 伊藤仁斎 (1627–1705) and posed him a number of "questions." Jinsai died in the following year, without having answered him, but in Hōei 4 (1707), his son Tōgai 伊藤東涯 (1670–1736) and others published *Kogaku-sensei ketsumei gyōjō* 古学先生碣銘行状 ("The Stele Inscription and Biography of Master Ancient Studies"),[27] which contained the letter from Sorai. As is well known, Sorai conceived an antipathy against Jinsai and Tōgai because they had published the letter without his permission. From compositions in *Sorai-shū*, one can get an impression of the twisted feelings Sorai had towards Jinsai and his son. They seem to have grown stronger in his final years.[28]

Sorai will have reacted the way he did because Tōgai had chosen to ignore that Sorai, too, was already entertaining doubts about Zhu Xi and had begun to conceptualize an "Ancient Learning" of his own; he had treated him like someone who had been converted by Jinsai. As is told in *Senkō Shūnan-sensei gyōjō* 先考周南先生行状 ("Biography of my Father, Master Shūnan"), by the time when, in Hōei 2 (1705), Yamagata Shūnan 山県周南 (1687–1752) from Chōshū entered his school, Sorai was already lecturing on "restoring antiquity" (*fukkogaku* 復古学). Sorai himself reminisces that Shūnan's father Ryōsai 良斎 (dates unknown), who was an adherent of Zhu Xi, did not let his principles get in the way, but allowed his son to enter his school.[29] This indicates that Sorai himself was also aware of the fact that he was moving away from Zhu Xi and was establishing his own, original teaching. It is unclear how many students Sorai had at this time, but from two sets of essay questions,[30] which he assigned to his students and which, putatively, stem from Hōei 4 (1707), we can infer that he was going ahead with his criticisms of Zhu Xi and of Jinsai's "Ancient Meaning." These students included Shūnan, Andō Tōya, and Tanaka Seigo 田中省吾 (1668–1742; *KGS* no. 2969).

On the basis of a statement by Usami Shinsui 宇佐美灊水 (1710–1776), which appears in *Ken'en zatsuwa* ("Random discussions from the Miscanthus Garden"), Sorai's encounter with the poetry and prose of Li Panlong 李攀龍 (1514–1570) and Wang Shizhen 王世貞 (1526–1590) is assumed to have taken place in Hōei 2 (1705). The story emphasizes the accidental character of the event, for the books were part of a collection that Sorai had bought as a whole ("the whole storehouse")

---

[27] *NKSM* mentions Kitamura Tokusho 北村篤所 (1647–1718) as the second author.

[28] See e.g. Sorai's *Ya-sei Raku e yuku o okuru no jo* (see above, note 18), or his *U Ki-shi ni okuru no jo* 贈于季子序 ("Preface sent to Uno Shirō"), *Sorai-shū* 11:3a-5a (pp. 109–110); Tōyō Bunko vol. 880, pp. 173–197.

[29] See his *Ken-sensei hachijū no jo* 県先生八十序 ("Preface on Master Ken's Eightieth Birthday"), *Sorai-shū* 9:21b-24a (pp. 94–95), Tōyō Bunko 880, pp. 198–217.

[30] The titles are *Shigi sakumon ichidō* 私擬策問一道 and the *Shigi sakumon kijin ichidō* 私擬策問鬼神一道 (*Sorai-shū* 17:1a-3b; pp. 173–174), which would translate as "one" (*ichidō*) "policy question" (*sakumon*) that "I privately made" (*shigi*). *Sakumon* (Ch. *cewen*) formed one part of the Chinese examinations; they were questions about the interpretation of the Classics or about matters of policy. The words *kijin* in the second title means "ghosts and spirits."

from "a certain person." It can also be maintained, however, that he was destined to encounter them eventually, in view of his interest in spoken Chinese and "Ancient Learning."

The shift from the every-day, spoken language called *Tō-wa* or *baihua* 白話 to the highly cultivated expressions called "ancient words and phrases" may look like a big jump, but in fact both were the product of the phenomenon called "popularization" that occurred during the Ming. Information about Li Panlong and Wang Shizhen had already been brought to Japan before Sorai; it was one aspect of the dissemination, through Nagasaki to all parts of Japan, of the "popularized" scholarship and arts of the Ming. The possibility, therefore, that Sorai's interest in the spoken language would eventually have made him interested in "ancient words and phrases" was quite high.

As it turned out, Sorai *did* discover the "ancient words and phrases" within the massive amount of information about the popular culture of the Ming, but his real importance lies, first, in his intuitive appreciation that this method of composing poetry and prose would be an effective method for the intellectuals of Tokugawa Japan, even though it could not but lead to the loss of individuality on the part of the authors. Culturally, Japanese intellectuals were still lagging behind, but because, with this method, they only needed to imitate a very limited number of texts, even those who had not received a general education in their youth would still be able to write elegant poetry and prose. Second, Sorai's importance lies in the purposefulness with which he tried to give this method a form that would suit him and his students. Here lies hidden the key to the riddle why a popularized method of producing poetry and prose of the Ming became fashionable in Japan in the middle of the Tokugawa period as the symbol of the "high" culture. What also helped was a circumstance unique to Tokugawa Japan, i.e., that the higher warriors and merchants, living in the cities, together formed clubs around their common interest in literature and the arts. The central preoccupation was *renga* and *haiku*, but the fashion was also spreading to poetry and prose in Chinese.

In *Sorai-shū*, Sorai used the term "ancient words and phrases" for the first time in his *Tō Kanto ji setsu* 滕煥図字説 ("Explanation of the style of Tō Kanto"), which he composed in Hōei 4 (1707), and in his *Jikō no azana ni jo-shite kō ni okuru* 次公字敘贈行 of Hōei 5.[31] Of course, even if you know the writings of Li Panlong and Wang Shizhen and understand that these were written with the methodology of "ancient words and phrases" in mind, this does not mean that you are immediately able to imitate them. I think that Sorai became more confident in handling this method of literary expression around the time of *Kōshū-shi o okuru no jo* 送香洲師送 ("Preface for Seeing-off Teacher Kōshū"),[32] which he wrote in Hōei 6 (1709). A *Kōshū-risshi yūō o okuru no jo* 送香洲律師遊嶼序 ("Preface for Seeing-off the *Vinaya* Master Kōshū on his Trip to the North"), written by Andō Tōya at the same

---

[31] See *Sorai-shū* 16:1a-2a (pp. 160–161) for 滕煥図字説, and *Sorai-shū* 10:1a-3a (pp. 96–97), and Tōyō Bunko 877, pp. 57–73 for 次公字敘贈行.

[32] See *Sorai-shū* 10:7b-11a (pp. 99–101); Tōyō Bunko 877, pp. 91–115.

occasion, was highly praised by Sorai as being "in the style of Li Yulin" 李于鱗体.[33] This shows that Sorai's students had become quite competent at expressing themselves through the method of "ancient words and phrases." With the appearance of *Monsa kishō*, inserted into *Monsa ni-shu*,[34] which was printed in Shōtoku 2 (1712), his student Yamagata Shūnan, but also others such as Irie Jakusui 入江若水 (1671–1729), Akimoto Tan'en 秋元澹園 (dates unknown; *KGS* 115), and Andō Tōya, began to attract attention for their ability to produce poetry and prose according to this new method of "ancient words and phrases." In this sense, too, we may consider the period from the end of the Hōei to the beginning of the Shōtoku Era as the epoch-making period for Sorai and the students of his school, which was known as the Ken'en ("Miscanthus Garden") School.

3   Light and Shadow in the Second Half of Sorai's Life

The death of Tsunayoshi in Hōei 6 (1709) and the *de facto* downfall of Yanagisawa Yoshiyasu it occasioned, had a great impact on Sorai and others who, like him, served the Yanagisawa house, and of whom he spoke as "my party." Because of the downfall of Yoshiyasu, the teaching facility (*Bunbu Kyōjō* 文武教場) that had been set up in his residence in order to re-educate the pages who served Tsunayoshi, was closed down.[35] Hence, Sorai withdrew from the Yanagisawa residence, while Andō Tōya, Hattori Nankaku 服部南郭 (1683–1759) and others were forced to resign and had to live in poverty. Sorai's own his ties with the Yanagisawa were not severed, but after leavingt the residence he moved from one place to the next – first to Kayaba-chō, then to Ushigome, and then to Akagi. Because, in the form of "Ken'en," Sorai used Kayaba-chō in the titles of his books,[36] later generations are wont to use it as the name of Sorai's academy and school, but he lived there for only 2 years, from Hōei 6 until Shōtoku 1 (1709–1711) – a very short period of his life. In Ushigome, where he moved next, he lived 9 years (until Kyōhō 5, = 1720); in Akagi he lived 3 years (until Kyōhō 9, = 1723); in Ichigaya, which became his last residence, he lived 4 years. In other words, from his late forties onward, Sorai mostly lived in areas located to the west of Edo Castle, in the opposite direction from Kayaba-chō (Ken'en).

---

[33] Yulin is the style of Li Panlong.

[34] *Monsa ni-shu* 問槎二種 is a collection of poetry in Chinese (5 fasc., 5 vols; Sorai's preface and postface are dated Shōtoku 2); it was compiled by Irie Jakusui, Ajiki Rikken 味木立軒 (1650–1725; *KGS* 167) *et al.* Several copies of the printed edition are extant. In most of them, the *Monsa kishō* 問槎畸賞 is included. *Monsa kishō* itself (3 fasc., 3 vols) is an independent poetry collection, compiled by Sorai's disciples Yoshida Yūrin 吉田有鱗 (no details known) and Akimoto Tan'en, and contains poems by Yamagata Shūnan, Andō Tōya and others. It was finished in Shōtoku 1. For the circumstances of the compilation of these two anthologies, see underneath.

[35] Note that the facility was *not* intended for the vassals of the Yanagisawa; it was intended specifically for the pages of Tsunayoshi.

[36] The characters 蘐 (*ken*) and 茅 (*bō*) are two ways of writing *kaya* (sedge), a reed like plant used for covering roofs.

Just before Sorai was about to go forth into the world, brandishing his new methodology of writing poetry and prose called "ancient words and phrases," the shogunal succession occurred. It meant that the students of Kinoshita Jun'an now became the mainstream in the world of Confucian studies, with Arai Hakuseki 新井白石 (1657–1725) at the top of the list, followed by such scholars as Kinoshita Jun'an and Muro Kyūsō. For the students of the Ken'en School this was a great blow. Things came to a head when a Korean embassy visited Japan in Shōtoku 1 (1711).[37] At this occasion, Hakuseki had imposed restrictions on the exchange of poems and prose with the Korean envoys; it was forbidden to approach them without prior permission. Afterwards, Hakuseki made a compilation of the poems exchanged with the envoys, entitled *Keirin shōwa shū* 鶏林唱和集 ("Collection of poems exchanged with Koreans"; 15 + 1 fasc.; printed Shōtoku 2, = 1712), which included poems written by Hayashi Hōkō, Yamagata Shūnan, and Irie Jakusui. However, the next anthology, *Shichika shōwa shū* 七家唱和集 ("Collection of poems exchanged by seven poets"; 10 fasc.; printed Shōtoku 2), only contains poems exchanged between the envoys and seven members of the Kinoshita School. This caused a groundswell of resistance. The printing of the aforementioned *Monsa kishō* is seen as an effort on behalf of Sorai to promote his students of the Ken'en School, in cooperation with others who had been excluded by Hakuseki.

Of course, the Korean envoys of this time highly appreciated the products of the Kinoshita school, and especially those of Hakuseki, because he wrote poetry and prose in an elegant, lofty style, while they did not appreciate at all the "ancient words and phrases" of the Ken'en School. Korean envoys began to take an interest in Jinsai and, together with him, in Sorai and the Ken'en School only after Sorai's death, when thanks to Shundai and Shūnan the poetics of the Ken'en School and the debate that went with it had proliferated to all parts of Japan.

After Yoshiyasu's retirement, Sorai lived as a "private" Confucian scholar, teaching his students. These were also the days in which his fame gradually increased. One reason was the publication of *Yakubun sentei* and *Ken'en zuihitsu*. Another reason was the active promotion by disciples who had newly joined "his party" like Irie Jakusui from Settsu and Yamagata Shūnan from Chōshū. As a result, there were many people who wanted to visit him, coming even from such far-away places as Kumamoto and Fukuoka.

"Ancient words and phrases" had by now become an established a method for composing poetry and prose, but Sorai's methodological awareness developed further. After the manuscript of *Bendō* 弁道 ("Distinguishing the Way") had been completed (Kyōhō 2, = 1717), he developed *kobunji* into a methodology for the study of the Classics and political thought, which was called, in a broad sense, "the study of ancient words and phrases" (*kobunjigaku*) or "Sorai's teachings" (*Sorai-gaku*). In a

---

[37] The Korean embassy (*Tsūshinshi* 通信使) visited Edo in the eleventh month of Shōtoku 1 (1711), a in order to congratulate the new shogun. These embassies always were an occasion for Japanese scholars to exchange poems with the members of the embassy, in the hope of getting praised. (WJB)

letter to Tanaka Seigo,[38] dating from Kyōhō 5 (1720), he announces that he has read the Six Classics according to the method of "ancient words and phrases" and that he has understood the mistakes of the Confucians of the Song. We may, therefore, assume that by that time his "ancient philology" had been perfected, as a greatly advanced version of his "translation studies" or "Nagasaki learning." It was also in this period that he composed the drafts of studies of the Classics such as *Benmei* 弁名 ("Distinguishing the names"), *Rongo-chō* 論語徵 ("Proof of the Analects"), *Daigaku-kai* 大学解 ("Explanation of the Great Learning"), and *Chūyō-kai* 中庸解 ("Explanation of the Mean").

This, one would almost say precipitous, involvement of Sorai in the study of the Classics can, of course, be seen as springing from Sorai's own, deepened, methodological awareness and from his impatience with a world that hardly took notice of him, but we also need to take into consideration that he was strongly influenced by a feeling of competition with Jinsai, whose books were being published one after the other by the Kogidō in approximately the same period. Jinsai had already died, but his books, edited by his son Tōgai, were all printed between 1705 and 1720; the first was *Go-Mō jigi* 語孟字義 ("The Meaning of Characters in the Analects and Mencius") in Hōei 2 (1705), followed by *Dōji mon* 童子問 ("A Boy's Questions") in Hōei 4, *Rongo kogi* 論語古義 ("The Ancient Meaning of the Analects") in Shōtoku 1 (1711), *Daigaku teihon* 大学定本 ("Definite Text of the Great Learning") and *Chūyō hakki* 中庸発揮 ("Showing the Mean") in Shōtoku 4, and *Kogaku-sensei shibun-shū* 古学先生詩文集 ("The Collected Literary Works of Master Ancient-Studies") in Kyōhō 2 (1717).

From this list, Sorai had certainly read *Go-Mō jigi* (in a pirated edition) and *Rongo kogi*. Especially in his *Rongo-chō*, he structured the discussion in each of the sections around criticisims of the interpretations given by Jinsai's as well as by Zhu Xi. While criticizing Zhu Xi's teachings, he also condemned Jinsai's arguments as being similar to those of Zhu Xi, although Jinsai actually stood closer to Sorai that to Zhu. Sorai seems to have based this acrobatic interpretation of the *Lunyu* on a carefully considered strategy, involving not only the presentation of his own opinions, but also his censure of problematic points in Zhu Xi and Jinsai. By merely examining and comparing *Go-Mō jigi* and *Bendō* we will not understand these deeper layers. Sorai's antagonistic relation with Jinsai must be examined through a careful analysis of his commentaries on the Classics.

We can be sure that Sorai's preoccupation with problems relating to the metaphorical use of language ("tropes"), which notably appears in *Benmei*, was the result of the method of composing poetry and prose called "ancient words and phrases." His consciousness, however, of a "linguistic order," which is evident in his "*study* of ancient words and phrases," was new. It was born from the necessity to find a new principle of order inside the phenomena themselves. This necessity derived from the fact that, when he made his argument about an order based on Rites and Music, he had at the same time denied the existence of the principle, called *li* 理 by Zhu Xi, that lay *behind* the phenomena and was the *source* of order.

---

[38] *Fushun-sanjin ni atau* 与富春山人, 7th letter; see *Sorai-shū* 22:4b-5b (pp. 230–231).

Actually, we should understand Sorai in terms of a problematic that does not cor-
respond with the "ancient words and phrases" movement of the middle of the Ming,
but with an intellectual direction that appeared much later and is known as
Kaozhengxue 考証学 ("Evidential research") in Qing China, or *Sirhak* 実学
("Practical Learning") in Korea. In the modern period, both these currents of thought
have been interpreted as precursors of a West-European type of "modernity." The
reason is that they tried to find the principle of order in the real world. They were
different, however, from the West-European debate of the "social contract" type in
that they sought the foundation of the social order *outside* man or his assemblies as
they actually existed.

Sorai discovered the foundation of the social order in the evident relation between
the referential function of language – in Sorai's case, not only the written, but also
the spoken language – and its signifying agency, i.e., in its orderliness. When he
claims that this orderliness resulted from the fact that the Sages had imitated Heaven,
we can acknowledge that as a peculiarity of Sorai's "study of ancient words and
phrases." He considered the Sages as beings who are beyond the understanding of
ordinary men, so theoretically the "linguistic order" is relegated to a territory that is
impossible to reproduce. Nevertheless, Sorai maintained that proficiency in "ancient
words and phrases" would make it possible to retrieve the way of thinking of the
men who lived in the ancient world, when the order was upheld, and even, that society as such should be able recover this order. At this point, all vestiges of his empirical, positivistic reflection on human consciousness and feelings have completely
disappeared. A major role was played by a "leap" that greatly resembles the literary
method of "ancient words and phrases" or, more precisely, by the poetic function of
language. It is certain that Sorai's methodology was not a simple form of
"Reactionism"; there was too much "Archaism" in it to warrant that qualification.[39]

This same applies also to Sorai's argument about the system of Rites and Music.
Sorai states that, in the ideal society of antiquity, Rites and Music had been turned
into a system only in the form of practice, and that their textual fixation had been
accomplished in Confucius' school. This textual fixation was undertaken in order to
leave through language (in writing) to later generations the system that was about to
be lost. Details of that operation as it was carried out in Confucius' school are, in
Sorai's opinion, only fragmentarily preserved in the *Liji* ("Book of Rites") and the
Lunyu ("Analects"). Even of those texts, mistaken interpretations abound, and there
is hardly anybody who understands their true meaning. In that sense, the "Way" of
the Sages, i.e., the ideal society, lies far away, in ancient history, and it is well-neigh
impossible to reach it from the present.

In Sorai's chronology, it took a great many Sages and several thousands of years
to create the "Way," and during the several thousands of years that followed, that
"Way" collapsed again. In order to recreate that "Way" for a second time, while it
was still right in the middle of that process of collapse, several thousands of years
would be needed. Hence, it was not feasible to expect the "Way" to be created again.
Having acknowledged that, it was Sorai's task to think up something that, under the

---

[39] "Reactionism" is the translation of *fukko shugi*, so "the intent to restore antiquity"; "Archaism"
is the translation of *giko shugi*, i.e. "the attempt to imitate antiquity." (WJB)

circumstances, could be called a second-best policy. That is the status of Sorai's political theory and of his discussion of the social system. Therefore, it was not the ideal society of antiquity or the written texts in which that society was fixated (the Five Classics) that should be thoroughly analysed, but, on the contrary, present-day reality. Probably, this was one of the reasons why Sorai showed no interest in annotating the body of texts called the "Five Classics," but on the contrary turned his eyes toward such thinkers as *Xunzi* 荀子 and *Han Fei zi* 韓非子, who were the product of an age of chaos.

Let me return to Sorai's *curriculum vitae*. The accession of Tokugawa Yoshimune (1684–1716–1745–1751) as the eighth shogun and the downfall of Arai Hakuseki, who until then had held power, was good news for Sorai and others of the Ken'en School. Men who had been pages of Tsunayoshi, but who thereafter had been given the cold shoulder – *daimyō* like Honda Tadamune (Iran) 本田忠統・猗蘭 (1691–1757) and Kuroda Naokuni (Kinkaku) 黒田直邦・琴鶴 (1666–1735) – now reached positions that allowed them to participate in the *bakufu* government. These were signs indicating that for Sorai the opportunity had arrived to be active not just in poetry and prose, but in discussions about practical policy. We know that immediately after Yoshimune's accession Honda and Kuroda visited Sorai. It is a matter of conjecture, but scholars have often pointed out the probable connection between this visit and the writing of *Taiheisaku* ("A plan for the great peace") and of the memorandum on the school system *Gakuryō ryōken* 学寮了簡 ("My ideas about an academy").[40]

Scholars of the Kinoshita School like Muro Kyūsō, too, remained important in Yoshimune's eyes, and in Kyōhō 4 (1719) he ordered them to give lectures on Confucianism to a wide audience of warriors and ordinary people, in the Takakura mansion that he built for the purpose in Kyōhō 4 (1719), while the Hayashi lectured to the *bakufu*'s *hatamoto* and *gokenin* in their own academy. In view of the fact that Sorai's brother Hokkei participated in the lectures of the Hayashi, and later on also gave lectures in the Takakura mansion, we had best see all this as an initiative by Yoshimune to overhaul the educational system of the *bakufu*, and to employ a wide variety of Confucian scholars for the purpose. *Gakuryō ryōken* and the translation of *Liuyu yanyi*, mentioned above, may also have been part of the same initiative.

Scholars often point out the conservative tendencies in Yoshimune's "Kyōhō Reform," but Yoshimune was the one who lifted the ban on the import of Chinese translations of European books and in general exerted himself to further the import of elements of the Chinese system and of Chinese material culture. Because of his broad knowledge, not only of vernacular Chinese, but also of Rites and Music, Sorai received assignments like editing *Yuelü quanshu*[41] 楽律全書 ("Complete works on musical tuning") and *Minglü* (J. *Minritsu*) 明律 ("Laws of the Ming"), though the latter eventually was counted as an achievement of his younger brother Hokkei.

---

[40] Text in Nihon Jurin Sōsho vol. 3, separately paginated.

[41] *Yuelü quanshu* originally counted forty-two fascicles, of which only thirty-two have survived. It discusses matters of tuning and temperament, introduced the twelve-tone scale, but it also contains the scores of "village drinking songs." The text is contained in Sigu Tiyao 四庫提要. It was compiled by Zhu Zaiyu 朱載堉 (see Mor. VI: 14424:790, and VI: 15399–273). (WJB)

It will have helped that there were important *bakufu* officials with whom he had connections, but what really created the opportunity for Sorai to be active was his broad knowledge of Chinese scholarship and culture, beginning with the "popular culture" of the Ming.

Sorai had always been liable to illnesses, but in the winter of Kyōhō 3 (1718) he suffered from an illness so severe that he realised he might die, and again, in Kyōhō 4, fourth month, Andō Tōan, who was the student of whom he had expected most – more a comrade than a student – died at the young age of thirty six. In other words, he was confronted with situations that forced him to become aware of clouds hanging over himself and his Ken'en School. Because he had to concentrate on curing his disease, quite likely he had to pass up opportunities that came his way immediately after Yoshimune's accession. Fortunately, his illness was cured, but then, in Kyōhō 5, he lost his only surviving daughter Masu 増, born from his first wife, *née* Miyake 三宅. Five children had been born to Sorai and his first wife, whom he married in Genroku 9 (1696) at the age of thirty. Three of them died in infancy; their gender is not known. The others were his second daughter Masu and his son Kuma 熊. There was also one daughter who seems to have been born from a concubine. With his second wife, *née* Sasaki 佐々木, whom he married in Shōtoku 3 (1713) and who died in Shōtoku 5, he had one daughter, but apart from Masu, all died at a young age.

When Masu died, Sorai had already become fifty five, so it must have been quite a shock to realise that his direct bloodline had died out. Likely, this was the reason why he decided to adopt the son of his elder brother Shunchiku 春竹 (d. 1747), called Sanjūrō (Kinkoku) 三十郎・金谷 (1703–1776). Of course, all this will have made him more conscious of his own physical decline. In compositions of this later period that are included in *Sorai-shū* he often expresses emotions such as that he is inclined to illness, that he is close to retirement, or that he is already old. At least in his own perception, Sorai's situation in the Kyōhō Era was not one of "under full sail, and with the wind in his back."

One of the emotions Sorai' experienced during these later years must have been a certain irritation or impatience with the lack of appreciation he received for his "study of ancient words and phrases" and for his innovative scholarship, which corrected the mistakes of Zhu Xi and Jinsai – a scholarship, in Sorai's view, that "correctly" understood the intents of the former kings and of Confucius. Most of the people who visited him had read books from his "translation studies" days such as *Ken'en zuihitsu* and did not expect much more of him than criticisms of Jinsai; they were almost completely unaware of his own, original method of "ancient words and phrases," through which he felt he had surpassed Zhu Xi and Jinsai.

Sorai's reaction was to explain his methodology through correspondence and, at the same time, to publish popularizing books that would introduce his teachings. These efforts finally bore fruit in Kyōhō 12 (1727), when, in the first month, his *Gakusoku* 学則 ("School Rules") was published, and in the fifth, his *Sorai-sensei tōmonsho* 答問書 ("Master Sorai's responsals"), which was written in Japanese.[42]

---

[42] These books had been brought to the press thanks to the exertions of Honda Tadamune, who at the time held the office of *wakadoshiyori*, i.e. member of the second-highest governing body of the Tokugawa *bakufu*.

Sorai added five extra letters in *Kanbun* to *Gakusoku*, in which he explained the main points of his "study of ancient words and phrases," while *Tōmonsho*, of course, consists of letters only.

He fully realised, however, that that alone would be insufficient. It seems likely that next he planned to publish texts that really came close to the heart of his studies, such as *Bendō* and *Benmei* and commentaries like *Rongo-chō*, which he kept revising as he fought his illnesses. If these had been published during Sorai's lifetime, they would have shown a Sorai completely different from the scholar who wrote *Yakubun sentei* and *Ken'en zuihitsu*, and who composed a commentary on *Liuyu yanyi*. We might even have witnessed a highly interesting situation in the intellectual history of Tokugawa Japan as criticisms of Sorai and Sorai's answers to these would unfold, for Sorai's classical scholarship really stood out in the scholarly world of Confucianism, not only of Japan, but of the whole of East Asia.

It was not to be. In the summer of Kyōhō 12, after he had participated in a boat outing on the River Sumida, which was organised by Yamagata Shūnan and in which many members of the Ken'en School participated, Sorai's health suddenly took a turn for the worse, and in the first month of 1728 (Kyōhō 13) his life ended. If we take into consideration that the Ogyū family was long-lived (his father Hōan and his elder brother Hokkei both lived on until over eighty), we cannot but say that Sorai died too soon.

An even greater problem than that Sorai's classical learning was hardly known during his lifetime, was the fact that he had to meet his end while his political theory regarding the contemporary political situation remained unfinished. While he was still alive, only a few of his arguments, that were recorded in *Sorai-sensei tōmonsho*, were known. It is quite true that his most famous political essay, *Seidan* 政談, written in his final years, between Kyōhō 10 (1725) and the seventh month of Kyōhō 12, was undertaken at a request for advice from Yoshimune, but it did not show the complete range of Sorai's political thought. As far as his political thought was concerned, therefore, it should rather be seen as an "unfinished" book.

For instance, in Kyōhō 11, as he was writing *Seidan*, he also wrote *Taimon*[43] 対問 ("In answer to a question"). He wrote it in response to a request for advice from a high official of the *bakufu*, helping the latter to touch up the inscription on the stele that had been erected on the bank of the River Sakawa for the sacrifice to Yu 禹祀 (*U shi*). In this composition, Sorai expressed the opinion that Shinto and Buddhism are useful devices in governing. Again, among the compositions and letters from Kyōhō 10 (1725) and later, included in *Sorai-shū*, we also find accounts of Christianity[44] and of the system of Shinto priests for the worship of ancestors.[45] All these afford glimpses of his interest in religious policy.

---

[43] Text in *Sorai-shū* 17:8b-10b (pp. 176–177).

[44] See his *Kijin jippen batsu* 畸人十篇跋 ("Postface of Ten Pieces about Eccentrics"); text in *Sorai-shū ishū*, pp. 358–360 (N.B. The *Ishū* is in manuscript, so not paginated).

[45] These are *Shō Shikin shinnshu seido o tou ni kotau* 答松子錦問神主制度 ("In answer to Shō Shikin's questions about the system of Shinto priests"), text in *Sorai-shū* 28: 17a-21b (pp. 308–310), and *An Tanpaku ni fuku-su, dai-go sho* 復安澹泊第五書 ("Answer to An Tanpaku, fifth letter"), text in *Sorai-shū* 28:10b-12b (pp. 304–305). The first text is dated Kyōhō 8/9/22 (1723).

Just at that time, from Kyōhō 8 (1723) until Kyōhō 17 (1732), Sorai's patron Kuroda Naokuni was *sōjaban* ("Master of Ceremonies") and *jisha bugyō* ("Superintendent of Temples and Shrines"). When we take that into account, we can no longer conclude that Sorai's interest in religious affairs resulted from his private curiosity. In the same way, his writings on the military arts such as *Kenroku* (see above), quite possibly, were not the outcome of the heightened "love for military lore" that Hattori Nankaku lamented. It is not clear whether he had in fact been consulted, but it is quite conceivable that Sorai foresaw future consultations and that, before he started on *Seidan*, he had been envisaging a new political system and had, with that system in mind, been thinking about military and religious matters.

It is unlikely that Sorai's audience with Yoshimune in the fourth month of Kyōhō 12 marked the end of his career; it should rather have assured him of the beginning of a rapid rise. Because of his death, however, his ideas on politics remained unfinished and disappeared into the obscurity of history even more promptly than his studies of the Classics.

Sorai's life certainly did not go smoothly. Although favourable occasions did come along for him to present to the world his "study of ancient words and phrases" and his "political theory" ("Sorai's Teachings"), he had to let them pass by on account of changes in his environment or because of his illnesses. If "unfortunate" is the word, he had an unfortunate life. After his death, however, Sorai's scholarship became known throughout the whole of Japan, and even in the Korean kingdom and in Qing China, thanks to the exertions of his disciples of the Ken'en School. And his unfinished political thought, precisely because it *was* unfinished, came to be highly appreciated in the modern age as the precursor of "Modernization." If we think of it in this way, maybe we will have to call Sorai a "fortunate thinker," who was blessed in his disciples and readers.

Bibliography

Hiraishi Naoaki 平石直昭. 1984. *Ogyū Sorai nenpu kō* 荻生徂徠年譜考. Tokyo: Heibonsha.

Kornicki, Peter. 2014. "From *Liuyu yanyi* to *Rikuyu engi taii*: Turning a Vernacular Chinese Text into a Moral Textbook in Edo-period Japan." In Matthias Hayek, and Annick Horiuchi, eds. *Listen, Copy, Read. Popular Learning in Early Modern Japan*. Brill's Japanese Studies Library 46, 205–225. Leiden: Brill.

Ogyū Sorai 荻生徂徠. 1978. *Gakuryō ryōken* 学寮了簡. Nihon Jurin Sōsho 日本儒林叢書 vol. 3. Rpt. Tokyo: Ōtori Shuppan.

Ogyū Sorai. 1986. *Sorai-shū* 徂徠集. Hiraishi Naoaki, ed. & intr. Kinsei Juka Bunshū Shūsei 近世儒家文集集成 vol. 3. Tokyo: Perikansha.

Sawai Keiichi 澤井啓一, Okamoto Mitsuo 岡本光生, Aihara Kōsaku 相原耕作, Takayama Daiki 高山大毅, trans. & annot. 2016. *Sorai-shū, Jo-rui* 徂徠集 序類1. Tōyō Bunko 東洋文庫 877. Tokyo: Heibonsha; id. *Jo-rui 2*. 2017. Tōyō Bunko 880. Tokyo: Heibonsha.

Yakazu Dōmei 矢数道明. 1982. *Kinsei Kanpō igakushi: Manase Dōsan to sono gakutō* 近世漢方医学史―曲直瀬道三とその学統. Tokyo: Meicho Shuppan.

Chapter 11
Sorai's Theory of Learning

Kojima Yasunori

1 Introduction

Why do people study? They do it in order to become a Sage. As Zhu Xi (1130–1200) taught, "One can become a Sage through study." In other words, every human being can reach the level of "Sage" through the medium of study. The reason is that "Principles" (*li* 理) are present in all things of the outside world, but are also equally present within the human heart. If we continue our efforts to investigate, on the one hand, the "Principles" that are within the things of the outside world (*kakubutsu kyūri* 格物窮理) and, on the other, to concentrate our minds and to scrutinize the "Principles" that are present within our hearts (*kyokei* 居敬, *zonshin jikei* 存心持敬), then, eventually, the highest "Principle," that keeps the whole of this cosmos together, will become clear.

Zhu Xi had changed the meaning of the concept "Sages," which originally referred to a ruler who was an ideal king, into "a man of character," which could be reached by anyone through study. One aspect of Zhu Xi's way of thinking was that it stimulated each person's individuality and awakening. The reason was that, basing oneself on Principle, one could from there relativize everything else. It is, for instance, exemplified in the following statement of Satō Naokata 佐藤直方 (1650–1719), who was a follower of Zhu Xi.

> When scholars do not believe their own principles, they are not true scholars. It is all right, as far as it goes, to believe in the Sages and Wise Ones, but that is not as important as believing in one's own principle.[1]

---

[1] See Satō Naokata, *Gakudan zatsuroku* 学談雑録 (*Unzōroku* 韞蔵録 3; *Satō Naokata zenshū* vol. 1, p. 126).

Kojima Yasunori (✉)
International Christian University, Mitaka, Tokyo, Japan
e-mail: kojima@icu.ac.jp

© Springer Nature Switzerland AG 2019
W. J. Boot, Takayama Daiki (eds.), *Tetsugaku Companion to Ogyū Sorai*,
Tetsugaku Companions to Japanese Philosophy 2,
https://doi.org/10.1007/978-3-030-15475-2_11

Here, basing oneself on "one's own principle," i.e., on the "principle" that one has grasped oneself, is regarded as taking precedence over the belief in the Sages and Wise Ones.

As if he had foreseen the doctrinal possibilities of this trend of Zhu Xi's teachings and the dangerous situation that they would cause when realized, Ogyū Sorai observed:

> Confucians of later generations revered knowledge and did their best to investigate Principle, and thus the Way of the Ancient Kings and of Confucius was destroyed. The harm of investigating Principle is that one regards Heaven and the spirits as not worthy of fear, and that thus one arrogantly establishes oneself [as an] independent [entity] between Heaven and Earth. This is the common illness of the Confucians of later generations. [Is there any other word for it than] "Above Heaven and below Heaven, I alone am worthy of respect?[2]

In other words, in the attitude of dealing with the world by basing oneself in everything on Principle, Sorai discerned a tendency to fall into self-centredness in the bad sense of the word. He feared that such a self-centred way of looking at things would slight the authority of the Sages; that it would eventually negate the belief in "Heaven" as the highest reality in the cosmos, and in the "spirits," who were presented as "the people's wisdom"; that, in the end, it would destroy "the Way of the Ancient Kings and of Confucius" (the Confucian culture). When you asked Sorai, it was impossible for each individual to give his own judgment in regard to Principle and to prove objectively that that judgment was not "a private opinion" or a "supposition." He concluded that "there is no fixed criterion for Principle."

In this way, Sorai rejected Zhu Xi's scholarly method, the core of which was "the investigation of things." In its stead, he advocated a scholarly approach in which one "made affairs affairs" on the basis of the "things" that were presented objectively, as conditions of the "teachings of the Ancient Kings."

> Methinks, the teachings of the Ancient Kings dealt with things 物, and not with principles. He who teaches with the help of things, will necessarily regard affairs as affairs 事事.[3]

In the present essay, I see it as my task to reconstruct the nature of Sorai's scholarship, which "regarded affairs as affairs," and to make a number of observations from a philosophical point of view about the problems it involves. One of the reasons is that the nature of "studying," as proposed here by Sorai, brings into the limelight something important that we, submerged as we are in our modern information society, have lost sight of.

---

[2] *Bendō* 21 (*Ogyū Sorai*, NST vol. 36, p. 206a, p. 30; cf. Tucker, *Philosophical Masterworks*, p. 159). Sorai allowed himself a little joke. As everybody knew, these words were spoken by the Buddha at the moment of his birth. (WJB)

[3] *Bendō* 16 (*Ogyū Sorai*, NST vol. 36, p. 205a, p. 26; Tucker, *Philosophical Masterworks*, p. 155).

2 "Virtue" As Bodily Knowledge

"With 'study' 学 we mean the study of the Way of the Ancient Kings"[4] is how Sorai defines "study." When he simply says "study," without specifying an object, the object that should be studied can only be "the Way of the Ancient Kings." The contents of "the Way of the Ancient Kings" were, concretely, the *Shijing, Shujing*, Rites, and Music. The tasks of the students of the "Way of the Ancient Kings" were, first, "to get for oneself" a classical erudition covering the songs of the men of old, the traces of the Ancient Kings, the rites and etiquette for all manner of situations, and the refined music of olden times; second, to try to perfect one's "virtues"; and third, to fulfil a social role commensurate with these virtues.

How did Sorai imagine the situation of someone who had absorbed a classical education and whose "virtues" had been perfected? Let us examine this point with help of a comparison Sorai made with Confucius. *Analects* 9.4 says: "There were four things of which the Master had rid himself. He had no foregone conclusions, no arbitrary predeterminations, no obstinacy, and no egoism."[5] In the Iwanami pocket edition of the *Analects*, this *passus* is explained as follows: "The Master had cut off four things. He did not have selfish feelings, he did not try to push things through, he did not cling [to the *status quo*], and he did not insist on being right."[6] This interpretation is based on Zhu Xi's annotation of the *Analects*. Most of the annotations current today have a similar translation, although the wording may be different. Apparently, it is a *passus* for which it is difficult to discover alternative interpretations. In his *Lunyu jizhu* 論語集注 ("Collected Annotations of the Analects"), Zhu Xi annotates the *passus* as follows: "*Yi* 意 means 'one's private opinions'; *bi* 必 means that 'one expects that something will certainly happen'; *gu* 固 means 'clinging to something'; *wo* 我 means 'one's own person'." In short, Zhu Xi, regarding Confucius as a man of flawless virtue, interpreted Confucius as someone who had no egoistic interests or desires, and who never flaunted his ego.

Sorai, however, separated this *passus* from Confucius' character and disposition, and regarded it as a description of a scene in which Confucius was practising the rites. He thus arrived at a truly unique interpretation, holding that "someone who does marvellously well in one or other art" has reached an appropriate mental state, and that this *passus* tells of the mental state of self-forgetfulness that Confucius reached when he executed the rites, of which he had complete mastery.

> *Yi* refers to the first stirrings of thought. It is something no man can avoid. With the Sages, too, it is the same. In such instances as 'not having any foregone conclusions' in the *passus* 'the Master had cut off four things,' the word *yi* specifically refers to Confucius' execution of the rites. Confucius' heart had become one with the rites; therefore, when he executed these rites,

---

[4] See *Benmei* 2 (*Ogyū Sorai*, NST vol. 36, p. 249a, p. 164; cf. Tucker, *Philosophical Masterworks*, p. 312).

[5] In Chinese the *passus* reads: 「子絶四、毋意、毋必、毋固、毋我」. The English translation is based on Legge's translation of the *Analects*.

[6] See Kanaya Osamu 金谷治, trans. & ann., *Rongo*, Iwanami Bunko, 1963, p. 117.

it was as if he acted without volition. [The *passus*] merely describes a person *all of whose movements, in his countenance and at every turn of his body, are exactly what is proper.*[7]

Yi refers to the first stirrings of thought. Everyone has these, including the Sages. Therefore, "without thought" in the present *passus* must be interpreted as restricted to the scene of Confucius execution of the rites. It describes how all of Confucius' actions are in agreement with the "Rites" and how completely he has become one with them.

> When things happen, we respond to them through the rites; [this response] seems to be [automatic, and] not to pass through thought. Therefore, it says 'without volition.' When [things] change, then the rites change accordingly. We did not expect [to have to change] beforehand, and we do not stick to [the previous rite] afterwards. Therefore, it says 'without arbitrary predeterminations, or obstinacy.' The only thing that exists is the rites of the Ancient Kings. There exists no Confucius anymore. Therefore, it says 'no ego'.[8]

When a certain situation manifested itself, Confucius reacted to it efficiently through the rites. His reaction did not first have to be made conscious; his actions followed without thought, easily. Therefore, it says "without thought." If the situation changed, the rites changed, too, and he reacted to the new situation with these changed rites. Because he was not captive of a consciousness that dictated that, within the continuous stream of the execution of a rite, this should come next, and then that, it says "without arbitrary predeterminations." Because he was not preoccupied with the question, after his action had been finished, whether he had done well or not, it says "without obstinacy." Because Confucius has become one with the rites – because only the rites of the Ancient Kings were there and a being called "Confucius" had disappeared, it says "without ego." It truly is an original interpretation.

What Sorai tries to say here reminds one of what Herrigel tells in his book *Yumi to zen* ("The Bow and Zen"[9]). By his teacher, Awa, Herrigel is taught to shoot his bow "without intent" (*mushin*), but time and again he is criticized because he is "intentionally without intent." Though Herrigel is troubled by this, he throws himself into his training, and eventually he learns how to be "without intent." He gives an impressive description of his state of mind at that moment: "Is it I who pulls the

---

[7] Quotation from *Benmei* 2, (*Ogyū Sorai, NST* vol. 36, p. 244a, p. 148; cf. Tucker, *Philosophical Masterworks*, p. 294). The final characters 「動容周旋中禮者」 are quoted from *Mencius* VII.B 79. Legge translates the complete section as follows: "Mencius said, 'Yao and Shun were what they were by nature; Tang and Wu were so by returning to natural virtue. *When all the movements, in the countenance and every turn of the body, are exactly what is proper,* that shows the extreme degree of the complete virtue. Weeping for the dead should be from real sorrow, and not because of the living. The regular path of virtue is to be pursued without any bend, and from no view to emolument. The words should all be necessarily sincere, not with any desire to do what is right. The superior man performs the law of right, and thereby waits simply for what has been appointed.'"

[8] Quotation from *Rongo-chō: Shikan* 論語徵: 子罕 9, *Ogyū Sorai zenshū* 4, p. 375.

[9] This is the Japanese translation of Eugen Herrigel (1884–1955), *Zen in der Kunst des Bogenschiessens*. The first Japanese translation appeared in 1969; a third, revised edition appeared in 1981.

bow? Or is it the bow that draws me to the full? Am I the one who aims at the target? Or is it the target that hits me?"[10]

In all kinds of activities, not only in rites and etiquette, but also in the martial arts, sports, acting, or musical performances, you stumble when you are seized by sundry thoughts and consciousness. In order to reach the stage wherein you are liberated from consciousness and are able to execute a complete action or series of gestures without intent, there is no other option than, as the popular phrase says, "to learn with your body" – not through understanding with your head, but through practice. For instance, when you have learned, as knowledge, the sequence of ritual acts for making and serving tea, it will not turn into flowing, naturally beautiful behaviour, if this string of ritual acts has not, through unremitting practice, been turned into bodily knowledge. In this sense, "learning" as Sorai uses the word, implies practice, as is suggested by such related words as "exercise" (*keiko*) and "training" (*shugyō*).

In the case of Sorai, "knowledge" and "action" must be taken as simultaneous and united; he was clearly convinced that "knowledge" deepened precisely through the accumulation of "action," and that this was the way to arrive at true "knowledge." Sorai says:

> "Action" means the energetic practice of something. When we have energetically practised something for a long time and have attained perfect mastery, only then we will have true knowledge of it. Therefore, knowledge does not necessarily come first, and action does not necessarily come last.[11]

In Chinese, there are words like "to obtain corporally" or "to know corporally," and in Japanese we have the expression "it adds itself to the body" (*mi ni tsuku*). Sorai took up this problem of learning things corporally with greater self-awareness than any other Confucian scholar in early modern Japan.

He carried this through admirably in his explanation of the word "virtue." In his *Collected Commentaries on the Analects*, Zhu Xi glosses *de* (德 "virtue") as *de* (得 "to obtain"), and glosses this as "it means to obtain in the heart." In the chapter *Xiangyin jiuyi* 鄉飲酒義 ("The Meaning of the Drinking Festivity in the Districts") of the *Liji*, there is a passage that says "virtue one obtains in the body."[12] Zhu Xi interprets the word "virtue" in this passage as something that has to do with the concept of "personality," and goes out of his way to replace the character *shen*身 ("body") with the character *xin*心 ("heart"). Sorai, on the other hand, follows the original "virtue one obtains *in the body*" of the *Liji*, and criticizes Zhu Xi's interpretation "to obtain in the heart."

> Zhu's commentary that 'The word "virtue" means "to obtain"; one practises the Way and obtains it in one's heart' is different like heaven and earth, when one compares it with the [original phrase in the] *Liji*, which says 'When one has obtained the Rites and Music in one's body, one calls this "virtue".' The character *shen* ("body") in the ancient books always

[10] See *Yumi to Zen*, Inatomi Eijirō & Ueda Takeshi, trans., p. 109.

[11] *Benmei* 2 (*Ogyū Sorai*, NST vol. 36, p. 250a, p. 167; cf. Tucker, *Ogyū Sorai's Philosophical Masterworks*, p. 316).

[12] *Liji* ch. 45, 6. The operative words are 「德也者, 得於身也」, which Legge less than convincingly translates as "Virtue is that which is the characteristic of the person." (WJB)

refers to the self. The Buddhists posited [the difference between] "body" and "heart," and [since then] scholars have disliked the simplicity [of the ancient usage]; that is all there is to it. The Rites and Music are the arts of the Way. The arts of the Way are on the outside. Through study, we perfect virtue in ourselves. Therefore, it says 'to have obtained it in the body.' This shows that one must not change even one character in the words of the ancient books.[13]

First, Sorai here claims that the way of thinking that separates *shen* and *xin*, attaching importance to the "heart" that is distinguished from the "body," and considers the heart to be the substance of the self, has emerged from Buddhist theory. Confucian scholars, too, got caught in this dualistic way of thinking in terms of "body" and "heart"; they came to regard the "heart" as important and to dislike the "superficiality" of the "body." "Anciently," however, "no one ever used body and heart as opposite terms."[14] In the ancient terminology, body and heart were understood as being one unified whole, and "body" in this sense was called "the self." And he, Sorai himself, followed this sound way of thinking as demonstrated in the ancient terminology. "Virtue should never be talked of separately from the heart. If, however, one only talks of it only in terms of the heart, how could it be sufficient to be regarded as virtue?" This is how Sorai understood the relation between the two. It shows that he was clearly aware of the problem of corporality. "Virtue" means that we have "studied," "made our own," and "obtained in our body" a cultural norm ("Rites and Music") that objectively exists outside ourselves. When we speak of "virtue" on this level, we speak of empirical facts that are obtained once we have mastered set routines (*kata*) or skills (*waza*), and that cannot be fully expressed in words. It should be called corporal, wordless knowledge,[15] carved into our bodies.

There exists a character 躾, which in Japanese is read *shitsuke*. It is not a Chinese character, but a character made in Japan – a combination of the characters "body" and "beautiful." What it shows is deeply meaningful. The word *shi-tsuke* means to teach manners and etiquette to someone in such a way that, as the word says, they "cleave to the body." The character became common with the spread of warrior etiquette, at the end of the Middle Ages (1192–1600) and in the beginning of the Early Modern Period (1600–1868). The invention of this character was inspired by the idea of coordinating the movements of the *body* in a *beautiful* way, but on a deeper level the intention will have been to mould the inward side of humans through the beautiful coordination of the movements of their bodies. In this sense, the "teaching of Rites and Music" that Sorai emphasized accurately corresponds to this *shitsuke*.

In the above, Sorai interpreted "virtue" not as something one obtains "in the heart," but as something obtained "in the body." As regards the method to accomplish

---

[13] See *Rongo-chō: Isei* 為政 2, *Ogyū Sorai zenshū* vol. 3, p. 409.

[14] See *Benmei* 1 (*Ogyū Sorai*, NST vol. 36, p. 212b, p. 50; cf. Tucker, *Philosophical Masterworks*, p. 182).

[15] Regarding the nature of this kind of knowledge, which is "carved into the body," Gilbert Ryle's "knowing how" as opposed to "knowing that" (*The Concept of Mind*, 1949), or Micheal Polanyi's "tacit knowing" (*The Tacit Dimension*, 1966) contain useful suggestions.

this, the key words Sorai emphasizes are "imitation" (*mohō*), "intensive practice" (*shūjuku*), and "thought" (*shiryo*). Below, I will consider these terms.

3 Imitation, Practice, Thought

How *can* one turn Rites and Music into corporal knowledge? Sorai maintained that "imitation" (倣傚 *hōkō*; 模倣 *mohō*) was the beginning and the foundation of learning anything. "Rites and Music" are intrinsically beautiful. Humans will try to imitate beautiful things. The Sages, having perceived this human urge for imitation, created "Rites and Music." Through the attractiveness of these beautiful archetypes they attempted to influence the people from the inside, without the people noticing it or knowing it: Do not argue, just follow the archetypes that "Rites and Music" are pointing at and imitate those. "When Confucius, joining both hands in front of his breast, put his right hand on top, his disciples, too, put their right hands on top."[16] Confucius called this "a desire to learn" (a "wish to imitate," in Legge's translation).

Those who learn calligraphy do the same. They always "imitate" the examples in Wang Xizhi's *Lantingxu* and *Huangtingjing*.[17] They do not do this with the intent to produce a forgery, they do it because this is the intrinsic nature of "the way of study." In calligraphy, and in painting, too, you cannot begin by producing calligraphy in an original style, or unique paintings. That only becomes possible through a process of persistent copying and sketching, in order to acquire the necessary skills and techniques. As is expressed in the words "You enter into a frame and emerge from the frame; then, for the first time, you will attain freedom,"[18] creativity only blossoms after a learning process during which one humbly trains oneself in the traditional styles.

In his account of the study of Rites and Music, Sorai, too, emphasizes the importance of this kind of imitation. In the first stage of your studies, it does not matter that you "plagiarize and imitate." When, "for a long time," you have imitated the examples, you will naturally "change" into the mould of the example and what was

---

[16]Reference to *Liji*, ch. 3: *Tangong* 檀弓 1; Legge translates as follows: "Confucius was standing (once) with his disciples, having his hands joined across his breast, and the right hand uppermost. They also all placed their right hands uppermost. He said to them, 'You do so from your wish to imitate me, but I place my hands so, because I am mourning for an elder sister.' On this they all placed their left hands uppermost (according to the usual fashion)."

[17]Wang Xizhi 王羲之 (303–361) is a famous calligrapher. His compositions *Lantingxu* 蘭亭序 ("Preface of [the poems composed in] the Orchid Pavilion") and *Huangtingjing* 黄庭経 ("Classic of the Yellow Garden"), as written in his own hand, are examples of the semi-cursive and square styles of calligraphy.

[18]Quoted from *Soō kuketsu* 祖翁口訣. The words are attributed to Matsuo Bashō 松尾芭蕉 (1644–1694).

an "external" mould will become "one with me." "Therefore, those who regard imitation as a disease do not understand the way of studying."[19]

In this way, Sorai made others aware of the meaning of imitation – as a method to imprint the "mould" of the example onto one's own body and to internalise it. His awareness of the importance of imitation stemmed from his own experiences, gathered as he advocated the method of "ancient words and phrases"; as he insisted that the Japanese way of reading Chinese should be abolished and that Chinese should be read according to the Chinese syntax; and as he exerted himself at learning Chinese as a second language.

How thoroughly imitation was practised in Sorai's school, even in the creation of poetry, is shown clearly in the following quotation:

> If you want to study the poetry of the Tang, you must divide the words of the poems of the *Tangshixuan* 唐詩選 ("Selection of Tang poems") into categories and extract them. If you want to study the poems of the *Wenxuan* 文選 ("Selection of literature"), you must divide the words of its poems into categories and extract them. Keep each [category] in a different box, so that they cannot be mixed up. If you want to write a word, take it out of those boxes, and if it is not there, give up. You must not look for it elsewhere. Do this for a long time, and [your poems] will naturally resemble [the Chinese ones].[20]

When you want to study the poetry of the Tang, do not pursue such vague things like the spirit of Tang poetry; write poems that in appearance and formal aspects resemble the "words" of the poems of the Tang. "The way to learn to write poetry and prose is to make the words resemble [the Chinese models]; that is the best."[21] Daily extract the "words" that are used in the poems of *Tangshixuan*, string these together, and in that way compose your poems. If someone criticizes this as "plagiarism and imitation," he is "someone who does not know the way of studying."

Such poetry and prose, in Sorai-style and full of patches, was sarcastically described by Ōta Nanpo 大田南畝 (1749–1823) as "cuttings of ancient words and phrases."[22] If, however, we trace back Nanpo's own scholarly affiliation, it turns out that he was connected to Sorai.[23] Precisely because Nanpo himself had received a training in the "school of cuttings of ancient words and phrases," he, of all people, had been able to become the central figure of that mad verse boom of the Tenmei Era. For instance, in his *Tsūshisen shōchi* 通詩選笑知 Nanpo makes really clever parodies of *Tangshixuan*; here, the strengths of the "school of cuttings of ancient words and phrases "are fully displayed.[24]

---

[19] Quoted from Sorai's first letter to Hori Keizan 堀景山 (1688–1757), 答屈景山 (*Ogyū Sorai*, NST vol. 36, p. 531a).

[20] See *Yakubun sentei*, *Ogyū Sorai zenshū* vol. 2 (Misuzu Shobō), p. 561.

[21] *Sorai-sensei tōmonsho*, *Ogyū Sorai zenshū* vol. 1 (Misuzu Shobō), p. 470.

[22] Quoted from the preface of Ōta Nanpo 大田南畝, *Neboke-sensei shokō* 寝惚先生初稿. See *Neboke-sensei bunshū*, Shin Nihon Koten Bungaku Taikei, p. 4. Nanpo not only wrote "mad verse" 狂歌 in Japanese, but he also led the boom of writing "mad Chinese poems" 狂詩 of the Tenmei Era (1781–1789).

[23] The scholarly affiliation is: Ogyū Sorai > Dazai Shundai > Matsuzaki Kankai 松崎観海 (1725–1775; *KGS* 4076) > Ōta Nanpo.

[24] See my "'Seijin no michi' to 'Shikidō'," *Ajia bunka kenkyū* 16, separate volume (2007).

What philosophical meaning, then, will "imitation" have had for Sorai? Of importance in this connection is Sorai's warning against the folly of abstracting the "meaning" from the "form" and of concentrating only on understanding the "meaning." As the reader will readily see if he considers the intellectual operation that we execute when we understand a foreign language after having translated it into our mother tongue, understanding an object through its "meaning" implies that we understand the object while maintaining our own logical structure and framework of thought, and stay inside that framework. Contrarily, the methodological attempt to try and make the "form" of the words resemble the original, implies that we reject our own, already established logical structure and intellectual framework, and follow the structure and framework of the other, whether we like it or not.

One aspect, therefore, of radical imitation is that it automatically forces us to demolish our own frameworks. The true meaning of radical imitation is *not* that we establish a position of subject *versus* object, and from that standpoint imitate the object, *but* that we abandon such subjective standpoints and become one with the object itself; that we abandon that by which we stand, slip into and stay within the object, and try and become one with it. It must have been philosophically meaningful considerations like these, that were at the back of Sorai's emphasis on imitation.

Imitation makes no sense when it is not repeated and habitual. Thus, at the same time as imitation, Sorai emphasizes "practice" and "exercise." In *Yakubun sentei*, Sorai explains the meaning of the character 習 ("to practise") as: "To practise continuously. ... 学習 ("to learn and practise") means to practise something many times and become adept at it." Again, the meaning of the character 慣 ("to get used to") he defines as "get used to doing something through doing it often. It has the same meaning as he character 習." In other words, Sorai interpreted *narau* 習 ("to [practise and] learn") as *nareru* 慣 ("to get used to").

The word *xi* (J. *narau*) occurs in the very first phrase of the *Analects*, where it says 学而時習之, Sorai did not interpret this as "to display from time to time what one has learned"; he went further and interpreted it as always "placing oneself bodily within the teachings of the Ancient Kings," getting used to and becoming familiar with them, and turning them into one's own routines. "Practice" was a continuous process through which one habituated one's "body" to the "teachings of the Ancient Kings" and waited ("It will become clear naturally") for experience to mature.

Through this type of "practice" it was possible to invite the "things" that extend themselves endlessly beyond the logic of language, i.e., the concrete archetypes ("Rites and Music") that the Ancient Kings presented as the "conditions of teaching,"[25] into "one's own body" and to make them "one's own." After you have "practised for a long time," the "things" that extend themselves outside of the self will naturally come to you and become "your own"; this is the interpretation Sorai and his school give of "going to the things and extending one's knowledge":

---

[25] In the annotation of this phrase in *Benmei* (*Ogyū Sorai*, NST vol. 36, p. 179), "conditions" (*jōken*) is explained as "the concrete content; things and affairs."

Having practised those things for a long time, what we [seek to] preserve will be perfected. This is meant with the phrase 'things will come to us.' When we first receive instruction, we do not yet possess the things within ourselves. This is compared with [things] that still are over there and have not yet come here. Once [our practice] has become perfect, the things become our possessions. This is compared to [things] that have come to us from over there. This means that we do not need to exert ourselves. Therefore, it says 'things come [to us].' The character 格 means 'to come.' When we obtain the concrete contents of the teachings in ourselves, then knowledge will naturally be clear. This is meant [with the words] 'knowledge arrives.' Again, this means that we do not need to exert ourselves.[26]

Zhu Xi read the characters *gewu*[27] as "to go to the things," which he interpreted as inquiring into the principles of things and affairs. Wang Yangming (1472–1528) read them as "to rectify things," which he interpreted as making things and affairs correct. Sorai, on the other hand, gives his own, original reading of "things have come." This reading of Sorai's deserves attention. In the first stage of learning something, "the things are not yet present inside ourselves," i.e., the "things" have not yet adhered to our "body." However, "after we have practised for a long time, they become our own," i.e., in the end, when we have become proficient, the objects of our study, which were outside, have become internalised inside our bodies. That is the meaning of "things come to us." Once the outside "things" that we must learn have been internalised inside our bodies, an opening-up of new knowledge will come to us "naturally"; that is meant with "knowledge comes to us."

What in the *Great Learning* is called *gewu* just means that one studies and practises something, becomes proficient at it, naturally obtains one or other thing, and that then knowledge arises.[28]

This is how Sorai argued the importance of "imitation" and "practice" within the process of learning "Rites and Music." In his words: "How great is practice! It is the one thing in which man is superior to heaven!"[29] If you imitate the archetypes that the Rites and Music of the Ancient Kings point at, and "practise these for a long time," then, in due time, "habits will become heavenly nature" – i.e., habits will form a second nature. Sorai regarded the force of habits as extremely important.

Generally speaking, when we become accustomed to a certain state of affairs, it turns into a habit that has, for us, an ambivalent significance. On the one hand, that habituation increases and perfects our natural powers. On the other hand, habituation invites mental laziness and brings forth stereotype ideas. As Montaigne lamented: "Whichever way I want to go, I will have to break down one or another fence of habits. That is how closely habits obstruct our way."[30] Sorai was fully aware that within the whole of human mental activities, habituation has an ambivalent

---

[26] Quoted from *Benmei* 2 (*Ogyū Sorai*, NST vol. 36, p. 254a, p. 179; cf. Tucker, *Philosophical masterworks*, pp. 330–331).

[27] *Ge wu* 格物 is the last (or the first) of the Eight Wires of *Great Learning*.

[28] Quoted from *Benmei* 2 (*Ogyū Sorai*, NST vol. 36, p. 250a, p. 167; cf. Tucker, *Philosophical masterworks*, p. 317).

[29] *Ken'en zuihitsu* 4, *Ogyū Sorai zenshū* vol. 17 (Misuzu Shobō), p. 306.

[30] See Montaigne, *Essais*, Livre I, Chapitre 36, first sentence.

character, and that, therefore, in cases when it functions negatively, it can also cause humans to formulate prejudices. For that reason, Sorai regarded the role that habits played as even more important than our innate, heavenly nature ("How great is practice! It is the one thing in which man is superior to heaven!").[31] He was on his guard, however, against the inertia that habit induces, having realised that it led to "tightly glued practices," "solidified conventions," and "harmful habits."

The element in Sorai's theory of learning that allowed one to avoid the habitualization of practice was "reflection." Together with "persistent practice," Sorai also regarded the working of "reflection" as extremely important. In Sorai's theory of learning, it is "reflection" that prevents "practice" from becoming routine and from solidifying, and that prompts a continuous renewal of "practice." Let us, at the end of this article, reflect more deeply on this point.

On the one hand, custom heightens our capabilities, but on the other, it invites mental ease and sloth. Sorai had remarked that the routinization of habit led to "tightly glued practice" and "harmful habits." For that reason, he emphasized the necessity of "thinking" – of reflecting subjectively on the meaning that was contained within Rites and Music, instead of studying and practising them aimlessly.

> The way of scholarship regards thinking as precious. ... Mencius said: 'To the mind belongs the office of thinking.' The reasons why man is man, is just his ability to think. Because later Confucians had no profound thoughts, they thought that 'thinking three times' was too much. They are talking nonsense.[32]

The words "... they thought that 'thinking three times' was too much" in the above quotation are based on the following section in the *Analects*: "Ji Wen thought thrice, and then acted. When the Master was informed of it, he said, 'Twice may do.'"[33] Zhu Xi comments on this passage as follows: "Gentlemen exert themselves at the investigation of principle and esteem decisive action. They have no high regard for thinking too much to no purpose."[34]

Sorai proposes an interpretation that is the complete opposite. It was not to be expected that Confucius, who held "thinking" in such high esteem, would say that thinking thrice is thinking too much. In Sorai's interpretation, Confucius intended to say: "Ji Wen is not someone who can think thrice; at best, he will manage to think twice." He adds the following comment: "In the case of small things close at hand, it is all right, even if you do not think at all, but about great and far-reaching matters one may think a hundred or a thousand times. Why should it necessarily be two or three times?"[35]

As this interpretation indicates, Sorai regarded reflection as important, and imposed it both on himself and on his disciples. He loved using phrases like "I think

---

[31] *Ken'en zuihitsu*, *Ogyū Sorai zenshū* vol. 17, p. 306.

[32] *Benmei* 2 (*Ogyū Sorai*, NST vol. 36, p. 244a, p. 149; cf. Tucker, *Philosophical Masterworks*, pp. 294–295). The reference to Mencius is to *Mengzi* 6A.15; the translation is Legge's..

[33] *Lunyu* 5.20; the translation is Legge's.

[34] See *Lunyu jizhu* 3:7b.

[35] See *Rongo-chō* 5, *Ogyū Sorai zenshū* vol. 3, p. 546.

about it, think about it, and then think about it again. If I think about it and do not get it, then the gods and spirits will get it,"[36] or "Doubt and reflection steamed in turn will give rise to wonderful wisdom."[37] They tell to what extent Sorai was a man of thought. The image of Sorai thinking will have been a frightening sight; in the words of the modern philosopher Nishida Kitarō 西田幾多郎 (1870–1945): "He truly thought as a thing, and acted as a thing."[38] According to one of his important disciples, Dazai Shundai 太宰春台 (1680–1747), "thinking too much" had been the cause that shortened his master's life, who, when in good health, worried twice as much as other people.[39]

Sorai held that "the instruction in Rites and Music" would induce people to "think"; in his words:

> Well now, when you speak to them, they understand. When you do not speak to them, they do not understand. Although, in the case of Rites and Music, there is no speech, why is it that they are superior to language for [the purpose of] instructing people? The reason is that they transform them. When people have practised them and reached proficiency, they have already, secretly, changed their minds and bodies into [their likeness], even though they have not yet understood them. What, if in the end they do not understand? [Does it matter?] When you speak to people and thus make them understand, they think that the meaning [of these words] is all there is to it. They do not reflect on what remains [unsaid]. The harm [words] do lies in that they cause people not to think; that is all. Because in the case of Rites and Music there is no speech, people will not understand them, unless they reflect upon them themselves. If, perhaps, someone has thought about them but has not understood, [it is a case of] "I can indeed do nothing with him"; he [should] extensively study the other rites. When his studies are extensive, and he has polished his knowledge of various [rites], then, in a natural way, he will come to understand.[40]

This quotation shows how Sorai truly thought of everything. Changing people through "Rites and Music" is superior to preaching to them with words (here, Sorai was probably thinking of the moralistic discourses of the orthodox Neo-Confucian school). The reason is that, "when one has practised them and reached proficiency," one's body has already agreed to them, bypassing the dimension of linguistic understanding. Moreover, pointing out things through language has the harmful effect that it does not make people think of other things, apart from what has been pointed out, because it is so clear. "Rites and Music," on the other hand, do not say anything, and therefore you have to piece together yourself what they mean. "Rites and Music," which are "a teaching without words," stimulate man's inclination to reflect. If you have reflected and still do not understand, you should extensively study other rites; having studied them, you should think about them, and having thought about

---

[36] *Guanzi* 管子 49 (Neiye 内業), 6.

[37] 「疑思交蒸、靈慧以生」, quoted from *Yakubun sentei, Ogyū Sorai zenshū* vol. 2, p. 546.

[38] Quoted from Nishida Kitarō, *Nihon Bunka no mondai*, p. 121: 「真に物となって考へ、物となって行ふ」.

[39] See *Shishien manpitsu* 紫芝園漫筆 9.

[40] *Benmei* 1 (*Ogyū Sorai*, NST 36, p. 219, pp. 70–71; cf. Tucker, *Philosophical Masterworks*, pp. 205–206). The phrase between quotation marks is quoted from *Lunyu* 9.24 and 15.16. The final clause of both sections is 「吾末如之何也已矣」; the translation is Legge's.

them, you must study them. In a continuous process of alternating between "study" and "thought," you will reach understanding naturally. "The way of scholarship [implies that] one desires to reach understanding oneself."[41]

The type of study we see here is different from present-day education, which provides excessive service to the pupils and teaches them every step of the way. It is, rather, a very thorough-going variant of the unkind (?) type of education that formerly prevailed in the world of the traditional performing arts such as Nō and Kabuki, or of traditional craftsmen. There, the master did not teach anything at all, and the pupils were expected to steal the master's art through observation and imitation.

Summarizing the above, the strong point of Sorai's "teaching of Rites and Music" – by him presented in the form of "affairs" and "things" – was that it urged students to start thinking for themselves. Sorai most certainly did not think that all humans qualified as subjects who could think for themselves. Statements like "The intelligent persons will think and get [the rites], and the stupid persons will follow [the rites] without understanding them,"[42] or "a gentleman [who follows the Way of the Sages] will thereby perfect his virtue, and a small man will thereby perfect his customs"[43] demonstrate that Sorai made a distinction between intelligent persons (gentlemen) and stupid persons (small men). He acknowledged that men of the first category had a conscious, active involvement with Rites and Music, but he was not prepared to acknowledge that the latter category had an involvement that was more than passive and routine. Such a view of man is in many respects problematic, but if we forget about that for the moment, one extremely important point remains, and that is that Sorai insisted that people should "reflect" personally about the "affairs" and "things" that had been put before them, and should "get for themselves" their meaning and the interrelationship between them.

The task Sorai imposed on the student was to immerse his "body" into the "Rites and Music of the Former Kings," to be "tranquil and contented"[44]; he was to be "calm and relaxed" while waiting for "practice to become nature," and for "maturity" to come about spontaneously. At the same time, however, he did not think that those who sought to involve themselves actively with learning should be satisfied with merely entrusting themselves to the routine behaviour of "practice." The indispensable pillar, which gave Sorai's learning its form and shape, was "reflection," in the sense of an awareness of the inner meaning of "practice" that had become one with the "body," and in the sense of a guarantee of uninterrupted renewal of "practice" from a lower to a higher plain.

---

[41] *Rongo-chō* 7, *Ogyū Sorai zenshū* vol. 3 (Misuzu Shobō), p. 610.

[42] *Bendō* 22 (*Ogyū Sorai*, NST vol. 36, p. 207a, p. 32; cf. Tucker, *Philosophical Masterworks*, p. 162).

[43] *Bendō* 22, ibid.; *Gakusoku* 5 (*Ogyū Sorai*, NST vol. 36, p. 257b, p. 193; cf. Minear, "Ogyū Sorai's Instructions for Students," p. 24).

[44] *Sorai-shū* 24, here quoted from *Ogyū Sorai*, NST vol. 36, p. 512a.

4 Closing Remarks

Above, we have examined the meaning of "imitation," "persistent practice," and "reflection" from the viewpoint of an understanding of the body, and we have examined the nature of Sorai's ideas about "study" through an exploration of the inter-relations between these terms. Simply put, Sorai understood "study" as "acquiring in one's body" certain fixed patterns (= the Way of the ancient kings) through "imitation," "persistent practice," and "reflection."

If one defines the nature of "study" in such a way, one invites the criticism that scholarship should be something different from adding to one's "body" an established system of knowledge; that true scholarship is characterised by intellectual courage and a free, critical spirit, which have liberated themselves from all dogma's and continuously undermine the foundations on which these stand.

In some sense, this criticism is correct. Nevertheless, having acknowledged that, I still maintain that the insight contained in Sorai's understanding of "study" as I have examined it in the present essay is important. Its importance lies in the fact that it urges us to reconsider the present-day situation of scholarship and education, which start from the consciousness of individual and all too rashly wants to turn the self into an autonomous subject who perceives and criticizes, while it shows hardly any interest in *forming* a self by internalising all kinds of cultural standards through the study of a classical culture.

Bibliography

Dazai Shundai 太宰春台. 1927–1935. *Shishien manpitsu* 紫芝園漫筆. In *Sūbun sōsho* 崇文叢書, 44–48. Tokyo: Sūbun'in.

Herrigel, Eugen. 1948. *Zen in der Kunst des Bogenschiessens*; (Japanese translation) *Yumi to Zen*. Inatomi Eijirō & Ueda Takeshi, trans. 1956. Tokyo: Fukumura Shoten.

Kanaya Osamu 金谷治, trans. & ann. 1963. *Rongo* 論語. Iwanami Bunko. Tokyo: Iwanami Shoten.

Kojima Yasunori 小島康敬. 2007. "'Seijin no michi' to 'Shikidō'" 「聖人」の道と「色道」, *Ajia bunka kenkyū* 16, separate volume, 33–56.

Minear, Richard H. 1976. "Ogyū Sorai's Instructions for Students: A Translation and Commentary." *Harvard Journal of Asiatic Studies* 36: 5–81.

Nishida Kitarō 西田幾多郎. 1940. *Nihon Bunka no mondai* 日本文化の問題. Iwanami Shinsho. Tokyo: Iwanami Shoten.

Ogyū Sorai 荻生徂徠. 1973–1987. *Ogyū Sorai zenshū* 荻生徂徠全集, vols 1–4, 13, 17–18. Tokyo: Misuzu Shobō.

Ōta Nanpo 大田南畝. 1993. *Neboke-sensei bunshū* 寝惚先生文集. Nakano Mitsutoshi, Hino Tatsuo, Ibi Takashi, eds. Shin Nihon Koten Bungaku Taikei, vol. 84. Tokyo: Iwanami Shoten.

Polanyi, Micheal. 1966. *The Tacit Dimension*. Garden City, N.Y.: Anchor Books.

Ryle, Gilbert. 1949. *The Concept of Mind*. London: Hutchinson.

Satō Naokata 佐藤直方. 1979. *Satō Naokata zenshū* 全集. 3 vols. Tokyo: Perikansha.

Tucker, John A., ed. & trans. 2006. *Ogyū Sorai's Philosophical Masterworks. The Bendō and Benmei*. Asian Interactions and Comparisons. Honolulu: Hawai'i University.

Yoshikawa Kōjirō 吉川幸次郎 et al., eds. 1973. *Ogyū Sorai* 荻生徂徠. Nihon Shisō Taikei vol. 36. Tokyo: Iwanami Shoten.

Chapter 12
Gods, Spirits and Heaven in Ogyū Sorai's Political Theory

Olivier Ansart

He wrote history, poetry, literary criticism, philosophical commentaries, treatises on language, translation, even on strategy, but Ogyū Sorai is mainly remembered today for his writings about the Way of the Ancient Kings. Those constitute – since for him the Way was the set of institutions that make the good society – what we now call a political or moral theory. Of this theory scholars, from his contemporaries to ours, have offered various interpretations, and few issues illustrate this diversity better than the understanding of the place and function of gods, spirits and heaven in his exposition of the Way.[1] This aspect of his thought is the subject of the present chapter.

I shall start by presenting the reasons some scholars have found to stress the religious dimension of his doctrine. Sorai indeed states and repeats that it would be folly to deny the existence of gods and spirits, that these are the "mind of heaven," upon which the Way cannot but be founded, and that humans need to respect all those entities with the deepest reverence (section 1). While the textual evidence to support such a "religious" reading seems plentiful, it quickly runs, I will suggest, into serious issues.

Firstly, there is the fact that all the descriptions of gods, spirits and heaven by Sorai seem to exclude the possibility that even the most gifted legislators – the ancient Sages or early Kings –, can find any indications as to what the good society ought to be, any blueprint of the Way, any prescriptive do's and don'ts (section 2).

---

[1] I shall talk of *the* Way to refer to the generic idea of *the* good society, and of *a* Way to refer to concrete incarnations of this idea. Sorai makes clear that the Way existed in different versions during the Chinese antiquity (Tucker 176; *Benmei* 211 §2), all as good as the others (*Rongo-chō*, I- 95, 117–118; *Tōmonsho*, 213; *Ken'en shichihitsu* 355).

O. Ansart (✉)
Department of Japanese Studies, University of Sydney, Camperdown, NSW, Australia
e-mail: olivier.ansart@sydney.edu.au

© Springer Nature Switzerland AG 2019
W. J. Boot, Takayama Daiki (eds.), *Tetsugaku Companion to Ogyū Sorai*,
Tetsugaku Companions to Japanese Philosophy 2,
https://doi.org/10.1007/978-3-030-15475-2_12

We shall also see that other passages of Sorai's writings suggest that gods and spirits, not to mention the Way itself, etc., are all human inventions, devised for the practical purpose of keeping society in order. There will appear a curious distinction between natural truths and validity. Finally, we shall ponder the fact that discussions of gods, spirits and heaven are very unevenly distributed in Sorai's writings. While they are constant in his commentaries on the Chinese Classics, themselves obviously replete with such discussions, they are almost totally absent when he talks about a Way for contemporary Japan – what he calls a System (*Seido*) (section 3).

The complexity that then appears should give us reason to try to understand better the place of gods, spirits and heaven in Sorai's political theory. While some scholars have been content to stress the tensions, or even the contradictions in his doctrine, I shall endeavour to produce a unified reading, capable of assigning a meaningful place to all the relevant statements. Starting with an analysis of the notion of "respect" as the respect due to non-normative constraints imposed on humans by nature or "super-nature," I argue that there are two voices, or two perspectives on the Way in Sorai's writings, that he can shift from one to another, but that he cannot announce the shift. One is the "external" perspective of the Sages, from which they can contemplate the (super)natural world outside and before the Way. This non-human world is made of the materials, beings, things and circumstances that must all be integrated in a Way – lest it quickly crumbles – so that they realize their potential and abilities in harmony. The other is the "internal" perspective of the inhabitants of a Way, where respect is only due to whatever the Sages have integrated in their Way, including, in some cases, institutions organizing the cult of gods and spirits.

Sorai takes this second, internal, perspective whenever he comments on the Canons that presented the Way, and defends, sometimes after some reinterpretation, whatever they claim. Ostensibly taking the first, external, perspective, was however, in the Confucian tradition, tantamount to a crime of *lèse majesté*, since the perpetrator was exposing himself to the accusation that he was usurping the role of the Sages. Sorai indignantly rejected this possibility, but this is exactly what he could not but do when he was outlining a radical reform of Japanese society. Obviously, pronouncements on gods, spirits and heaven will vary according to the perspective chosen. From the external perspective, gods and spirits are institutions *valid* inside the Way, but not necessarily corresponding to a *truth* outside the Way (section 5).

Lastly, I offer some suggestions on the possible reasons for the emergence of a scheme, that can look – in an obviously paradoxical or misleading way – modern or even postmodern, in that it separates the notion of truth or natural facts from that of validity. If in a Neo-Marxist way we can certainly see in this positivism a useful strategy for the *bushi* group in order to justify a power that no hard fact could justify anymore, we should also see here an example of what Max Weber called "elective affinity." I mean by this that the *bushi* society in which Sorai lived was replete with fictions or masquerades that could only discreetly be recognized as such but had to be publicly respected. Very far from the realm of the production of political theory, daily life in *bushi* society offered thus this *trope* of the separation of what was true and what was valid, that could not but find echoes in some political theories (section 6).

It should thus appear that the argument is not over a word. After all, why would the putative religious views of Sorai matter so much? My point is rather that, by naively using such an ambiguous concept, we miss the complexity of this religious dimension – and the most interesting aspect of his political theory.

1   The Seemingly Compelling Reasons for a Religious Reading

Let us call, for the sake of convenience and brevity, the interpretations of Sorai's moral and political theory that take at face value its affirmations of the existence of the ghosts and spirits, its injunctions to respect them, and its claims that the Way is founded upon them, the "religious readings." Such interpretations were already aired by Sorai's immediate or near contemporaries. Nakai Chikuzan 中井竹山 (1730–1804) and Yamagata Bantō 山片蟠桃 (1748–1821) both remarked, with little sympathy, Sorai's apparent fascination for gods and spirits. Much more recently such seems to have been the interpretations of several amongst the most respected students of Sorai's work,[2] – even if it is unclear whether the alleged religiosity is Sorai's or his theory's.

Granted, scholarly analyses of Sorai's religion or religiosity are typically not accompanied by any definition of those terms. This is unfortunate, for it would be hard to find a term as ambiguous as "religion" – a term, of course, that Sorai did not use. For the sake of the argument we will have to assume that those analyses see "religion," in a vague but common understanding, as the affirmation of a transcendent, supernatural or spiritual dimension from which value and significance for human lives and societies can be derived

In this understanding the textual evidence that supports the qualification of Sorai's thought as "religious" is so clear that it cannot be glossed away. Sorai states "Discussions of gods and spirits have been muddled to no end simply because of debates over whether or not there are any. [but…] How could anyone doubt them?" (Tucker 272; original in *Benmei* 237 §11).[3] Indeed, it is a folly to deny the existence of gods and spirits, or of the mind of heaven (*Sorai-shū* 514). Not only they exist,

---

[2] Classical examples are Yoshikawa 1975, p. 243; Bitō Masahide 1982, p. 48; Minamoto Ryōen 1984, pp. 9, 16; Kojima 1987, p. 12; Hiraishi 1988, p. 98; Tahara 1991, pp. 113–23, 127. Such "religious" reading is especially strong among Western specialists, as is suggested by the cases of Najita (1998) and Yamashita (1994, pp. 16–25), although others seem to stay on the fence. J. A. Tucker, in his masterful translation and commentary of *Benmei* and *Bendō*, does not take stance, but seems to favour a non-positivist reading (Tucker 2006, 126); I. J. McMullen (McMullen 2007, 130–131) mentions "the paradoxical assumptions concerning the status of the Way," but does not delve on the issue of the foundations of the Way.

[3] When using Tucker's translations, I have replaced "spirits" with "gods," and "ghosts" with "spirits." Sorai, following the Canons, defines *kishin* as "heavenly deities" (*shin*) and "human spirits" (*ki*) (*Benmei* 237 § 9). Heaven (*ten*) is the sky, and, when associated with earth, nature, but this nature is a cosmos, impregnated with meaning.

but we even seem to be able to grasp their intentions: "Divination transmits the words of gods and spirits. If they were no gods and spirits, neither would there be divination." (Tucker 271, 278; *Benmei* 237 §9, 239 §11) Most importantly, the existence of gods and spirits has an immediate bearing on the Way that is the central notion of his political theory. As the Sages recognized, "everything was due to the decrees of gods and spirits." (Tucker 276; *Benmei* 239 §14) Thus, not only humans cannot do anything without heaven's help (Yamashita 81; original in *Tōmonsho* 198), but the Way is entirely grounded on gods, spirits and reverence for heaven:

> The Way of the early kings includes nothing that is not grounded in reverence for heaven and reverence for gods and spirits. There are no exceptions to this. (Tucker 159; *Bendō* 206 §21)

> The various old teachers of the Song forgot that the way of the early kings deems reverence for heaven and making people secure as its foundations. (Tucker 268; *Benmei* 236 §6).

This reverence must be understood in the strongest meaning possible – not merely as respect for the awe-inspiring power of gods, spirits and heaven, but as the faithful obedience to a pattern (*hō*), and to its prescriptive dimension: "Sage emperors and enlightened kings have made heaven their model (*hō*) in governing all below it." (Tucker 263; *Benmei* 235 §1) Not surprisingly humans, each and every one of them, have to accomplish the tasks heaven assigns them (*Rongo-chō* I: 20, 33, II: 313),

The evidence thus seems unequivocally to support the conclusion that Sorai's political theory, his defence of the Way, is infused with a strong religious dimension, in the sense that gods, spirits and heaven provide its normative content.

2   The Problem of the Impossible Access to the Normative Dimension of Ghosts, Spirits and Heaven

Be this as it may, as soon as we try to place those discussions in the broader context of Sorai's statements on the Way, and even of other statements on gods, spirits and heaven, the issue of religion appears in fact to be far from settled. The first thing that should be said concerning Sorai's alleged religiosity is that, if "religion" is there, it is of a very puzzling kind.

One first assertion that Sorai repeatedly made is that gods, spirits and heaven are not objects of knowledge. We cannot know what they are. "Yet heaven is incomprehensible, as are gods and spirits." (Tucker 274; *Benmei* 238 §12) "Is this heaven? Is this a god? Is it one, or is it two? Such matters cannot be known." (Tucker; *Benmei* ibid.; see also *Rongo-chō* I: 83)

Granted, we may wonder whether this inability extends to the Sages, or Ancient Kings, and whether these wise founders of the Way may have been able to obtain some insight on gods and spirits. Sorai certainly states: "Because the Sages comprehended (*chi, shiru*, know) the nature (*jōjō*, circumstances, facts) of gods and spirits, they founded the rites of the abstruse and the intelligible, of life and death." (Tucker; *Benmei* ibid.) However, a careful reading of Sorai's statements will demonstrate that, while the Sages may have understood what *sort of entities* were named "gods and spirits" or "heaven," and even their role in the production of the circumstances of human lives, they were certainly not able to decipher any intentions, prescriptions or plans these may have concerning the building of a Way. For gods and spirits to provide the inspiration, if not the blueprint, for the Way, humans, or more likely Sages, must be able to read their intentions, likes, dislikes, commands or prescriptions. Sorai, however, steadfastly rejects such insight, as impossible. While often, when he talks about "humans" it is unclear whether Sages – who are mortal humans, only of extraordinary abilities – are included, he will ultimately deny knowledge of gods and spirits even to Sages.

The reason for their opacity appears in other discussions about the "mind" of gods, spirits, that is, heaven: "Gods and spirits, they are the heart of Heaven" (*Chūyō-kai* 422). The problem is that, not thinking or acting in the way humans do, this "mind" is definitely not endowed with agency: "Heaven and earth do not have deliberative, striving minds" (Tucker 231, 275; *Benmei* 226 §1, 238 §13). "Heaven's mind," thus, cannot be understood as we understand the mind of our fellow humans:

> Heaven is not akin to humanity, just as humanity is not akin to the birds and beasts. For this reason, if humans tried to scrutinize the mind of birds and beasts, what could we possibly gain? Nevertheless, we cannot deny that bird and beasts have minds. Alas! How could the mind of humans possibly resemble that of heaven? Heaven cannot be fathomed. (Tucker 264; *Benmei* 235 §1; a few pages later we read "Now, spirits are unfathomable" – Tucker 270; *Benmei* 237 §8)

All this seems to clearly exclude, for those yet ill-defined "humans," the possibility of a rational, logos-centred approach in the neo-Confucian fashion, where they would scrutinize a mind structured like theirs. Sorai will indeed close, one by one, all possible access to some content in gods, spirits and heaven from which prescriptions could be derived.

Looking for another mode of access, we could thus imagine that some intuitive, or mystical understanding could allow humans or Sages to fathom what are the normative requirements of gods, spirits and heaven. But this option is also flatly rejected by Sorai who intensely disliked subjective knowledge as is shown in his discussion of the neo-Confucian notion of principle (*li* 理):

> Principle has no form. Therefore, it has no standards. To consider the mean as the principle that ought to be, however, simply [permits] people to have their own perspective on thing. Perspectives differ from person to person. Each and every person will use his own mind and then conclude that his thoughts express the mean, or that they [convey the principles] that ought to be. (Tucker 157; *Bendō* § 19, 205)

Subjective intuition, without the objective markers that are rituals, is in fact a mark of folly.

> Apart from rites, discussions of the way of controlling the mind are all far-fetched fabrications of personal wisdom. Why? The one that controls is the mind, but it is also the mind that is being controlled. Trying to use our mind to control our mind is like a crazed person personally trying to control his own craziness thereby. (Tucker 157; *Bendō* §18, 205)

Divination could be another path to the inscrutable intentions of gods, spirits and heaven. Sorai, we have seen, certainly endorses it in several places; but he also takes pains to assert that the purpose of divination cannot be to understand the will, or the plans of gods, spirits and heaven. Various forms of divination seem only to be a psychological device used by the ruler who wants to give his people the necessary confidence that their enterprises will succeed: "All are ways of uniting the minds of the ignorant masses and getting them at a task." (Yamashita 81–83; *Tōmonsho* 198)

Neither rational understanding, nor intuition or divination can provide humans with insights into the will of gods, spirits and heaven, but could such insights be attainable *ex post facto* so to speak? Maybe enterprises that have the assent of gods, spirits and heaven will be successful; maybe those that do not will meet failure and punishment. Sorai sometimes uses the terms "divine retribution" (*tenbatsu*) or "natural principle" (*tenchi no dōri*). They are however emptied of religious substance, as this retribution is seen as the natural outcome of a disregard for natural facts (Lidin 218–220, original in *Seidan* 365)

The last possible access to the normative content in gods, spirits and heaven is the very mysterious notion of *tenmei*, the "heavenly mandate," in the usual translation of the term, or "fate" as I shall call it. Did not Sorai claim that gods, spirits and heaven are the source of whatever happens, of all the circumstances of human lives? (Yamashita 50, 81; *Tōmonsho* 181, 198). This could entail that, while humans can know neither the nature nor the intentions and plans of gods, spirits and heaven, they can see what these mysterious entities impose upon them, and understand from this what they want them to do. This option does not, any more than the previous ones, survive a close analysis.

What heaven, and its mind (that is, gods and spirits) ordain for humans is a huge and complex set of constraints. Among them are first the nature (*sei*), abilities and disabilities, skills or propensities that humans are born with:

> What heaven imposes (*tenmei* 天命) is what is called human nature (*sei* 性). Humans differ in their nature; their natures differ in their qualities (*toku* 徳). (*Gakusoku* § 7, 258)

Others are the situations that impose themselves upon human beings:

> To be in the countryside, without friend or master, such is fate (*tenmei*). To be of a poor family and without books, such is fate (…) To be an officer, overworked and without leisure, such is fate. (*Gakusoku* §7, 258)

At a higher level, what heaven ordains are all the circumstances of the life of humans (Tucker 276; *Benmei* 239 §14): their habitat, the climate, the natural resources of their environment, their history. All those are aspects of the huge "given" that is imposed on humans.

But here is the crucial point: in all discussions by Sorai of the diverse aspects of this given, it appears that those constraints never show what humans *ought* to do. In other words, those constraints do not have the normative import we would expect if they were part of a religious worldview, at least in the common understanding of the term. Clearly aware of the distinction between what we can conceptualize as "material constraints" and "normative constraints," Sorai is at pains to stress the point in a discussion of the given materials used to make artefacts:

> While other trees cannot be made into cups and bowls, the nature of the willow allows for [the making of] cups and bowls. But how could cups and bowls be considered a natural expression of the willow wood? (Tucker 137; *Bendō* § 1, 200)

This is such a crucial idea for Sorai that it is repeated in the fourth section of same work (and found also in his commentary of the *Mean – Chūyō-kai* 440).

> We can compare this [a discussion on human nature precisely] to cutting down trees to build a palace: the builders must simply follow the nature of the wood in constructing it. Yet how could the palace be said to reside naturally in the wood? (Tucker 142; *Bendō* § 4, 201)

Artisans who make pieces of furniture, carpenters who make houses, sword-smiths who make swords, etc., have to use certain materials, and no others. One type of wood is good for cabinets, another for beams, or wheels; one type of iron is good for blades, another for nails. But in none of those cases does the wood, or the metal, contain inside themselves the normative design of cabinet, beams, nails or swords. It is not the case that, in order to fulfil some grand plan in nature, specific materials, woods, or metals have to be used towards such and such a specific end. It just happens that if you want to make beams, you will use a suitable type of wood, and that if you want to make a cabinet you will use other types. The materials given by fate do not tell us how we *ought* to use them. It is hard to see, in this awareness of the importance of "materials constraints" imposed by heaven any religious dimension.

It is then time to go back to the suspicion that Sages may have access to what is forbidden to ordinary humans. The passages quoted above did not indeed distinguish between the abilities of ordinary beings and that of the Sages. However, when he squarely addresses the problem, Sorai does not leave room for ambiguity:

> "Sages were not able to fathom (again, *chi, shiru*, know) heaven" (Tucker 264, 266; *Benmei* 235 §1, 4), "[simply because] Heaven cannot be fathomed." (Tucker 266; *Benmei* 236 §4)

The most reasonable conclusion that can be drawn from this is that what the Sages could understand was the fact that powerful forces existed – which they called gods, spirits and heaven – and that these had to be pragmatically respected. They could not, however, obtain any insights into their intentions, into what they wanted humans to do, nor into their plans for them. The first problem that a religious reading of Sorai's political theory of the Way confronts must be clear by now: There is no way, for humans and even for the best of them, the Sages, to understand the normative content, if any, in gods, spirits and heaven, no way to take them as guides for doing certain things and not others.

3 The Creation of Gods and Spirits, and Their Dispensability

The two other serious problems for the religious reading will require less elaboration. One appears in the form of a statement that asserts that "gods and spirits were created by the Sages." (*Benmei* 221 §11).

Plausibly enough, this is usually understood as meaning that Sages created the *institutions* of gods and spirits, or the *words* "gods and spirits" (see Tucker 272) – for all their extraordinary gifts the Sages were probably not able to literally create gods and spirits. But even if we leave aside the somewhat *ad hoc* aspect of this interpretation – after all, why did not Sorai write "institutions" or "words"? –, it seems that the translation of the passage as "created the *words*," or "created the *institutions*" of gods and spirits" sanitizes it too quickly. It certainly brushes aside without much reflection the intriguing possibility that had appeared that, in some sense and form, gods and spirits did not exist before Sages created them.

A first step to show that this last interpretation is indeed quite plausible is to remark that it offers a convincing echo to other famous provocative statements. Sorai certainly asserted that the Way was founded upon gods, spirits and heaven, but he even more famously stressed, without the least ambiguity, that the Way is not the Way of heaven and earth, but a creation (Tucker 318, *Benmei* 250 §5; Yamashita 41; *Tōmonsho* 176; *Sorai-shū* 510), and that the Sages have invented the rituals, the norms and the institutions of the Way without any "higher authority" (Tucker 214; *Benmei* 220, §1).

Such statements may be called "positivist" in the sense that the adjective has in legal philosophy, where it refers to a conception of norms as existing without foundations in a natural or supernatural dimension, and as valid only because of their coherent insertion in a system of other created norms. Granted, there may exist no contradiction between the idea that the Sages created the Way and the claim that the same Way was founded upon gods, spirits and heaven. It may simply have been founded upon heavenly principles while not pre-existing there prior to its creation by the Sages. However, such an attempt to empty the positivist statements of much meaning fizzles when we remember the remarks made above on the non-normative dimension of heaven and of fate: the "foundation" was clearly a purely practical, or pragmatic one, similar to the one of the artisan who "founds" his artefacts on the characteristics of the materials he uses.

A second argument to give plausibility to the idea of a creation of gods and spirits is to stress that the positivists statements are confirmed, and even radicalized, by others which bring us back to the question of gods, and suggest a break between truth outside of the Way, in the natural or supernatural dimension, and validity within the way. The break can be suspected when we encounter a curious statement on the possible inexistence of *shintō*:

> We have to revere the *kami* (the gods of Japan), even if there was no *shintō* ("way of the kami" - *shintō wa naki koto*). (*Taiheisaku* 452)

One may think that the supposition of the "inexistence of *shintō*" merely means the inexistence of a doctrine about indigenous gods – an inexistence that would not invalidate the need to respect them. However, more interesting things soon appear. In the previous sentence Sorai has indicated that his concern was the disbelief of some in the existence of *kami* or gods. In the following one he argues that the reason why Japanese people must follow *shintō* practices of reverence is that "for people born in Japan, to respect the local deities is what the Way of the Sages requires" (*ibid.*). Thus, here, as is usual whenever he discusses the existence of gods and spirits, Sorai's argument is that respect for gods is required not because gods truly exist, but because the Sages have made provision for them in the Way (also see Tucker 272; *Benmei* 237 §11). Disbelief is an insult, not to the gods, but to the Sages. Faith is always "faith in the Sages," not in the gods (*ibid.*).

The idea that seems to appear here is that cults and institutions are valid within a Way without being necessarily true, or backed by some reality outside this Way. The same intuition is expressed when Sorai states that, even if some teaching of the Sages appeared wrong and false, he would still ultimately accept it because it is part of the Way (Yamashita 105; *Tōmonsho* 208)

Bold as it seems this paradox is decisively confirmed by its corollary when he affirms without ambiguity that, by the same logic, truths are not necessarily valid: talking about the transmigration of the soul asserted in some Buddhist writings, he states:

> For a thing that is not present in the teaching of the Sages, for example transmigration, even if it existed, I think it still would not mean anything. (*Tōmonsho* 192)

A radical break between facts of nature and value has clearly emerged. Gods and spirits must be respected because they are institutions in the Way, not because they may be natural or supernatural beings.

The last problem for any religious reading of Sorai's political thought, a problem that precisely illustrates the break between facts of truth and validity, is the fact that his apparent obsession with gods, spirits and heaven is only manifest in his comments and explanations of those Canons of ancient China. Those expound the Way of the ancient Kings, and are replete with mentions of gods, spirits and heaven. Whenever, despite all his disclaimers, Sorai assumes the role of a Sage and sets upon designing the institutions and system of a better society for his times, such remarks almost totally disappear (the sole exception is his comment on *shintō* reported above – which led us to the break between truth and validity).

In his two political programs, submitted with little success to the *shōgun*, the *Seidan* and the *Taiheisaku*, discussions of gods, spirits and heaven are few, far between, and typically rhetorical. There, "way of heaven" refers prosaically to the natural course of things (against which the Way is built, stresses Sorai!) (Lidin 220, *Seidan* 365); and "lack of respect for the way of heaven" (Lidin 236, *Seidan* 382), rather curiously, to the interdiction made to lowly people to freely express their views. This alleged lack of respect, and its purely secular content, are explained by Sorai when he points out that "lowly people" (let us understand by this, not the illiterate peasants or palanquin bearers, but the lower strata of the *bushi* group) train their talents more than those born in a privileged position – it is a poor use of talents to shut them down. Elsewhere he may state that whenever people look for men of talent, they will be helped by heaven, but he only means by this our "Heaven helps those who help themselves." Lastly the rare mentions of temples and shrines in the policy proposals are all made from the point of view of an administrator desirous to check the anarchic proliferation of unauthorized constructions. Thus, an Inari shrine on his property is found not to have been built according to the rules, and is promptly destroyed (Lidin 207, *Seidan* 356). As in the discussion above about the inexistence of *shintō*, it seems that gods and spirits can exist only, under various forms and degrees, as regulated institutions within a Way. In the Way for contemporary Japan, well established beliefs and practices would thus have to find a place – after all Sages had to make a place in their Way for erroneous and stupid practices (Yamashita 81; *Tōmonsho* 197) – but they most likely would not play the crucial role they played within the Way of ancient China.

4   Reconciling the Contradictions

Having just as many reasons to accept as to reject the religious reading, we seem to have reached a dead end. Sorai certainly vehemently rejects any doubt as to the existence of gods and spirits, states the necessity to respect and revere them, and affirms that the Way is founded on, or patterned after, heaven, whose mind are those gods and spirits. However, he also writes that gods and spirits are inventions of the Sages, who could not follow any anterior and higher authority; he suggests that the possible inexistence in nature or 'super-nature' of those entities is not a reason not to respect them; and he states squarely that, conversely, some things may exist in nature and yet not be accounted for in the Way. Typically, he limits his remarks on gods and spirits to commentaries on the Classics that discuss them, and shows very little interest for them when outlining his proposals for a better world.

It is not easy to reconcile the two readings. Interpretations of Sorai's thought seem indeed to have been split from the beginning. If some of Sorai contemporaries, as mentioned earlier, drew attention to the importance he seems to give to the mysterious dimension of gods and spirits, another, Muro Kyūsō 室鳩巣 (1658–1734), in his *Shundai zatsuwa* 駿台雑話, was more impressed, albeit not favourably, by Sorai's insistence that the Way had been created by men. Maruyama Masao quotes a student of Sorai, Miura Heizan (Atsuo) 三浦瓶山・淳夫(1725 (1715?) – 1795; *KGS* 4193), who declared that whoever affirmed that institutions were all invented was a disciple of Sorai, and that whoever denied it was an opponent (Maruyama 1952, p.92). The break we have discovered between validity and truth is obviously not a reconciliation of the two possible readings; because the articulation between those two notions is as yet unclear, it merely restates the opposition.

One can of course conclude that Sorai's doctrine is riddled with contradictions – and this has indeed been said (Kojima 1987, p. 12). I believe, however, that it is possible to truly reconcile the two strands of statements, and, in doing so, explicate the articulation between truth and validity. For this we need to revisit the notion of respect: "respect for heaven," "respect for gods and spirits," and especially "respect for fate." All those notions are inextricably intertwined in Sorai's doctrine. "Respect for heaven," or for its mind, "gods and spirits," upon which the Way is founded, can only mean *in fine* "respect of *tenmei*," since this fate – the facts of our lives, all the things and circumstances that surround us – is the only tangible manifestation of gods, spirits and heaven. Indeed "respect for heaven" is said to mean ultimately "to respect every single thing" (*Benmei*, 227 §2); or even more straightforwardly: "The foundation of the Way resides in revering the decree of heaven" (Tucker 145; *Bendō* § 7, 202).

This consideration immediately sends us back to Sorai's discussion of the treatment of the materials imposed on us by the fate of *tenmei* (section 3). We saw then that he took pains to stress that the constraints they present are only practical. They do not tell us in a normative way what we *ought* to do with them, only what we *can*, and *cannot*, do. We could then understand that, just like carpenters and swordsmiths need to "respect" in this pragmatic sense the characteristics of the wood or metals they will use, the builders of a Way will need to respect the materials that the Way is made of: the humans with their history, their culture, and the physical circumstances of their habitat. Such respect is needed because one cannot hope to impose, in a sustainable way, violence on the materials. If some deep-seated habits, mentalities, needs of humans, or constraints of nature were ignored, they would come back to haunt and undermine the system that excluded them. All this should suggest how fundamental is the distinction between what exists, as valid institutions, regulations, practices, within the Way, and what exists outside a Way: materials of all sorts, devoid of normative import, each with their characteristics, their possible and impossible uses, that all need to be incorporated, integrated into an effective system. At the same time, all this should also make clear the articulation between truth outside the Way and validity inside: valid institutions cannot but take account of the facts of nature, but this "taking into account" is merely pragmatic; facts of truth never tell us what we should do.

Needless to say, only Sages are able to make use of all those materials, to find them a meaningful place. This all-inclusive dimension is the hallmark of a true Way (*Gakusoku* §6, 258; also Tucker 187, *Benmei*, 214 §1). Its coherence and solidity, when all materials have been put to use, assigned place and role, in a closely interconnected and interdependent fashion (Yamashita 323; *Tōmonsho* 191), also means that whatever has found place in a Way is *ipso facto* justified (*Gakusoku, ibid.*). Ordinary humans, for their part, should certainly not attempt to build Ways. Ordinary humans live inside a Way – and must accept everything that is presented to them inside this Way. Only Sages, builders of a Way, can stand outside it, when they consider the given of fate, its possible uses and functions.

Here lies the key to a coherent reading of Sorai's writings: two perspectives exist there on the Way – the internal perspective of ordinary humans, and the external of the Sages. The impression of tension that we have surveyed above between two opposite interpretations, religious and positivist, comes from the fact that Sorai sometimes talks from the first perspective, and at other times from the other.

Sorai speaks from the internal perspective whenever he expounds the Way of ancient China as the Canons describe it. There he stresses the indubitable existence of gods and spirits, and accepts whatever has a place in a Way. From this perspective the Way may have been created, but this creation followed some heavenly pattern.

But he speaks from an external perspective whenever he draws what he calls a system (*seido*) for contemporary Japan, or when he takes a meta-view of the old Ways. From this last perspective it can appear that gods, spirits, even Heaven, while they refer to phenomena outside the Way, were created as specific entities or institutions by its builders. From this perspective, and from this perspective only, it appears that not all Ways need to give to those institutions the importance that was theirs in ancient China. History, knowledge, existing cultures and mentalities, etc., might impose a different treatment. The practices of divination played a crucial role in the Ways of ancient China, but are absent in the system that Sorai proposes for his country. From this perspective, the creators of a Way can see what is before and outside a Way. The origins of things are hidden, even to the Sages, but they can see those things and how they can contribute to a good society. They can order the chaos of the given to build a Way.

Of course, between the two perspectives the separation could not be total. Some statements could be made from either – for example the idea that the Way is not the Way of heaven and earth, although ensuing precisions would naturally veer toward one or the other. Besides, while the two perspectives are typically characteristic of two types of writings – commentaries of the Canons for the internal, political propositions, or letters for the external –, glimpses of the other can be found in writings largely oriented toward its opposite. As a political thinker, Sorai could probably not refrain for too long from taking the external perspective; and as a defender of the Way he could not consistently refrain from affirming the absolute convictions that exist within a Way. However, he could not, in the common sense of the Confucian tradition, openly state he was taking the external perspective. Not only this might have weakened the other, but this was tantamount to usurping the position of the Sages. Still, Sorai took this position often enough to expose himself to the accusation of *lèse-majesté*, and his indignant denunciations of those of who did so probably were attempts to fend off this accusation (Yamashita 105; *Tōmonsho* 208). The shift to and fro between the perspectives could not be announced, but only this unspoken double perspective explains the surprising distinction between truth (in the external perspective) and validity (in the internal).

5   Sorai's Reasons

Some words of conclusion on the reasons of this most striking distinction are in order. How was Sorai led to an idea that looked so modern to Maruyama Masao and that may even look postmodern, since the absence of foundations seems to be a favourite trope of political post-modernity?

The resemblance with modern or postmodern conceptual schemes, as fortuitous as it is, can be explained by several factors. The first might be that a positivist or conventionalist political theory – arguing that the regulations should stand and be obeyed simply by virtue of already being there, and not because of some grounding in reality – was in the interest of the *bushi* group, to which Sorai was assimilated. It was not the actual merits and qualities of its members that could justify the fact that they were monopolizing power, as Yamaga Sokō 山鹿素行 (1622–1685), for example, well recognized. Indeed, Sorai argues many times that existing regulations should be respected, not because they are intrinsically better than alternatives, but because, even if bad originally, they have become part of a whole system that it is always very dangerous to modify (Yamashita 323; *Tōmonsho* 191). In such position we already see the break between the validity of social and political systems and the natural truth (say, here, the fact that *bushi* were not necessarily the best suited to administrative work and responsibilities, or that specific pieces of regulations, reverence for old families, etc., were not warranted by their intrinsic qualities – Lidin 220; *Seidan* 365).

More intriguingly, we should also notice the fact that thinkers like Sorai, or Sokō, were living in a *bushi* society – whose practices illustrated daily the rupture between truth and validity. Examples of this rupture abound.

The genealogies that justified the status of the warriors were often, in common knowledge, false and always embellished – but they were nevertheless validated in the 1640's *Genealogies of the Military houses, Kan'ei shoka keizu den* 寛永書家系図伝 (Spafford 2016).

The reports made by the *daimyō* to the shogun were routinely full of lies, but were accepted as valid (Roberts 2012). Even the signature of the shogun could be falsified in diplomatic correspondence, with very little consequences when the trick was exposed (Tashiro 1983).

Bushi were posing as warriors, but their sabres were more status symbols than the weapons that had won battles (firearms had, but took a back seat in the displays of authority).

They were identifying themselves by the cardinal virtues of loyalty and honour, but in the new circumstances they could not accumulate honour nor demonstrate loyalty by martial feats. At best they were obedient, and using embellished or invented genealogies as social capital. More often than not the pretences of loyalty and honour were masks, poorly dissimulating self-interest and greed, but they were still the norms and, if found violated, warriors had to take the blame. We do not count now the number of plots and strategies directed toward the *daimyō* by their retainers (Kasaya 2006).

Even the most defining moment, the most powerful symbol for the popular imagination of the *bushi* condition – the *seppuku* – was often a fake disembowelment, a decapitation enacted on a sign of the condemned warrior – as even the forty seven *rōnin* showed (Watanabe 1975, 250. 257; Yamamoto 2003, 51, 93). *Bushi* life was a careful performance of many impostures, a masquerade that managed the delicate co-existence of masks and realities.

In such circumstances, is it surprising that Sorai could apply the trope to political theory? We seem to have here a case of those elective affinities that Max Weber invokes in his study on the origins of capitalism – only to forget it soon, I think. The pattern of dissociation between truth and validity existed in contemporary life, in a realm far from that of political theory, but it found echoes there, partially explaining one of the most intriguing political doctrines of pre-modern Japan.

Bibliography

1. Primary Sources/Sorai's Works

Bendō 弁道 (*Distinguishing the Way*), in Yoshikawa Kōjirō, et al., eds., *Ogyū Sorai*. 1964. NST vol. 36. Tokyo: Iwanami Shoten.

Benmei 弁明 ("Distinguishing names"), NST 36.

Chūyō-kai 中庸解 ("Explanation of the Mean"), in In Imanaka Kanji and Naramoto Tatsuya, eds., *Ogyū Sorai zenshū*, vol. 2. Tokyo: Kawade Shobō Shinsha (below OSZ).

Gakusoku 学則 ("Precepts for learning"), NST 36.

Ken'en zuihitsu 蘐園随筆 ("Essays of Ken'en"), OSZ 1.

Rongo-chō 論語徴 ("Notes on the Analects"), Tōyō Bunko. Heibonsha (no 575–76).

Seidan 政談 ("Discourse on government"), NST 36.

Sorai-shū 徂徠集 ("Collected Writings of Sorai"), NST 36.

Taiheisaku 太平作 ("Measures for the Great Peace"), NST 36.

Tōmonsho 答問書 ("Responsals"), OSZ 6.

2. Translations

Lidin, Olof G. 1999. *Ogyū Sorai's Discourse on Government (Seidan)*, Harrassowitz Verlag.

Tucker, John, A. 2006. *Ogyū Sorai's Philosophical Masterworks*. Honolulu: University of Hawai'i Press.

Yamashita, Samuel Hideo. 1994. *Master Sorai's Responsals: An Annotated Translation of* Sorai Sensei Tōmonsho. Honolulu: University of Hawai'i Press.

3. Secondary Sources

Bitō Masahide 尾藤正英. 1982. "Kokkashugi no sokei toshite no Sorai" 国家主義の祖型としての徂徠. In Bitō Masahide, ed. *Ogyū Sorai*. Tokyo: Chūō Kōronsha.

Hiraishi Naoaki 平石直昭. 1988. "Sorai-gaku no sai-kōsei" 徂徠学の再構成. *Shisō*, 766.

Kasaya Kazuhiko 笠谷和比古. 2006. *Shukun "oshikome" no kōzō* 主君「押込」の構造―近世大名と家臣団. Tokyo: Heibonsha.

Kojima Yasunori 小島康敬. 1987. *Sorai-gaku to han-Sorai* 徂徠学と反徂徠. Tokyo: Perikansha.

Maruyama, Masao 丸山眞男. 1952. *Nihon seiji shisōshi kenkyū* 日本政治思想史研究. Tokyo: Tōkyō Daigaku Shuppankai.

McMullen, James. 2007. "Reinterpreting the Analects: History and Utility in the Thought of Ogyū Sorai." In James C. Baxter and Joshua A. Fogel, eds. *Writing Histories in Japan*, 127–174. Kyoto: International Research Center for Japanese Studies.

Minamoto, Ryōen. 1984. "Senkuteki keimō shisōka Bantō and Seiryō" 先駆的啓蒙思想家蟠桃と青陵. In Minamoto Ryōen, ed. *Yamagata Bantō, Kaiho Seiryō* 山片蟠桃・海保青陵. Nihon no meicho 23. Tokyo: Chūō Kōronsha.

Najita, Tetsuo. 1998. *Tokugawa Political Writings*. Cambridge: Cambridge University Press.

Roberts, Luke. 2012. *Performing the Great Peace*. Honolulu: University of Hawai'i Press.

Spafford, David. 2016. "Handed Down in the Family: The Past and Its Uses in the Kan'ei Genealogies of 1643." *The Journal of Japanese Studies*, Volume 42, 2, pp. 279–314.

Tahara Tsuguo 田原嗣郎. 1991. *Sorai-gaku no sekai* 徂徠学の世界. Tokyo: Tōkyō Daigaku Shuppankai.

Tashiro Kazui 田代和生. 1983. *Kakikaerareta kokusho: Tokugawa, Chōsen gaikō no butaiura* 書き替えられた国書—徳川・朝鮮外交の舞台裏. Chūkō shinsho. Chūō Kōronsha.

Watanabe Yosuke 渡辺世祐. 1975. *Seishi Akō gishi* 正史赤穂義士. Kōwadō.

Yamamoto Hirofumi 山本博文. 2003. *Seppuku* 切腹. Kōbunsha Shinsho.

*Translation of Yoshikawa Kōjirō. 1975. *Jinsai, Sorai, Norinaga* 仁斎・徂徠・宣長. Tokyo: Iwami Shoten.

Yoshikawa, Kōjirō. c1983. *Jinsai, Sorai, Norinaga: Three Classical Philologists in Mid-Tokugawa Japan*. Tokyo: Tōhō Gakkai.

Chapter 13
Ogyū Sorai and the Forty-Seven Rōnin

John A. TUCKER

1 Introduction

This paper explores Ogyū Sorai's 荻生徂徠 (1666–1728) thinking on the most sensational and controversial incident of eighteenth-century Japan, and perhaps the most well-known in all Japanese history, the forty-seven *rōnin* incident of 1701–1703. Viewed in relation to his lifework, Sorai's views on the incident are significant insofar as they reveal the extent to which his philosophical thinking was occasionally shaped decisively by neither ancient Chinese nor later Confucian texts, Neo- or otherwise, but instead by formative life-experiences he had as a youth living in exile. No doubt, Confucian and Neo-Confucian notions, which Sorai knew in-depth, helped him filter, epistemologically, events, issues, and most importantly what he understood to be righteous and just behaviour in a polity. Yet ironically enough, Sorai's thinking on the *rōnin* incident shows that however philosophically erudite, cosmopolitan, and urbane he was as an intellectual, his appraisals of things sometimes harked back to rural experiences he had early on with some of the most primitive and foundational expressions of human agency, civilization, and socio-political ethics in early-eighteenth century Japan. In the process, Sorai's essay reveals, through its later resonance with some Meiji thought, how his views on those same primitive expressions remained relevant even in modern contexts.

Maruyama Masao's 丸山眞男 (1914–1996) *Studies in the Intellectual History of Tokugawa Japan* (*Nihon seiji shisōshi kenkyū* 日本政治思想史研究), published in 1952, made the topic of Sorai's thinking on the *rōnin* incident a popular one.[1]

---

[1] Maruyama's work, *Nihon seiji shisōshi kenkyū* 日本政治思想史研究 (Tokyo: Tokyo University Press, 1952), was translated into English by Mikiso Hane as *Studies in the Intellectual History of Tokugawa Japan* (Princeton: Princeton University Press, 1974), and into French by Jacque Joly as *Essais sur l'histoire de la pensée politique au Japon* (Paris: Presses universitaires de France,

---

J. A. TUCKER (✉)
Department of History, East Carolina University, Greenville, NC, USA
e-mail: tuckerjo@ecu.edu

© Springer Nature Switzerland AG 2019
W. J. BOOT, TAKAYAMA Daiki (eds.), *Tetsugaku Companion to Ogyū Sorai*,
Tetsugaku Companions to Japanese Philosophy 2,
https://doi.org/10.1007/978-3-030-15475-2_13

Because so many have been influenced by Maruyama's interpretations of Sorai, this paper first critically assesses Maruyama's grasp of Sorai's position on the incident, showing that at the very least, his analyses were textually questionable. Yet rather than dismiss Maruyama, the study agrees with his conclusions about the modern nature of Sorai's thinking on the incident but does so for very different reasons than Maruyama himself offered. Rather than concur that Sorai's thinking reflected modern tendencies *vis-à-vis* the independence of the private and public domains, the study suggests that Sorai's take on the *rōnin* incident was modern in a more *de facto* way insofar as it anticipated the early-Meiji and surely modern views of Fukuzawa Yukichi 福澤諭吉 (1835–1901) on the matter. Fukuzawa's thoughts in turn echoed, in part, the analyses of another modern thinker, the American ethicist Francis Wayland (1796–1865), regarding unjust laws and people's obligation to obey them. Strikingly, Sorai, Fukuzawa, and Wayland successively praised the course of ultimate yet non-violent remonstration rather than the vengeful, feuding ethic of retribution and murderous vendetta so evident in many of the early modern discussions of the socio-political ethics relevant to the *rōnin* incident.

The study emphasizes that Sorai's ideas on the incident percolated at a time in his life when his thinking was more consistent with the Confucian philosophy of the Song master, Zhu Xi 朱熹 (1130–1200; J. Shushi 朱子) than his own later advocacy of the study of ancient words and phrases (*kobunjigaku* 古文辭學 C: *guwencixue*).[2] Admittedly, even as Sorai advanced a quasi-modern, Song Confucian inspired expression of civil disobedience, he appealed implicitly to East-Asian paradigms of principled disobedience harking back to the legendary fringes of ancient Chinese myths. Sorai's perspective thus might be viewed as either timeless, spanning the ages, or as a Janus-faced, look back into antiquity even while pioneering a distinctively modern way forward. The latter interpretation seems most appropriate. Apparently Sorai found, in the ancient past and in contemporary peasant life, avenues around the samurai values of his day, and towards a more civil if simplistic society wherein the basics of culture, civilization, and righteous integrity were honoured over martial birth and imagined paths of righteous samurai valour and honour.

1996). Joly's translation, rendered into English as *Studies on the History of Japanese Political Thought*, is the more accurate. Rather than intellectual history, Maruyama's focus is on the history of political thought; also, rather than the Tokugawa period, the analyses address modern times as well. The essays comprising the volume were first published in *Kokka gakkai zasshi* 国家学会雑 誌, between 1940 and 1944.

[2] Sorai traced his method, fully evident in his *Discerning the Way* (*Bendō* 辨道) and *Discerning Names* (*Benmei* 辨名), to the Ming dynasty writings of Li Panlong 李攀龍 (1514-1570) and Wang Shizhen 王世貞 (1526-1590), who in turn had earlier advocated a return to ancient words and phrases (*guwencixue* 古文辭學). With Li and Wang, however, "ancient words and phrases" referred to the writings of the Han and Tang dynasties, not to the allegedly ancient classics of the Zhou dynasty. Also, for Li and Wang, the return was primarily stylistic in nature, not a profoundly philosophical one. Sorai's return to ancient words and phrases was both literary and most importantly, philosophical in nature.

As will be emphasized here, Sorai's authentic writing on the rōnin incident drew decisively on his ties to Kazusa, the place to which he, as an adolescent, lived in exile along with his father and family for nearly a decade. Gido Ichibei 義奴市兵衛, the crucial exemplar of loyalty and righteous remonstration whom Sorai extolled above all others came not from the ranks of ancient Chinese Sages, nor from the later philosophical ferment of Song Confucianism, but instead from Kazusa's rustic peasantry. Gido Ichibei's elevation in Sorai's thoughts on the *rōnin* incident reveals that regardless of Sorai's overall admiration for Chinese language and learning, he remained in many respects a thinker deeply grounded in the local lore of the Kantō region. Yet there again, as with Sorai's seeming obsession with the past, he seems to have found in his rural encounters with peasant life, as well as later reports about the same, a portal providing an alternative vision of ethical virtue, courage, and justice in action. In short, *via* what he deemed to be exemplary expressions of socio-political ethics issuing from the rural peasantry, Sorai envisioned what would later come to be recognized – though he never understood it as such – as one of the most widely admired ethical expressions of political thought and action associated with modernity.

2 Overcoming the Legacy of Maruyama's Misconceptions

Post-war understandings of Ogyū Sorai's thought have been decisively shaped, perhaps even warped, by Maruyama Masao's *Studies in the Intellectual History of Tokugawa Japan*. Rather than interpret Sorai entirely on his own terms and in light of his own times, Maruyama offered a quasi-Hegelian philosophical narrative wherein Sorai's supposedly purist grasp of ancient Chinese texts anticipated, ironically enough, the dialectical quickening of a "modern" consciousness within Japanese political thought. In Maruyama's view, the distinguishing feature of modernity was "the independence of the public sphere" (*kōteki na ryōiki no dokuritsu* 公的な領域の獨立) and "the liberation of the private sphere" (*shiteki na ryōiki no kaihō* 私的な領域の解放) (Maruyama 1974: 103, 1952: 107).

Simply put, this view of modernity implies that the polity exists as a political entity independently of the personal concerns of those governing it. It is not their possession, nor are those who dwell within it the property of those governing. Individual autonomy, both of the ruling elite and the ruled, is recognized within this conception of modernity. The premodern mentality, however, was one wherein the ruler claimed not only authority over the polity, but personal possession and ownership of it, disallowing distinctions between him as a person, his values, and supposedly his polity. Also disallowed would be any claims to autonomy on the part of those governed. Instead, the people belonged, in premodern conceptualizations, to those ruling them. According to Maruyama, Tokugawa Japan's movement toward realization of this kind of modern political consciousness was furthered though not finalized by Sorai's views on the relative independence of the public (*kō* / *ōyake* 公)

and private (*shi / watakushi* 私) spheres. Within that context, Maruyama highlighted Sorai's thinking on the forty-seven *rōnin* incident of 1701–1703, as purportedly set forth in a text known as the *Giritsusho* 擬律書 ("Legal Precedents").

Maruyama's interpretations are appealingly counterintuitive because according to nearly all accounts of Sorai's thought, Sorai distinguished himself in Tokugawa intellectual history with his thoroughgoing call for a return to antiquity, at least as antiquity was imagined to have existed in the so-called words and phrases of remote Chinese mytho-history. Sorai expressed no ultimate admiration for seemingly progressive political leaders of more recent generations or even contemporary times. Instead, he praised the long clichéd "early kings" (*sennō* 先王 C: *xian wang*),[3] whom he identified, along with a few other pivotal figures of ancient Chinese legends, as "Sages" (*seijin* 聖人 *shengren*).[4] Sorai lauded these men (all of them Chinese) – including Yao 堯, Shun 舜, Yu 禹, Tang 湯, Wen 文, Wu 武, and the Duke of Zhou 周公[5] – as "creators," "makers," or, put differently, "founders" (*sakusha* 作者),[6] of the basics of cultured, civilized existence as known to history. Sorai

---

[3] References to the "early kings" (*xian wang* 先王) appear in the *Book of Poetry* (*Shijing* 詩経) six times, including one poem, "Tian Bao 天保," which asks how debauched rulers might expect to succeed without extensively studying the early kings. In the *Book of History* (*Shujing* 書経), *xian wang* appears forty-two times in thirty-two paragraphs, beginning with the "Books of the Xia" (*Xia shu* 夏書) and the justification of the impending Shang 商 conquest of the Xia 夏 dynasty. There, the early kings referred largely to the early kings of the Xia dynasty. They are described as having been attentive to the warnings of heaven (*tian* 天), makers and recipients of sacrifices, concerned with the foundations of social unity, founders of states, compassionate to those distressed and in suffering, and devoted to the cultivation of virtue (*de* 徳). Later rulers were advised to follow their models.

[4] References to "the Sages" (*shengren* 聖人) only appear twice in the *Book of Poetry*, and not once in the *Book of History*. Sagacity as an attribute (*sheng* 聖) does occur twenty-two times in the *History*, typically as a characteristic of exemplary rulers. In the *Book of Changes* (*Yijing* 易経), however, "the Sages" (*shengren*) appears thirty-eight times in twenty-two paragraphs. Therein they are described as masters of action and inaction, and as the crucial formulators of concepts and ideas that enable others to comprehend things. By shaping the understandings of humanity, the Sages provided for harmony in the world below heaven.

[5] Yao is the first ruler described in the *Book of History*. He was elevated by the people around him as their ruler due to his virtues, not military conquest or claims of divine appointment. Yao later turned authority over to Shun, the second ruler described in the *History*. Shun ruled wisely, and eventually turned governance over to Yu, the third major ruler of the *History*. Yu founded the Xia dynasty, perhaps the most remote in Chinese antiquity (though its authenticity remains questionable). Tang overthrew the Xia dynasty and founded the Shang, claiming – according to the *History* – to have received the decree of heaven in doing so. Wen, Wu, and the Duke of Zhou presided over the end of the Shang and the beginning of the Zhou dynasty. Sorai typically cites these figures as Sages, and sometime includes other figures as well such as the Yellow Emperor, the Divine Farmer, and Fu Xi, the supposed inventor of writing. Sorai does not readily acknowledge Confucius, however, as been a Sage. He denies such status because Confucius claimed to be a "transmitter" (*shu* 述) rather than a "creator" (*zuo* 作) of culture.

[6] The term "founder" (*zuo zhe* 作者 *sakusha*) appears in the *Analects* (*Lunyu* 論語 *Rongo*) of Confucius (7/1), but there in reference to "worthies" rather than "Sages." The *Book of Rites* (*Liji* 禮記 *Raiki*) chapter, "Records of Music" (*Yue ji* 樂記), does, however, state, "Those who founded (things) are called Sages" (*zuo zhe zhi wei sheng* 作者之謂聖).

saw these leaders as the formulators of an expansive and unrivalled if not universal civilization born from their foundational efforts and further developed over millennia. Because of their epic contributions to the core, fundamental essentials of the civilized order, which seemed, even in Sorai's day, secure if not utterly unchallengeable, he extolled them in quasi-religious terms as Sages.

Sorai claimed that accounts of these figures were documented, historically, in "the words and phrases" (*kobunji* 古文辭 *guwenci*) of the ancient classics of Chinese literature, the so-called "Six Classics" (*rikkei* 六経 *liujing*), including the *Book of Historical Writings* (*Shokyō* 書経 *Shujing*), the *Classic of Poetry* (*Shikyō* 詩経 *Shijing*), the *Classic of Change* (*Ekikyō* 易経 *Yijing*), *Records of the Rites* (*Raiki* 礼記 *Liji*), and the once extant but long since lost *Classic of Music*. Had Sorai been aware of the oracle bones, he might have advocated a return to them or other writings purportedly in the primordial tadpole script. Sorai thus seems historicist in orientation, yet even in his day the authenticity of the texts he privileged had been questioned. As documents, they were hardly of impeccable antiquity, making any claims to his historicism potentially spurious, even in his, Sorai's, own day. That notwithstanding, the Sages, those revered philosophical heroes of Sorai's theoretical *Weltanschauung,* were still widely regarded as founding figures – invariably fathers – of civilization as it had unfolded by Sorai's time. Although today it might be called "East-Asian civilization," in Sorai's mind, it was not one among many, but simply "civilization." Though he had some inkling that there were other models of civilization, given Japan's sixteenth and early-seventeenth century contacts with Western explorers, traders, and missionaries, plus the long presence of Central-Asian and Islamic minorities in China, other models were scarcely understood and hardly revered.

Sorai's call for a return to ancient Sagely models, and most especially, the words, phrases, and meanings of Chinese antiquity, might easily and not inaccurately be viewed as a conservative, possibly reactionary revival of the archaic basics of East Asian foundations and the essentials of what had made Japan, within that civilizational complex, a distinctive historical entity. Sorai's later suggestion, made in his *Seidan* 政談 (*Political Discussions*) and *Taiheisaku* 太平策 (*Plan for an Age of Great Peace*) – that urban-dwelling samurai be returned to the countryside to live alongside peasant farmers – even suggests that he longed to turn time back to a more idyllic moment in the increasingly distant and all but irretrievable past. To see within such calls for a return to antiquity the beginning of modernity of any sort is as intriguing as it is counterintuitive.

Maruyama's analyses drew on Western narratives of modernity and politics, ones that would, in many circles, now be considered *passé*. He noted, for example, that in the West, Niccolo Machiavelli's (1469–1527) *The Prince* was recognized as having completely exemplified this trend of separating the public and private spheres. Just as Machiavelli had the "honour of having established political science as a science in modern Europe," so might it be, in Maruyama's view, appropriate "to call Sorai the 'discoverer of politics' (*seiji no hakken* 政治の発見) in the Tokugawa feudal system" (Maruyama 1974: 83, 1952: 83–84). If on no other count, Maruyama's understanding of "modernity" seems questionable for its very reliance on now dated, somewhat textbook accounts of the topic in the history of Western political thought.

Maruyama made his case for comparing Sorai's thinking and Machiavelli's by noting that the division of the public and private can readily be seen, without imposition, in Sorai's writings on the *rōnin* incident. Maruyama cited a work that he attributed to Sorai, the *Giritsusho*, which supposedly dates from shortly after the 1701–1703 vendetta. There are, however, at least three questionable aspects of Maruyama's analyses of Sorai's thinking on this count. First, if Sorai's thoughts on the incident were actually recorded in the *Giritsusho* dating from circa 1703, his ideas would need to be situated within the context of his time as a Confucian philosopher advancing, for the most part, the ideas of the Zhu Xi school of thought, not that of his later, so-called "learning of ancient words and phrases" (*kobunjigaku*), largely postdating his service to Yanagisawa Yoshiyasu 柳沢吉保 (1658–1714), chamberlain and trusted advisor to the reigning Shogun, Tsunayoshi (1646–1709).

Second, Sorai's distinction between the public and private found in the *Giritsusho* was by no means unprecedented in East Asian or even Japanese thought. It easily traces back to the philosophical writings of the late-Zhou dynasty, the Warring States' Period, and to an extent to passages in the Six Classics. In Japan, the distinction is evident early on, appearing in the "Seventeen Clause Constitution" (*Jūshichijō kenpō* 十七条憲法) attributed to Prince Shōtoku 聖徳太子 (574–622), and dating from the seventh century (*Shōtoku taishi shū* 1975: 21).

Finally, and no doubt most significantly, the *Giritsusho* is of questionable authenticity. Tahara Tsuguo 田原嗣郎 (b. 1924) and others addressing Sorai's involvement in the debates over the forty-seven rōnin incident, have noted that the *Giritsusho* was not included in the earliest compilations of Sorai's writings (Tahara 1978: 65–69). Oddly enough, copies of the text are only known to have existed in collections transmitted by the Hosokawa 細川 *daimyō* line of Kumamoto domain. Tahara therefore concludes that the text was questionable, and though written in Sorai's style and drawing on Sorai's ideas, falsely attributed to him. Pointedly, he asked why a document written by a promising, prominent young Edo scholar such as Sorai would have ended up exclusively in the possession of a distant line of "outer lords" (*tozama*) like the Hosokawa (Tahara 1978: 68).

Also noteworthy is that while Yanagisawa Yoshiyasu, according to his memoir, the *Yanagisawa hikki* 柳沢秘記, asked Sorai for his thoughts about the *rōnin* incident, Sorai is reported to have only responded verbally. Yanagisawa subsequently discussed the vendetta with shogunal officials, but without mentioning the existence of a text by Sorai, or as far as is known, Sorai's views. Tahara suggests that on the basis of Yanagisawa's account, if Sorai's thinking reached the shogunate, it did so orally, and as mediated by Yanagisawa. Yet that Sorai's ideas indeed made their way to shogunal discussions of the *rōnin* incident is by no means clear. To imagine the *Giritsusho* was an authentic text by Sorai that decisively influenced the shogunate's verdict regarding the rōnin incident therefore seems, in light of Tahara's scholarship, rather farfetched (Tahara 1978: 68). It is difficult, then, to avoid the conclusion that Maruyama's analysis of Sorai's thinking on this important topic was based on a spurious text. Another matter worth mentioning is that if the *Giritsusho* is accepted

as a text written before the shogunate's sentence and the *rōnin*'s seppuku, it would
stand alone in that regard. All other texts in the debate post-date the deaths of the
rōnin, with Hayashi Hōkō's "On Revenge" (*Fukushū ron* 復讐論), coming first,
dating from shortly after the mass punishment in 1703.[7] While later texts mention
Hayashi's writing, subsequent participants in the lengthy, often self-referential
debate never mention the *Giritsusho*. If it was indeed Sorai's text, it seems that he
kept it a secret.

Even Maruyama allows that there is room for doubt about the importance of
Sorai's *Giritsusho* in deciding the matter, especially when one considers that there
is no mention of Sorai's thinking in the official chronicle of the Tokugawa shogunate as it records the incident and its legal resolution. Nevertheless, Maruyama
broadcast his claims about the supposedly probable importance of the *Giritsusho*
and coupled those claims with an earlier observation that Sorai's thinking on a previous legal issue had initiated his ascent as a Confucian scholar serving the inner
circle of Tsunayoshi's shogunate. This study, rather than concur that Sorai rose to
prominence because of the *Giritsusho*, emphasizes the very dubiousness of this
claim. While there can be no question that Sorai was a major Confucian thinker, the
contemporary importance of his thinking has been poorly assessed through exclu-
sive reliance on what was apparently a spurious text, coupled with a determination
to see in Sorai some kind of key legal role that, on this count at least, he apparently
did not seem to have had.

This study concurs then with recent scholarship by Tahara and others in concluding that the *Giritsusho* should not be deemed one of Sorai's authentic writings.[8] At
best, it might be considered an apocryphal work attributed to Sorai, and significant
for that reason. After all, authentic or not, the *Giritsusho* has been factored into at
least some channels of early modern Japanese intellectual history, especially those
influenced by Maruyama's writings, as an expression of Sorai's thinking on the
incident. This study emphasizes, on the other hand, that while Sorai did leave at
least one authentic text addressing the *rōnin* incident, his conclusions about the matter did not, as contemporary statements, circulate widely and did not become signature expressions of his thinking, regardless of the developmental stage from which
they emerged. Still, this does not necessarily make Sorai's thinking on the *rōnin*
incident any less significant.

Indeed, the paper suggests that the importance of Sorai's views needs to be
appreciated in relation to slightly later developments in Japanese intellectual history, specifically those of the early-Meiji period and most especially the ideas of
Fukuzawa Yukichi. Fukuzawa developed his thoughts on the *rōnin* incident most
famously in his *Encouragement of Learning* (*Gakumon no susume* 学問のすすめ),

---

[7] See Tahara Tsuguo, *Akō shijūroku shi ron*, pp. 62–63, for a listing of major texts in the vendetta
dates, and their dates. Tahara notes that all of the discussions occurred after the vendetta was done.

[8] For example, Ishii Shirō 石井紫郎, ed., *Kinsei buke shisō* 近世武家思想, NST Vol. 27 (Tokyo:
Iwanami Shoten, 1974), does not include the *Giritsusho*, but does present "Essay on the Forty-
Seven Samurai" (*Shijūshichi shi no koto o ron zu* 四十七士の事を論ず), as Sorai's authentic
contribution to the rōnin debates.

where he offered his reflections on the *rōnin* incident in relation to the question of a citizen's obligation to obey the laws of a state, even when those laws are considered profoundly objectionable. At the very least, there is a striking resonance between Sorai's authentic thinking on the *rōnin* incident and that of Fukuzawa, implying that whatever its significance might have been in Tokugawa times, Sorai's thinking fore-shadowed that of at least one modern Japanese intellectual, if it did not more directly and decisively impact them.

Without making grand claims about what, precisely, modernity and the intellectual development of a modern political consciousness consists in, this paper agrees with Maruyama in concluding that Sorai's thinking does resonate with modern Japanese thinking, especially to the extent that Meiji Japan as a historical period is almost universally considered, *de facto*, to have been the beginning of modern Japan. Yet the modern dimensions of Sorai's thinking, this paper emphasizes, have little to do with his advocacy of the study of ancient words and phrases, or his sup-posedly theoretical "dissolution" of the Zhu Xi mode of thought in Japanese intel-lectual history. Instead, curiously enough, Sorai's views seem to have issued from his personal familiarity with circumstances in the Japanese hinterlands generated by his early experiences, living in Kazusa (modern Chiba prefecture) with his family following the exile of his father from Edo by none other than Tsunayoshi, the sho-gun with whom he, Sorai, later enjoyed scholarly proximity.

3   The Forty-Seven Rōnin Incident and the Confucian Debate: The Altercation and Aftermath

Before proceeding, a summary of the *rōnin* incident and the debate it spawned is in order. The incident began in Edo, the shogun's capital, during New Year's ceremo-nies hosted in Edo Castle, the shogun's residence, sponsored by the shogun, Tokugawa Tsunayoshi, and including, as guests of honour, representatives of the emperor and retired emperor. These ceremonies occurred annually with shogunal emissaries first traveling to Kyoto to offer the shogun's New Year's greetings to the imperial court, followed by reciprocal ceremonies in Edo wherein representatives from the court responded with the emperor's greetings to the shogun. As the final day of the Edo ceremonies was about to begin, Asano Naganori 浅野長矩 (1667–1701), the young lord of Akō domain, suddenly attacked, with his ceremonial sword, for no clear reason, the shogunate's senior master of ceremonies, Kira Yoshinaka 吉良義央 (1641–1703). Although Kira was not killed, the incredible breach of etiquette brought the wrath of the shogunate down on Naganori. Within hours, he was ordered to commit *seppuku*, or ritual suicide.

Naganori's retainers in Edo immediately sent word of the shocking news to Akō domain. The Akō samurai, led by Ōishi Kuranosuke 大石内蔵助 (1659–1703), moved from initial shock to consideration of what course of action to follow. Of the roughly 300 samurai who had served the Asano lord, over two thirds soon departed.

Those remaining considered various options, including immediate suicide, a last stand defending Akō Castle, and an attack on Kira Yoshinaka, the man they blamed for provoking Naganori's attack. The *rōnin*, guided by Ōishi Kuranosuke, decided to surrender the castle peacefully in the hope that the Asano line, led by Naganori's younger brother, Asano Daigaku, might be allowed to continue. The *rōnin* thus yielded to the shogunate and within two months had quit the domain. Without necessarily denying that what their lord did was wrong, the *rōnin* felt that Kira Yoshinaka should have been punished equally. When the shogunate showed no leniency for the Asano line, the Akō *rōnin* decided to provide for justice in their own way. By doing so, they felt that they might finally console their deceased lord by completing his deed. Approximately eighteen months after Asano Naganori's attack and his *seppuku*, the *rōnin* invaded Kira's residence in Edo, tracked him down, and beheaded him. They then marched around the periphery of Edo, toward the Sengakuji, a Zen temple that was the family place of worship for the Asano family when in Edo, and the place where Asano Naganori had been interred in 1701. Even as the *rōnin* presented Kira's severed head at Naganori's grave, two members of the group had been sent to inform the authorities of their deed.

Although the *rōnin* had initially numbered forty-seven, one of them, for reasons that remain unclear, had parted company from the group, leaving only forty-six. The shogunate divided them into four groups and had four daimyō with mansions near the Sengakuji assume custody of them until a verdict was handed down. After two months in captivity, the shogunate decreed that because the *rōnin* had banded together in a league to commit murder, that of a former shogunal official, they would have to commit *seppuku*. On the appointed day in 1703, the forty-six men, one by one, at four different *daimyō* compounds, proceeded to their ceremonial death ritual. Within two hours, all were dead. Palanquins accompanied by a retinue of samurai guards subsequently transported their remains to the Sengakuji for burial. Clergy there cleared a special cemetery for the *rōnin*, just below the gravestone of their deceased master, Asano Naganori.

4 Discussion and Debate

Seeing that the *rōnin* vendetta was fraught with socio-political and ethical implications, Confucian scholars soon registered their thinking on the incident. Hayashi Hōkō 林鳳岡 (1645–1732), then head of the Tokugawa shogunate's Confucian academy, is recognized as the first to have authored an essay, "On Revenge" (*Fukushū ron*), conveying his judgment. Hōkō argued that while the *rōnin* had followed the course of *chūshin gishi* 忠臣義士, or "loyal retainers and righteous samurai," they had also broken the law. However admirable their loyalty to their lord might have been, their violation of law had to be punished. Hōkō even hinted that in their punishment by death, the *rōnin* would be completing their display of ultimate loyalty to their lord, dying on his behalf, even as they simultaneously upheld the integrity of the law (Hayashi 1974: 371–376). Another early writing, *Righteous*

Men of Akō Domain (*Akō gijin roku* 赤穂義人録) by Muro Kyūsō 室鳩巣 (1658–1734), praised the *rōnin* without equivocation as loyal and righteous samurai (Muro 1974: 272–273).

It is often at this juncture that Sorai's *Giritsusho* is introduced as a decisive statement upholding shogunal law even while recognizing that the *rōnin* had acted on the basis of a personal sense of loyalty and righteousness. Ultimately, however, Sorai affirmed the primacy of the law and the public interests of the state. Therefore, the *rōnin* had to die. Earlier it was noted that the *Giritsusho* is a questionable text because it only survived in the possession of the Hosokawa *daimyō* line rather than in shogunal archives or in the collections of Sorai's disciples. Even more telling, it seems, is the fact that unlike the writings of Hayashi Hōkō and Muro Kyūsō, which are often referred to critically in later essays, there is no mention of Sorai's *Giritsusho*, positive or negative, by other essays in the debate that followed. If the *Giritsusho* had been a crucial text in the decision-making process of the shogunate, one would have expected it to have had some impact on the debate. Sorai was, after all, a thinker who on other counts drew many critics. That the *Giritsusho* goes unmentioned suggests that it was possibly a later forgery, attributed to Sorai by someone familiar with his philosophy, but not written by him as a statement about the *rōnin* incident.

A third major statement on the incident came from Satō Naokata 佐藤直方 (1650–1719), a former student of Yamazaki Ansai's 山崎闇斎 (1619–1682) teachings. Although Ansai died well before the incident, Naokata was one of two of his disciples who wrote important, and, incidentally, diametrically opposed, essays on it. Naokata's "Notes on the Forty-Six Men" (*Shijūrokunin no hikki* 四十六人之筆記), argued that the *rōnin* were mistaken in considering Kira Yoshinaka as their lord's enemy. Naokata recalled that Kira had never attacked Asano Naganori. Accordingly, Naganori was sentenced to death, but Kira, who had delivered no blows, was deemed innocent. The *rōnin*, in viewing Kira as their lord's enemy, made an egregious mistake. Naokata adds that it is understandable why common people might err in declaring the *rōnin* "righteous samurai," but he criticizes Hayashi Hōkō in particular for having suggested as much. Naokata declares such a view the result of ignorance, and asks how the *rōnin* could not be considered lacking in righteousness (Satō 1974: 377–388). Naokata never mentions Sorai on any count, despite the fact that Sorai's *kobunjigaku* philosophy was considered anathema by virtually all followers of Ansai's teachings.

Ansai's other student who helped to define the contours of the debate, Asami Keisai 浅見絅斎 (1652–1712), offered a profoundly different perspective on the incident, repeatedly criticizing Naokata's views, referred to with vague contempt as those of "a certain person." Keisai's "Essay on the Forty-Six Samurai" (*Shijūrokushi ron* 四十六士論), argues that the *rōnin* were simply carrying out the intentions of their late master, Asano Naganori, in slaying Kira Yoshinaka. In doing that, they were acting on their sense of ultimate duty. In Keisai's view, they were undoubtedly loyal retainers and righteous samurai. Keisai compares the duty of the *rōnin* to that of a son whose father has been murdered. Regardless of the judgment of the authorities regarding the murderer, it is the son's responsibility to slay the murderer. Similarly, the *rōnin* were obliged to carry out their lord's work, incomplete and perhaps flawed though it was. In doing so, they exhibited complete loyalty and righteousness. For that reason, they deserved unmitigated praise as loyal and righteous samurai (Asami 1974: 389–398).

A representative of Sorai's school, Dazai Shundai 太宰春台 (1680–1747), entered the debate with what turned out to be the single-most controversial piece of all, "Essay on the Forty-Six Samurai of Akō Domain" (*Akō shijūrokushi ron* 赤穂四十六士論). In it, Shundai went well beyond Satō Naokata's earlier denunciation of the rōnin as utterly lacking in loyalty and righteousness. Shundai asserted that rather than attack their lord's real enemy, the Tokugawa shogunate, they instead targeted an innocent official, Kira Yoshinaka. Worst of all, in taking action against the master of ceremonies, the *rōnin* were motivated, according to Shundai, not by loyalty or righteousness, but rather by the desire for fame and profit (*myōri* 名利). Shundai added, quite critically, that after succeeding in their lethal attack and then presenting Kira Yoshinaka's severed head at their master's grave, the *rōnin* did not immediately commit suicide, but instead waited for the shogunate to take a decision on the matter. Shundai claims that in waiting, the *rōnin* revealed that they somehow hoped to be pardoned and then perhaps offered a stipend for their bold deeds (Dazai 1974: 404–412). This assertion, that the *rōnin* were out for fame and fortune rather than loyalty and righteousness, prompted a succession of counterattacks that extended the *rōnin* incident debate for decades to come. Yet in later years, relatively few Confucian scholars endorsed the line pioneered by Satō Naokata and furthered by Dazai Shundai condemning the *rōnin* as lacking in righteousness and loyalty. Nevertheless, these men were named and repeatedly criticized by later Confucians praising the *rōnin*. Yet later essays, as with those earlier, never mention an essay by Ogyū Sorai.

Shundai is one exception to this. He relates that after he began studying with Sorai, he took the opportunity to ask Sorai about his thinking on the rōnin incident. Implied in Shundai's remarks is that if Sorai had written an important essay on the topic such as the *Giritsusho*, he did not make it known to his disciples generally or Shundai would have at least heard about it and probably mentioned it in the context of his question. Yet Shundai's remarks suggest that without his, Shundai's, prompting, Sorai had not and would not have volunteered his thoughts about the matter. Shundai's study with Sorai began in 1711, a decade after Asano's attack and just eight years after the *rōnin* suicide, i.e., when memories of the events were still relatively clear and discussions just beginning to emerge in number. Had Sorai been a participant in the discussions, Shundai would have surely known about it. His question to Sorai suggests instead that Sorai had not expressed himself publicly on the matter.

As reported by Shundai, Sorai replied, "The Akō samurai did not understand righteousness. Their killing of Kira represented nothing but their study of Yamaga Sokō's military strategies." As if to minimize Sorai's involvement in the discussions, Shundai then added that Sorai had not yet written anything on incident (*mada roncho suru tokoro arazu*). Yet almost in passing Shundai also noted, quite significantly for this study, that Sorai had indeed written on the loyalty that the people of

Kazusa had shown to their master's family, but then added that Sorai, in doing so, had only tangentially touched on the deeds of Ōishi Yoshio and the *rōnin*. Though he seems not to have understood as much, Shundai's allusion to Sorai's writing on the displays of loyalty in Kazusa in fact was a reference to the one piece by Sorai that is widely considered to have been his authentic essay on the *rōnin* incident.

Shundai's remarks suggest that Sorai had said nothing of any consequence about the matter, other than to relate it – in ways that Shundai apparently did not grasp the significance of – to examples of loyalty found in Kazusa. No doubt, Shundai's assessment of Sorai's essay is superficial if not self-serving. Either the not so subtle points that Sorai meant to make escaped him or he, Shundai, minimized Sorai's essay mentioning Kazusa so as to magnify his own contribution to the discussions. There is, no doubt, considerable hubris in Shundai's essay, making it quite possible that he both failed to appreciate Sorai's thinking and also sought to inflate his own, even while claiming that everything he thought about the matter was consistent with what he had heard from Sorai on the topic. Thus, Shundai added, once again, that Sorai's thoughts were consonant with his own. Shundai further added that there was no change in Sorai's views thereafter. As if to minimize further impact of Sorai on the discussions, Shundai observed that since Sorai's passing down to his own day, no one – presumably indicating, among others, no one among Sorai's students – had offered the very insights into the matter that he, consistent with Sorai yet clearly going well beyond him, was setting forth (Dazai 1974: 406). Implied in Shundai's remarks is that if Sorai had said much about the matter, that some of his many other disciples would have reiterated or taken issue with those ideas. The very absence of the same, Shundai suggested, pointed to the marginal importance of the topic in Sorai's teachings.

Shundai's report on Sorai's thinking is interesting because it claims that Sorai's views on the incident "tallied perfectly with my [Shundai's] own conclusions." This would imply that Sorai was at one with Shundai not only in denying that the *rōnin* were loyal and righteous, but also in claiming that they had sought nothing more than profit and fame. Yet in none of the writings attributed to Sorai on the topic, authentic and apocryphal, is there any hint that Sorai saw the *rōnin* as driven by the desire for fame and profit rather than loyalty and righteousness. Nevertheless, Shundai's essay is noteworthy because it recognizes that Sorai wrote something on the incident which also was related to displays of loyalty by people in Kazusa, but that the essay, if important (and Shundai seems not to have recognized its importance), was not widely known. Eighteenth-century Confucian scholars were aware of one another's views, if they cared to have them known. Shundai's own essay is a case in point: like Naokata's it elicited a barrage of criticism, reflecting the extent to which ideas were circulating and being responded to. That Sorai's essay is never so much as mentioned in the debate indicates that either Sorai preferred to keep his thoughts private, or that his take on the matter was so out of keeping with other discussions of it that Sorai's views were simply disregarded. Perhaps both possibilities were realities with Sorai's essay insofar as its seemingly idiosyncratic central allusion to Kazusa loyalism was deemed beyond the pale of serious discussion, and therefore leaving the essay itself seemingly non-existent.

5   Sorai's Essay on the Forty-Seven Samurai Incident

Sorai's most authentic writing on the *rōnin* incident is entitled "An Essay on the Forty-Seven Samurai Incident" (*Shijūshichishi no koto o ronzu* 論四十七士事). Although this essay is not in *Sorai's Collected Works* (*Sorai shū* 徂徠集) first published in Genbun 5 (1740), it appears elsewhere, in a manuscript copy of *Gleanings from Sorai's Collected Works* (*Sorai-shū shūi* 徂徠集拾遺).[9] *Gleanings* mentions that Sorai's essay on the forty-seven samurai had been appended to another essay, "The Gido Ichibei Affair" (*Gido Ichibei no koto o shirusu* 記義奴市兵衛事), describing in detail the exemplary loyalism of a Kazusa peasant. It adds that the publisher removed the essay on the forty-seven *rōnin* from the twelfth fascicle where "The Gido Ichibei Affair" appears. Since the latter essay, of course, postdated the Gido Ichibei affair of Hōei 2 (1705), Sorai's writing on the *rōnin* vendetta, which mentions Ichibei, must have been written sometime later. Apparently the two pieces were paired in order to contrast approaches to loyalty and righteousness on the part of different groups of retainers serving, in ultimate ways, their lords: Gido Ichibei's path of patient, righteous remonstration eventually succeeded in restoring the holdings of his previously dispossessed lord, while the murderous path of the forty-seven failed in bringing about anything other than personal honour for them and spiritual solace for their lord, both achieved through bloodshed and death, but nothing close to their original objective, a restoration of the Asano line. As was typical of Sorai's writings overall, his sympathies were with the law-abiding rustic exemplars of simple honesty and persistent service, the likes of which he had surely encountered among the peasantry during his family's decade of exile in Kazusa. Although the forty-seven rōnin were also rustics, Sorai unequivocally condemned their lawless course as a "foolish undertaking" (Ishii 1974: 400; Yoshikawa 1973: 643–644; Yoshikawa 1983: 100–101).

6   Sorai's Account of the Gido Ichibei Incident

Given the pivotal significance of Gido Ichibei in Sorai's "Essay on the Forty-Seven Samurai Incident," Sorai's "The Gido Ichibei Incident" deserves attention. As noted earlier, Sorai's knowledge of Ichibei was a by-product of his decade in exile in Kazusa with his father, Ogyū Hōan 荻生方庵, a samurai-physician, after the latter, for unspecified reasons, incurred the wrath of the then future shogun, Tsunayoshi, in Enpō 7 (1679). Though a samurai by birth, Hōan had taken up the practice of medicine and was one of Tsunayoshi's attendants prior to his exile. His exile came as Sorai entered his mid-teens, with his family being banished from Edo to a

---

[9] Yoshikawa's "Sorai gakuan" 徂徠学案, in *Ogyū Sorai*, Yoshikawa Kōjirō et al., eds., p. 644, states that the copy of the *Sorai-shū shūi* that Yoshikawa cites is a manuscript (*shahon*) housed at Hiroshima University. Hiraishi Naoaki 平石直昭 has edited a modern edition, published as *Sorai-shū, Sorai-shū shūi* 徂徠集 · 徂徠集拾遺, Kinsei Juka Bunshū Shūsei vol. 3.

relatively remote countryside, barren of the profligate distractions emerging in the shogun's capital. Sorai remained in Kazusa until age twenty-five, when in Genroku 3 (1690), his father was pardoned and allowed to return to the capital. During his decade in exile, Sorai's father ensured that his son, seemingly of quick mind, read widely in Chinese and especially Confucian literature. As a result of his decade of focused study, Sorai re-entered Edo with a wealth of experiences rooted in peasant life, coupled with considerable mastery of Chinese texts. Unlike many in Edo who acquired their learning in temple schools, Sorai was home schooled and so had little contact with the Buddhist and Shinto worlds while in Kazusa. His direct experience of the capriciousness of fate likely prompted him to scepticism regarding the gods, Buddhas, and their supposed providential agency. Sorai thus returned to Edo as an unusually well-educated but independent-minded thinker with considerable knowledge of, and apparently admiration if not sympathy for the ways of the peasants, at least those he had encountered in Kazusa.

Sorai later spoke repeatedly of his time in Kazusa, from age fifteen to twenty-five, as decisive in his development. In a Sino-Japanese (*Kanbun*) letter written on the occasion of Okai Kōsen's 岡井孝先 appointment to service in Hitachi (present day Ibaraki prefecture), adjoining Kazusa, Sorai observed, "Today the Eastern Capital (Edo) is the greatest capital in the world below heaven. Needless to say, it far surpasses even the ancient capitals of the Shang, Xia, and Zhou dynasties. ... Neither Changan, Luoyang, Nanjing, nor Beijing compare. ... Yet every corner of the city serves as the hiding place of wickedness, iniquity, deception, and hedonistic pursuits." Sorai went on to say that his time in Kazusa turned out to be a positive one for him. He speculated that had he remained in Edo, he would never have amounted to much. But having spent his youth away from Edo's temptations helped to make him a scholar renowned throughout the land. As a result, Sorai suggested to Kōsen that his move to Hitachi might turn out to be a positive development in the long run (Sorai 1973a: 493–494). In his *Political Discourses* (*Seidan* 政談), Sorai similarly recounted his exile experiences as formative ones that had decisively shaped his intellectual growth (Sorai 1973b: 290; Lidin 1999).[10]

In addition to memories of his experiences in Kazusa, Sorai was apparently attentive to current events in that area as well. His knowledge of Ichibei, for example, was based on reports received well after his return to Edo and rise to scholarly power within Tsunayoshi's intellectual circle. Sorai's essay relates that Ichibei was a peasant farmer in the village of Anesaki 姉崎.[11] Ichibei's village headman, one Jirōbei 次郎兵衛, apparently had been exiled to Izu-Ōshima, a largely uninhabited volcanic island approximately 100 km southwest of Edo, following his wrongful implication in the murder of a fellow villager. Ichibei, viewing his village headman as his master, took it upon himself to help in providing for Jirōbei's family, even as he repeatedly, over an eleven-year period, asked that Edo officials restore to Jirōbei's

---

[10] Lidin, Olof, *Ogyū Sorai's Discourse on Government (Seidan)*, p. 4. Lidin mentions that Sorai referred to his early experiences in Kazusa in all four volumes comprising the *Seidan*.

[11] Waseda University's 1791 (Kansei 3) edition of the *Sorai-shū* (Osaka: Bunkindō), fascicle 12, pp. 12b–15a. (This edition can be consulted through the homepage of Waseda University Library.)

family the dwelling and rice lands that had been confiscated when Jirōbei was exiled. Ichibei even went so far as to stage, according to Yoshikawa, a "sit-in protest" (*suwarikomu*). With the latter, Ichibei's pleas were finally heard. During the long period of remonstration, Ichibei, thinking that if he fathered children he might be unable to provide sufficiently for Jirōbei's family, reportedly abstained from relations with his wife. He did this despite the fact that, as Sorai described their life, the peasantry laboured in the fields in the day, wove rope at night, ate beans, dressed in rags, and sat on nothing better than rush matting, with only conjugal relations as a source of pleasure. For Ichibei to have foregone that one source of happiness, not to mention his own family line, for the sake of Jirōbei was extraordinary. Finding accounts of Ichibei's devotion credible, Sorai praised him for having sacrificed out of loyalty and honest devotion to his lord (Ogyū 1791: 28b–30a; Yoshikawa 1973: 643–644, 1983: 100–101).

7 Sorai's Account of the Forty-Seven Samurai Incident

Sorai's essay on the forty-seven samurai incident opens with the remarks of "an unofficial historian" (*gaishi shi* 外史氏), i.e., none other than Sorai, narrating, in brief terms, the forty-seven rōnin incident. He related:

"On the fourteenth day of the third lunar month of Genroku 元禄 14 (1701), imperial emissaries (*tenshi* 天使) went down to the eastern capital (Edo). That day, the lord of Akō domain, Asano Naganori, due to a private resentment,[12] drew his sword and struck the major general of the Right Division, Kira Yoshinaka. [Kira] Yoshinaka was wounded but not killed. That evening, [Asano] Naganori was ordered to die [by *seppuku*], and his domain was abolished. [Kira] Yoshinaka remained as before.

Then, in the twelfth lunar month of the following year, forty-seven samurai including Ōishi Yoshio and other former retainers of Akō domain, broke into [Kira's] residence and killed him. However, after that, their hands were bound and they were placed in confinement. Then, in the second month of the next year, they were all made to die [by *seppuku*]. Everyone in the world seems to have thought that the forty-seven men had decided, following their master's death, to forfeit their own lives to achieve an act of loyalty without consideration of reward. People joined in unison proclaiming them righteous samurai." (Sorai 1974: 400–401)

Sorai's account omitted many details. Despite his philosophical emphasis on "rites and music" in the *Bendō* and *Benmei*, Sorai did not mention that Asano Naganori's attack on Kira Yoshinaka occurred in the midst of a high ritual occasion, arguably the highest of a calendar year, wherein imperial emissaries offered New Year's greetings from the reigning emperor and retired emperor to the shogun. This

---

[12] The words that Sorai uses to convey "private resentment" (*shitai* 私懟 C: *si dui*), appear individually in the *Classic of Poetry*. In characterizing Asano Naganori's feelings via these ancient terms, Sorai was unique in retellings of the incident, and faithful to his emerging emphasis on the use of ancient words and phrases. He found the latter more authentically meaningful than words and expressions of more recent vintage.

occasion had been preceded by one, held in the imperial capital, Kyoto, in which shogunal ceremonial officials had first offered the shogun's greetings to the emperor and retired emperor. During the latter, Kira Yoshinaka, the senior shogunal ceremonial official, led the shogun's emissaries in presenting greetings to the imperial family. Also, it was Kira Yoshinaka's responsibility to make sure that Asano Naganori, a minor *tozama daimyō*, was prepared to assist in hosting the imperial emissaries while they were in Edo. These details – which make Asano Naganori's attack on Kira Yoshinaka seem all the more egregious – are omitted from Sorai's account, despite his later emphasis on ritual as a key component of governing in accordance with the way. Given his proximity to shogunal activities, ritual and otherwise, through his service to Yanagisawa Yoshiyasu, Sorai surely knew these details and their importance overall to the incident as it unfolded. Even if Sorai's thinking is viewed more as an expression of Zhu Xi's Confucian philosophy, the latter also emphasized the importance of rites, ritual, and proper etiquette as the means by which one might be done with selfishness and thereby achieve a level of humane action. Thus, regardless of which philosophical moment one situates Sorai in at the time he wrote his essay on the rōnin incident, it is peculiar that he omitted mention of the high ritual setting of Asano's attack.

Sorai's account is also peculiar insofar as it attributed Asano Naganori's attack to a "private, personal resentment" (*shitai*), which otherwise goes unexplained. In doing so, Sorai endorsed the official line of the shogunate that Asano had had reasons, albeit of an unspecified sort, for his attack. Some who witnessed it first hand, however, suggested that Asano Naganori had simply lost his senses (*ranshin* 乱心), and in a moment of what might be called temporary madness, acted in an utterly irrational manner. Without a doubt, Naganori's attempt at murder was inept: he used a ceremonial sword meant for little more than show, and certainly nothing lethal, and did so while wearing awkward ceremonial robes and surrounded by numerous castle functionaries whose job it was to ensure that all went well, without incident of any kind. Simply put, if Asano Naganori meant to kill Kira Yoshinaka, he could not have chosen a less opportune moment or a more disadvantageous set of circumstances. Whether Naganori was sane was surely questioned and indeed questionable. Yet Sorai offers no hint that Asano was anything other than a rational agent acting on a private grudge, no matter how disturbed his actions might have seemed.

Sorai suggested that the forty-seven rōnin who took action against Kira Yoshinaka were those left by Asano Naganori. In fact, they were a decidedly minor fraction of the over three hundred retainers that Asano once supported. Sorai also noted that the retainers killed Kira, but he neglected to add the extent of the collateral carnage: sixteen of Kira's guards were also killed in the attack, and twenty-seven others wounded. Nor did Sorai mention the *rōnin* march across Edo unopposed and unpursued, surely a poor reflection on the shogunate and its ability to respond to violence within the capital. The presentation of Kira's head at the Sengakuji, the Asano family temple in Edo, home of Asano Naganori's grave, is similarly omitted from Sorai's account, as is the fact that the *rōnin* left a statement documenting their motives and intent to kill Kira, in effect providing a report of their crime to the authorities. Finally, Sorai suggests that the *rōnin* were bound and captured when, as things turned out, they essentially reported their own crimes, and peacefully surrendered themselves to the authorities, without resistance, verbal objection, or otherwise.

8 Sorai's Judgment

After giving his brief narrative and noting that popular opinion cast the *rōnin* as "righteous samurai," it might appear that Sorai is exhibiting a variation of what came to be his signature *kobunjigaku* methodology of appealing to ancient words and phrases by adding that "in his view" the *rōnin* were "akin to the five hundred retainers of Tian Heng 田横 who committed suicide *en masse* following the death of their master." However, Hayashi Hōkō also alluded to Tian Heng in what was seemingly the first essay on the incident, making the comparison of the forty-seven rōnin to the five hundred retainers of Tian Heng equally of Neo-Confucian provenance. In any event, the allusion is to an incident described in some detail in Sima Qian's 司馬遷 (145–86 BCE) *Historical Records* (*Shiji* 史記). Sima recounts that Tian Heng rose to prominence as a defender of the Tian line in the state of Qi 齊, even as Han (206 BCE–220 CE) dynasty forces were intent on conquering the same kingdom in the wake of the collapse of the Qin (221–206 BCE) dynasty. With the founding of the Han dynasty, Tian Heng feared persecution by the first emperor and so fled with five hundred of his retainers to an unidentified island off the coast of China. Later, the first emperor of the Han invited Tian Heng to the Han court for an audience, and even suggested that Tian Heng would be recognized within the new regime. After initially declining, Tian Heng proceeded to Luoyang, the capital. Suspecting that certain death at the decree of his former rival awaited him, he committed suicide along the way. At his request, his attendants presented his head to the Han emperor. The two attendants were subsequently allowed to commit suicide at Tian Heng's grave after the latter was buried, reportedly with the rites of a king. Later, the remaining 500 retainers, upon learning of Tian Heng's death, promptly committed suicide on the island to which Tian Heng had earlier fled. Commenting on this incident, Sima Qian praised the retainers as men of the "highest worth" (*zhi xian* 至賢), but also asked why none of the retainers, who were not unskilled in strategy and planning, had sought to chart an alternative course (Sima Qian ch. 94; Ogawa 1975: 56–64; Watson 1993: 200–202; Nienhauser 2008: 147–150). Presumably, Sorai, in likening the *rōnin* to Tian Heng's retainers, both admired them, but also wondered why, given the abilities they evidently had in planning and execution, could not have provided for a better outcome to events.

Sorai next argues that the forty-seven samurai had not taken revenge on their lord's enemy (*ada* 仇). Implied is that they had murdered an innocent man. Sorai reasons that Asano Naganori wanted to kill Kira Yoshinaka, but Kira Yoshinaka had no desire to kill Asano Naganori. For that reason, Sorai declares that Kira could not be deemed the enemy of Asano Naganori (*kimi no ada to iubekarazaru nari* 不可謂君仇也). Sorai further reasons that it was because the lord of Akō domain wanted to kill Kira Yoshinaka that his family's domain, Akō, was confiscated. Kira Yoshinaka had not, however, wanted to confiscate Akō. For that reason, Sorai again declared unequivocally that the *rōnin* attack on Kira could not be described as revenge on the enemy of their lord (Ogyū 1974: 400–401). In this respect, Sorai and Shundai did indeed share common ground, but Sorai never hinted that the *rōnin* should have viewed the shogunate as the real enemy of their lord, and so the proper target of their vengeance.

Sorai had little good to say about Asano Naganori. He explained, for example, that because of "one morning's anger" (*itchō no ikari* 一朝之忿), Asano Naganori forgot about his ancestors, stooped to the level of a rustic's rash courage (*hippu no yū* 匹夫之勇), and in the end, failed in his attempt to kill Kira Yoshinaka. For this, Sorai declared that Asano Naganori should be deemed "not righteous" (*fugi to iubeki nari* 可謂不義). Therefore, at best the forty-seven samurai could be praised for having brought to completion their master's evil intentions (*yoku sono kimi no jashi o tsugu* 能継其君之邪志). But Sorai then asked how can fulfilling the evil intentions of one's master possibly be considered an exemplification of righteousness? (Ogyū 1974: 400–401).

Somewhat sarcastically, Sorai observed that since the samurai were unable to save their master from his unrighteousness in life, they chose to complete "their master's unrighteous intentions" (*kimi no fugi no kokorozashi* 君不義之志) through their own deaths. Still, even when he tried to consider their circumstances and feelings, he asked how on earth the entire incident could not be deemed egregiously pathetic (*ōi ni awaremubekarazaran ya* 大いに憫むべからざらんや). For that reason, Sorai declared that he viewed the forty-seven samurai as comrades of the five hundred retainers of Tian Heng (Ogyū 1974: 400–401).

At this crucial juncture, Sorai introduced the case of Gido Ichibei, asking whether Ichibei's example was not superior to that of the retainers of Asano Naganori. Ichibei exerted himself with deference and modesty (*kikyū* 鞠躬) in following a path of loyalty to his master (*aruji ni chū taru no michi* 忠主之道), thereby doing well everything that he could and should have done. He was persistent, never giving up despite the years his loyalty to his lord consumed. His sincerity in purpose (*seishi* 志) ultimately moved the authorities to restore his master's family and their standing as good people. In this, did he not surpass, Sorai asked, by some degree the retainers of Asano Naganori? Although the circumstances Ichibei encountered were not the same as those of the forty-seven, when it came to Ichibei's sense of purpose, Sorai declared without equivocation that it was surely an expression of righteousness (Ogyū 1974: 400–401).

8.1 *Sorai Giritsusho*

As noted earlier, the *Giritsusho* is not included in Sorai's *Collected Works* (*Sorai shū* 徂徠集), or other compilations that purport to include his authentic writings and/or publications. It is included, however, in a late-Tokugawa anthology edited by Nabeta Sanzen (Shōzan) 鍋田三善・晶山 (1778–1858), *Writings on the Righteous Samurai of Akō Domain* (*Akō gijin sansho* 赤穂義人纂書), along with not a few other documents now viewed as apocryphal. Even in the *Akō gijin sansho*, the text is preceded by a note explaining that it is a copy of one stored in Kumamoto, where it was passed down by the Hosokawa family, *daimyō* of the former Tokugawa domain. It was supposedly Sorai's response to questions posed by the *bakufu* regarding how the Akō vendetta should be dealt with (Nabeta 1911: 150). The Hosokawa family was interested in the incident in part because seventeen of the *rōnin* – including Ōishi Yoshio – had been confined at the Hosokawa compound following their vendetta. And it was there that those seventeen were sentenced to death by *seppuku*, and there that the death ritual was carried out. The Hosokawa *daimyō* had treated the *rōnin* exceptionally well, and even declared in the wake of their deaths that they would be spiritual guardians of his domain's samurai. Although the *Giritsusho* does not praise the forty-seven without qualification, it is far more accommodating of them and their deeds than is Sorai's "Essay on the Forty-Seven Samurai Incident." That the *Akō gijin sansho* addresses the limited circulation of the *Giritsusho* hints at some suspicion on the part of Nabeta Shōzan and those who assisted in the compilation of the *Akō gijin sansho* that the document might be spurious. As noted previously, while a substantial debate occurred in the aftermath of the vendetta with scholars openly criticizing one another, none mention the *Giritsusho*. This, combined with its absence from official compilations of Sorai's writings, suggests that it was most likely a later fabrication attributed to the famous scholar.[13]

The *Giritsusho* first defines some basic ethical and legal principles that echo those found in Sorai's *Bendō* and *Benmei*. It states, for example, that "righteousness is the way that purifies the self (*onore o isagiyoku suru no michi* 己を潔くするの道), while laws (*hō* 法) constitute "the rules and regulations (literally, the compass and square, *kiku* 規矩) of the world below heaven." The text adds "we regulate our minds with rites (*rei o mote kokoro o sei shi* 禮を以て心を制し), while we manage our affairs with righteousness (*gi o mote koto o sei su* 義を以て事を制す). Applying these to the vendetta, the *Giritsusho* adds that the forty-six samurai, in taking revenge on the enemy (*ada* 讎) of their master, understood the shame that comes to those who serve as samurai and so, in pursuing a path that enabled them to purify themselves, their deeds were righteous. However, the *Giritsusho* adds,

---

[13] For a contrary view, see James McMullen, "Confucian Perspectives on the Akō Revenge: Law and Moral Agency," *Monumenta Nipponica*, 58:3 (2003), pp. 1, 6–7, 22. McMullen questions the authenticity of Sorai's "Essay on the Forty-Seven Samurai Incident," noting how it was omitted from the 1740 publication of Sorai's *Collected Works*. Like Maruyama, he accepts the *Giritsusho*, without, however, addressing the fact that the *Giritsusho* as we know it today traces to an obscure text that was only transmitted in the Hosokawa family in remote Kumamoto domain.

because this way of thinking only applied to samurai, the conclusion that the forty-seven acted righteously amounts merely to "a personal opinion" (*watakushi no ron nari* 私の論なり). The *Giritsusho* goes on to explain why this is so by noting that when he struck Kira Yoshinaka, Asano Naganori was in the shogun's castle, and so, in attacking the shogunal master of ceremonies, behaved outrageously, and his "wrongdoing" (*tsumi* 罪) was dealt with accordingly. Moreover, he attacked Kira Yoshinaka even though he did not have the approval of the shogunal authorities (*kōgi* 公義) in doing so, and as a result, caused a disturbance (*sōdō* 騒動) in the castle. The law does not permit this (*hō ni oite yurusazaru tokoro nari* 法に於て許さざる所也). The *Giritsusho* then observes that the crimes of the forty-six samurai were dealt with according to the samurai rite of *seppuku*. This resolution expressed, the *Giritsusho* states, the perspective of the public interest (*kōron to iubeshi* 公論と云うべし). The *Giritsusho* concludes dramatically by stating that "if private interests (*shiron* 私論) are allowed to harm public interests (*kōron* 公論), then it will not be possible to establish the laws of the realm (*tenka no ho* 天下の法)" (Nabeta 1911: 150). Although a powerful statement affirming the rule of law over private interests and inclinations, it does not seem to have been Sorai's own judgment on the matter, but instead, one fabricated and attributed to him.

9   Meiji Echoes: Fukuzawa Yukichi

More than with Tokugawa essays on the *rōnin* incident, Sorai's writings resonate with the early Meiji period writings of Fukuzawa Yukichi. Fukuzawa addressed the incident in *Gakumon no susume* as he sought to illustrate what he deemed to be enlightened, civilized thinking about how citizens should respond to unjust laws and despotic rule. Following ideas of an American philosopher, Francis Wayland, as developed in the latter's *The Elements of Moral Science* (1835), Fukuzawa explained that citizens have three options: (1) to obey the laws even if unjust, (2) to rebel against them, and (3) to remonstrate civilly with the authorities even to the point of martyrdom in order to lay bare the egregiousness of the injustice being protested. It is this final option that Fukuzawa, like Wayland, endorsed. In doing so, Fukuzawa was thus philosophically proximate to Sorai insofar as Sorai's authentic essay on the incident had extolled the path taken by Gido Ichibei in his unrelenting remonstrations with the authorities for the sake of his village headman, who had been in his, Ichibei's view, treated unjustly. Although Fukuzawa's analysis of how one should respond to unjust laws is based on Wayland, Fukuzawa contextualized the issues in relation to the *rōnin* incident, realizing that virtually all Japanese were familiar with it and would more easily appreciate his views if cast in relation to it. Fukuzawa surely understood that in commenting on the incident, he was in effect extending the *rōnin* debate into the early Meiji, even as he sought to expound American political ethics to his readers. Although there is no evidence that Fukuzawa meant to endorse or even paraphrase Sorai's writings on the incident, his conclusions are strikingly similar to Sorai's insofar as they condemn the approach of violent opposition, and instead extol that of patient, even martyr-like remonstration with the authorities in opposition to unjust laws and decrees.

Fukuzawa did not, however, suggest that the *rōnin* should have directed their efforts against the shogunate instead of the master of ceremonies, but instead, like Sorai, asked why the *rōnin* did not petition, civilly yet persistently, the shogunate for reconsideration of the matter. Fukuzawa went so far as to say that the *rōnin* should have been willing to die, one by one, in petitioning the shogunate on behalf of the Asano line, rather than resort to a private vendetta targeting Kira Yoshinaka.

Fukuzawa did not mention Gido Ichibei, but did offer as an example of the kind of behaviour that he deemed to be a civilized response to unjust laws, the case of a Tokugawa period figure, Sakura Sōgorō 佐倉惣五郎. Fukuzawa admitted that knowledge of Sakura Sōgorō was more the product of legend than historical scholarship, but insisted that Sōgorō was the only exemplar, in premodern Japan, of relentlessly protesting unjust laws as a means to change them rather than resorting to violence of a more vigilante sort. While it might be entirely coincidental, Sōgorō reportedly hailed from the same general area as had Gido Ichibei, that of the Bōsō Peninsula, modern day Chiba Prefecture. Fukuzawa did not go into these details, but the legend of Sōgorō holds that he directly and repeatedly petitioned the authorities on behalf of the interests of the peasantry of his village. Despite the non-violent nature of Sōgorō's petitions, they were in violation of the law. As a result, he was finally put to death, along with his family. Fukuzawa saw in Sōgorō's willingness to make, even if only in legend, the ultimate sacrifice, the kind of civil political behaviour that modern, civilized Japanese should take up in response to unjust laws. Admittedly, Fukuzawa never mentions Sorai in this context, but insofar as his reflections on the *rōnin* incident (1) suggested that the *rōnin* were not righteous, (2) advocated remonstrating with the authorities as a way of protesting unjust laws and decisions, and (3) elevated a peasant leader from the Kantō hinterlands as an exemplar of the non-violent path he endorsed, Fukuzawa's thinking at the very least echoed that of Sorai. Insofar as Fukuzawa's in turn drew on the thinking of a Western ethicist and was an expression of Japan's mid-nineteenth century version of modernity, so in turn do Sorai's rather similar views convey a decidedly modern air. Moreover, insofar as the course of non-violent civil protest remains one widely endorsed if seldom practiced even in contemporary times, Sorai's views continue to be relevant even today for those contemplating a civil response to unjust laws.

Bibliography

Asami Keisai 浅見絅斎. 1974. "Shijūrokushi ron" 四十六士論. In Ishii Shirō 石井紫郎, ed. *Kinsei buke shisō* 近世武家思想. NST, vol. 27. Tokyo: Iwanami Shoten.

Dazai Shundai 太宰春台. 1974. "Akō shijuroku shi ron" 赤穂四十六士論. In Ishii Shirō, ed. *Kinsei buke shisō*. NST, vol. 27. Tokyo: Iwanami Shoten.

Fukuzawa Yukichi 福澤諭吉. 1959. *Gakumon no susume* 学問のすゝめ. In *Fukuzawa Yukichi zenshū* 福澤諭吉全集, vol. 3. Tokyo: Iwanami Shoten.

Hayashi Hōkō 林鳳岡. 1974. *Fukushū ron* 復讐論. In Ishii Shirō, ed. *Kinsei buke shisō*. NST, vol. 27. Tokyo: Iwanami Shoten.

Ishii Shirō 石井紫郎, ed. 1974. *Kinsei buke shisō* 近世武家思想. NST, vol. 27. Tokyo: Iwanami Shoten.

Lidin, Olof G. 1999. *Ogyū Sorai's Discourse on Government (Seidan): An Annotated Translation.* Wiesbaden: Harrassowitz.

Maruyama Masao 丸山眞男. 1952. *Nihon seiji shisōshi kenkyū* 日本政治思想史研究. Tokyo: Tokyo Daigaku Shuppankai.

Maruyama, Masao. 1974. *Studies in the Intellectual History of Tokugawa Japan.* Trans. Hane Mikiso. Princeton: Princeton University Press.

McMullen, James. 2003. "Confucian Perspectives on the Akō Revenge: Law and Moral Agency." *Monumenta Nipponica* 58:3.

Muro Kyūsō 室鳩巣. 1974. *Akō gijin roku* 赤穂義人録. In Ishii Shirō, ed. *Kinsei buke shisō* 近世武家思想. NST, vol. 27. Tokyo: Iwanami Shoten.

Nabeta Shōzan (Sanzen) 鍋田晶山 (三善). 1910–1911. *Akō gijin sansho* 赤穂義人纂書. 3 vols. Tokyo: Kokusho Kankōkai.

Nienhauser, William H., editor. 2008. *The Grand Scribe's Records, Volume Three: The Memoirs of Han China, Part 1, by Ssu-ma Ch'ien.* Bloomington: Indiana University Press.

Ogawa Tamaki 小川環樹. 1975. *Shiki retsuden* 史記列伝, vol. 3. Tokyo: Iwanami Shoten.

Ogyū Sorai 荻生徂徠. 1791. *Sorai-shū* 徂徠集. Osaka: Bunkindō.

Ogyū Sorai. 1973a. *Sorai-shū* 徂徠集. In Yoshikawa Kōjirō 吉川幸次郎 et al., eds. *Ogyū Sorai* 荻生徂徠 (excerpts). NST, vol. 36. Tokyo: Iwanami Shoten.

Ogyū Sorai. 1973b. *Seidan* 政談. In Yoshikawa Kōjirō et al., eds. *Ogyū Sorai.* NST, vol. 36. Tokyo: Iwanami Shoten.

Ogyū Sorai. 1974. "Shijūshichishi no koto o ronzu" 論四十七士事. In Ishii Shirō, ed. *Kinsei buke shisō*. NST, vol. 27. Tokyo: Iwanami Shoten.

Satō Naokata 佐藤直方. 1974. *Shijūrokunin no hikki* 四十六人の筆記. In Ishii Shirō, ed. *Kinsei buke shisō* 近世武家思想. NST, vol. 27. Tokyo: Iwanami Shoten.

Shōtoku-taishi 聖徳太子. 1975. *Kenpō jūshichijō* 憲法十七条. In Ienaga Saburō 家永三郎 et al., eds. *Shōtoku-taishi shū* 聖徳太子集. Tokyo: Iwanami Shoten.

Sima Qian 司馬遷, "Tian Dan liezhuan" 田儋列傳, *Shiji* 史記, ch. 94.

Sorai Giritsusho 徂徠擬律書. 1911. In *Akō gijin sansho* 赤穂義人纂書, vol. 3. Nabeta Shōzan 鍋田晶山, ed. Tokyo: Kokusho Kankōkai.

Tahara Tsuguo 田原嗣郎. 1978. *Akō shijūrokushi ron: bakuhansei no seishin kōzō* 赤穂四十六士論: 幕藩制の精神構造. Tokyo: Yoshikawa Kōbunkan.

Watson, Burton, translator. 1993. *Records of the Grand Historian: Han Dynasty, Volume 1.* New York: Columbia University Press.

Yoshikawa Kōjirō. 1973. "Sorai gakuan" 徂徠学案. In Yoshikawa Kōjirō et al., eds. *Ogyū Sorai.* NST, vol. 36. Tokyo: Iwanami Shoten, pp. 629–739.

Yoshikawa Kōjirō. 1983. *Jinsai, Sorai, Norinaga: Three Classical Philologists of Mid-Tokugawa Japan.* Tokyo: The Tōhō Gakkai.

Chapter 14
"The Reception of Sorai's Thought in the Second Half of the Edo Period"

W. J. Boot

In modern Japan, Ogyū Sorai is the best-known Confucian thinker of the Edo Period (1600–1868). The question I want to address in this article is, whether Sorai was as famous before the opening of the country as he became after World War II, and what he was famous for in his own time. It is difficult to measure popularity and influence, but if we go by such indications as number and quality of disciples, number of books in print, and the number and contents of the critical reactions from contemporaries, it should be possible to get a fairly good idea – at the same time of the measure of someone's popularity (or notoriety) and of the nature of his appeal.

In this essay, I will explore two of the three avenues mentioned above: genealogies and critical reactions. Sorai's important writings are all treated in the "Introductions" (*kaidai*); hence, it will not be necessary to cover the same ground again, here.

1 Genealogies

A good impression of the *total* number of disciples and of disciples of disciples of Sorai is given by the early-Meiji source *Jugaku genryū* 儒学源流. If we count all the names listed there, we come to a total of 113 disciples in the first and later generations, which is appreciably more than the number for Itō Jinsai 伊藤仁斎 (1627–1705), who would be the nearest point of comparison; Jinsai only comes to 48.[1] For

---

[1] See *Nihon kyōikushi shiryō* vol. 8, resp. pp. 57–66 for Sorai, and pp. 53–57 for Jinsai. N.B. *Jugaku genryū* was compiled by Sugiura Masaomi 杉浦正臣; the *batsu* is dated Meiji 17 (1884). Masaomi studied with the Kyoto scholar Iwagaki Gesshū 岩垣月洲 (1808–1873; *KGS* 609). He is represented in *NKSM*) with two titles, undated; no further details are known.

W. J. Boot (✉)
Leiden Institute of Area Studies (LIAS), Faculty of Humanities, Leiden University,
Leiden, The Netherlands
e-mail: w.j.boot@hum.leidenuniv.nl

© Springer Nature Switzerland AG 2019
W. J. Boot, Takayama Daiki (eds.), *Tetsugaku Companion to Ogyū Sorai*,
Tetsugaku Companions to Japanese Philosophy 2,
https://doi.org/10.1007/978-3-030-15475-2_14

Sorai, *Jugaku genryū* lists forty direct disciples, fifty-eight disciples in the second generation, thirteen in the third generation, and two in the fourth. The largest numbers of disciples of the second and later generations (15 > 3 > 1) studied with Hattori Nankaku 服部南郭 (1683–1759). Nankaku is followed by Yamagata Shūnan 山縣 周南 (1687–1752), who had 13 > 3 > 1 disciples; Ōuchi Yūji 大内熊耳 (1697– 1776), who had ten direct disciples of his own, and one in the next generation; and Dazai Shundai 太宰春台 (1680–1747), for whom *Jugaku genryū* lists seven direct disciples, and three in the following generation.

Similarly, in the most important study of Sorai made before the war, Iwahashi Junsei (1883–1933) lists sixty-four direct, first-generation disciples of Sorai, nine of whom are Buddhist priests.[2] The most prolific of the disciples were Nankaku, who had twenty-two direct disciples, and nineteen in the second to fifth generations; Shundai, who had fifteen disciples in the first generation, and nine in the second and third; and Shūnan, who had seventeen direct disciples, and five more in the second and third generations. A good runner-up is, again, Yūji, who has ten direct disciples, and twenty more in the second, third, and fourth generations. A new name is the priest Daichō 大潮 (1676–1768), who has three direct disciples to his credit, and twenty-one more in the second and third generations, only two of whom are bonzes. Iwahashi also lists Sorai's direct (through his adopted son) descendants into the fifth generation; they were Confucians in the employ of the domain Kōriyama, which in 1724 had become the new fief of the Yanagisawa; they did not continue Sorai's school.[3]

Similar indications are given by other lists, such as the list made by Ichikawa Mototarō.[4] It gives the names of twenty-seven first-generation disciples, followed by twenty-nine in the second generation, eight in the third, and three in the fourth. Of these, again Dazai Shundai (6 > 5 > 1), Hattori Nankaku (7 > 23), Yamagata Shūnan (4 > 1 > 2), and Ōuchi Yūji (3) have the most disciples of their own. These modern lists fit with lists from the Edo Period such as the hand-written list *Itan Sorai gakka* 異端徂徠学家, which has thirty-two disciples in the first generation; of these, again, Nankaku, Shundai, and Shūnan have the most disciples of their own.[5]

It seems we may forget Ōuchi Yūji. Although he had the signal distinction of having taught the Mito scholar Tachihara Suiken 立原翠軒 (1744–1823), he wrote very little, and what he wrote was poetry.[6] The same would at first sight seem to

---

[2] They may have attended Sorai's school on the principle of "know thy enemy," but the more probable reason is that they wanted to learn Chinese in order to be able to compose Chinese poetry.

[3] See appendix in Iwahashi, *Sorai kenkyū*.

[4] See Ichikawa, *Jugaku shi* vol. 5, p. 239.

[5] *Itan Sorai gakka* (Seidō 120–6) is kept in the archive of the Confucius Temple in Nagasaki. It is undated and not signed. As one of the three third-generation students who are mentioned, Wakatsuki Taiya 若月大野 (*KGS* no. 4869), lived 1721–1790, this should put the *terminus post quem* for the completion of the list somewhere around 1755.

[6] *NKSM* lists six titles, four of which apparently are no longer extant. See also the printers' announcement of Genbun 2 (1737), that mentions two titles edited by him, next to *Sorai-shū*, *Bendō*, *Benmei*, and *Rongo-chō*; quoted Hiraishi, *Kaidai*, p. 16.

apply to Daichō, who produced *haiku*, Chinese poetry and prose, and four titles of Buddhist relevance.[7] However, through his disciple Uno Meika 宇野明霞 (1698–1745) he is connected with Katayama Hokkai 片山北海 (1723–1790) and Hokkai's disciple Bitō Jishū 尾藤二洲 (1747–1813), i.e., with the anti-Sorai movement that reared its head in the Kansai in the second half of the eighteenth century. Satō Issai 佐藤一斎 (1772–1859), follower of Wang Yangming and teacher at the *bakufu*'s academy of Confucian studies, the Shōheizaka Gakumonjo, is also listed as a disciple of Meika (through the priest Daiten 大典, 1719–1801). Not only Jishū and Issai, but also Daiten had connections with the *bakufu*. The latter had been "in charge of the correspondence with Korea," i.e., been stationed at the Iteian 以酊庵 on Tsushima as Iteian *rinban* 輪番, and was known to, and appreciated by Matsudaira Sadanobu 松平定信 (1758–1829) himself.[8]

So, when we conclude that from the genealogies Dazai Shundai, Hattori Nankaku, and Yamagata Shūnan emerge as Sorai's most prolific disciples we merely restate the *communis opinio* that they are his most *important* disciples. It goes without saying, that this consensus was not reached on the basis of a nose count, but on more subtle mechanisms of social negotiation within Sorai's school, and between later scholars. We will come to this in one of the following sections. It is interesting, nevertheless, to see to what extent the consensus is underscored by the relative attraction these disciples had on young intellectuals. It also leads to the question, why some of Sorai's other disciples are left out of the list, though they, too, scored rather well on popular attraction.

2 Assessments

A fairly non-partisan assessment of Sorai is given by the Kyushu schoolmaster Hirose Tansō 廣瀬淡窓 (1782–1856) in his *Jurin-hyō* 儒林評 ("An evaluation of the Wood of Confucians"; 1836).[9] In his opinion, "Sorai was a unique personality in our country, past and present. It is because of his many merits that in those days Japan's scholarship greatly flourished. The poisons he poured into the empire, too,

---

[7] *NKSM* lists fourteen titles s.v. "Daichō."

[8] After it had become public knowledge that on Tsushima they were doctoring the state letters exchanged between Seoul and Edo (the so-called Yanagawa Incident, 1635), the *bakufu* sent a priest selected from the large Zen monasteries in Kyoto to Tsushima to keep an eye on the diplomatic correspondence and other contacts with Korea. The office goes by a number of names: *Chōsen shūbun shoku* 朝鮮修文職, *Chōsen shokei goyō* 書契御用, or *Taishū shoyaku* 対州書役. Because the monks were stationed on Tsushima for periods of one to two years, the system is known as the Iteian *rinban* 輪番 system. Daiten was located in the Shōkokuji (Kyoto), so he probably met Sadanobu during the latter's visit to the Kansai in 1788.

[9] *Jurin-hyō*, quoted from Nihon Jurin Sōsho vol. 3, separately paginated. A comparable account is given in Nawa Rodō 那波魯堂, *Gakumon genryū* 学問源流 16b-28a.

were very many.[10] In someone's evaluation, he was 'The Head of the Meritorious and the Leader of Sinful' 功首罪魁. This is truly how it must have been."[11]

"That Sorai appeared in our country," he continues, "was because he was generated from the heat and steam of the compressed hegemonic spirit of that period. In those days, it was Sorai amongst the Confucians, and Hōtan[12] 鳳潭 (1654–1738) amongst the Buddhists. In daring and boldness, both were superior to [anyone else,] now or formerly. They chided the Sages and rebuked the wise; they abolished the Buddha and ignored the patriarchs; vociferously, they occupied their independent positions between heaven and earth. Their actions and temperaments were all [the result of] the hegemonic spirit. If the hegemonic spirit had not been vigorous throughout the state, how could it possibly have brought forth men like these? As regards their plusses and minuses, their good and bad points – when a knowledgeable person looks at them, they will be clear, without debating them in depth."[13]

"Sorai was someone who excelled in literary scholarship (*bungaku*). He had realized that moving important people was not his *forte*. Although he served the new favourite [of Shogun Tsunayoshi], Lord Yanagisawa [Yoshiyasu] 柳沢吉保 (1658–1714), he did not become a senior vassal, but held an exclusively scholarly appointment. Although he came very close to Jōken'in 常憲院 (= Tsunayoshi) and also had an audience with Yūtokuin 有徳院 (= Yoshimune), in the end he did not receive an appointment. If you had put Banzan or Hakuseki in his position, I think they would have been somewhat more inventive."[14]

Tansō also discusses three of Sorai's pupils – Shundai and Nankaku briefly, and Shūnan at some length. Shundai he calls "a straight and stern person," whose "scholarship is based on Sorai's, but as a person, he did not resemble him at all; in character he was close to Cheng Yichuan 程伊川 (1033–1107)," one of the Song patriarchs of Neo-Confucianism. Of Nankaku he says, on the authority of Shūnan's student Nagatomi Dokushōan 永富獨嘯庵 (1732–1766; *KGS* 3210), that "he stood highest amongst Sorai's students." "He disliked arguing with people; he had a temperament [suited] to amusing himself leisurely in this world."[15]

Of Shūnan, he writes: "In the evaluation of Kamei Shōyō 亀井昭陽 (1773–1836; *KGS* 1421), Shūnan was the first of Sorai's students. Outwardly, he was warm and

---

[10] Tansō does not explain what poisons he had in mind, but the remark will at least partially refer back to what he wrote earlier: "In those days students of Ancient Studies went in for frivolity and debauchery; this was exclusively a vice of followers of Sorai." (Nihon Jurin Sōsho vol. 3, p. 4.)

[11] Hirose, *Jurin-hyō*, p. 5. Who the "someone" is, is unclear.

[12] Hōtan studied at the Enryakuji and was ordained as a Tendai monk. He wanted to travel to China and India, but that was, of course, impossible in those days. Instead, he studied widely in various monasteries in the Kansai. He took an interest in the Kegon 華厳 School and spent the remainder of his life trying to revive it. From 1704 till 1723 he was in Edo, teaching Kegon doctrine and writing about it. In 1723, he returned to Kyoto and founded the Daikegonji in Matsuo. He continued to be active in his discussions with monks of other sects, esp. those of the Pure Land and Nichiren Sects. In *NKSM* he has fifty-two titles to his name.

[13] Hirose, *Jurin-hyō*, pp. 5–6.

[14] Hirose, *Jurin-hyō*, p. 6.

[15] Hirose, *Jurin-hyō*, p. 6

friendly; inwardly, he was very talented. He did not seem to believe particularly in the ancient words and phrases (*kobunji*); he had discernment, and thus, as a rule, he was not led astray by his teacher's theories."[16] To this, Tansō adds his own evaluation: "When I read Sorai's *Collected Works* 徂徠集, I knew that Shūnan was loyal to his teacher. In Sorai's *Collected Works*, there are a great many inscriptions of pavilions and prefaces [in honour of] old age that he wrote in response to requests from every province, but there is not even one that he wrote for anyone from Suō and Nagato.[17] What we have [for those two provinces], are all discussions (*ron* 論) of the Way, written on request. This is because Shūnan was the intermediary and made the introductions [to Sorai]. We must say that a man like Shūnan really knew how to honour his master. Those who are disciples of others should take Shūnan as their example."[18]

Tansō also mentions the monk Daiko 大湖 from Hizen, who had never been a disciple of Sorai, but who had been in contact with him and had studied literature through the theories of Sorai. "After Sorai died, his reputation moved the empire. People in Kyushu heard of his method; they all longed for it and studied his theories through Daiko."[19]

Apart from playing up the Kyushu angle and underscoring Sorai's intrinsic importance, Tansō says three things: Sorai was not very adept in interpersonal relations, which explains why he found it hard to get a decent appointment after Yanagisawa Yoshiyasu's 柳沢吉保 fall from power; second, that the students of his school were inclined to profligacy, which made him and his school notorious, rather than famous; third, that Shūnan stood highest among his disciples.

The criticism of the profligacy of his school's students peaked in the *Kansei igaku no kin* 寛政異学の禁 ("Prohibition of heterodox teachings") of Kansei 2 (1790). In this prohibition, Matsudaira Sadanobu indicted the head of the Hayashi family, Hayashi Kinpō 林錦峯 (1767–1792), for falling short in supervising the students of Confucianism. This was hardly his task, of course, and Sadanobu had ulterior aims with his accusation, but the indictment repeated the by then standard criticism of the students from Sorai's school, that they "studied various new-fangled teachings, that heterodox studies were popular, and that there were those who injured morals."

---

[16] Hirose, *Jurin-hyō*, pp. 6–7.

[17] The point is that Shūnan came from Nagato and was the rector of the fief academy Meirinkan in Hagi.

[18] Hirose, *Jurin-hyō*, p. 7.

[19] Hirose, *Jurin-hyō*, p. 8.

3 Disciples

From the above, it is clear that Dazai Shundai, Hattori Nankaku, and Yamagata Shūnan were generally recognised as Sorai's most important students and the mainstays of his school. If, however, one therefore assumes that they spent their time spreading their teacher's doctrine, one is on the wrong track. The point is that the implication "X studied with Y, *therefore* he preached Y's doctrines," does not really hold in early modern Japan. The fact that one had studied with Master Y gave a general indication of quality and area of specialization. Between master and disciples there existed bonds of friendship, of patronage, and of loyalty, but doctrinal purity would be too much to expect.

A blot on his disciples' reputation is Sorai's *Bunshū*, his "Collected Literary Works" in Chinese.[20] Tradition prescribed that such a work was to be compiled after the Master's death by his grateful sons and disciples. Sorai's disciples, too, undertook the task, and the work appeared, eventually. It is not *too* voluminous, counting seven fascicles of poetry and twenty-three of prose.[21] Compilation was led by Hattori Nankaku, but nowhere is his name, or the name of any of the other collaborators mentioned, not even at the beginning of the individual fascicles, where one would expect, next to 物茂卿著 ("written by Butsu Mokei"), a reassuring 南郭校 ("edited by Nankaku") or something along those lines.

Compilation seems to have begun in Kyōhō 17 (1732). In this year, "On the basis of Nankaku's collation of the writings left by Sorai, they were divided into [sets of] one or two fascicles each, and clean copies were made by Sorai's disciples."[22] Some of Sorai's texts were edited, and there was some discussion among the disciples about which texts to include. There was, in other words, a measure of collaboration, so the standard assumption that Nankaku decided everything has to be reversed.[23] It was Nankaku, however, who seems to have done his best to weed out printer's errors, pointing out mistakes in the *printed* books for the next edition.[24]

The *Sorai-shū* was published in three stages (1735: poetry; 1737: prose; 1740: letters), with two different publishers. It does not contain any biographical accounts (*nenpu* 年譜 or *gyōjō* 行状) of Sorai. The most amazing thing, however, is that it has only one preface and not even one postface. The preface is written by Honda

---

[20] I use the facsimile edition in Kinsei Juka Bunshū Shūsei vol. 3, edited and introduced (*kaidai*) by Hiraishi Naoaki.

[21] Compare this with Hayashi Razan 林羅山, whose sons published a *Shishū* and a *Bunshū* of seventy-five fascicles each, or with his son Gahō 鵞峰, whose Collected Works count 150 fascicles of poems and 150 of prose.

[22] The source is *Ken'en zatsuwa* 蘐園雑話, quoted by Hiraishi, *Kaidai*, p. 9. Hiraishi mentions by name Nankaku, Shundai, Miura Chikkei 竹渓 (1689–1756; *KGS* 4189), one Kentaku 堅卓, Takami Sōkyū 鷹見爽鳩 (1690–1735; *KGS* 2657), and Tanaka Ranryō 田中蘭陵 (1699–1734; *KGS* 2535) as the students who collaborated on the compilation of the *Bunshū*. See also his conclusion, ibid., p. 17.

[23] Hiraishi, *Kaidai*, p. 10.

[24] Hiraishi, *Kaidai*, p. 2, pp. 18–19.

Tadamune 本多忠統 (1691–1757), who mainly asks himself (in the preface) whether he is the one who should have written it.[25]

To me, all this argues lack of organization, lack of manpower, and lack of money, in short, a lack of cohesion within Sorai's school. The most probable reason why Tadamune wrote the preface was that he, as a *daimyō*, had put up the money to make publication possible, as he had also composed the text inscribed on the stele on Sorai's grave, and probably paid for that as well.[26]

No one will deny Shundai, Nankaku, and Shūnan broadly stood within the tradition of Sorai. They all privileged the more ancient forms of classical Chinese, were in favour of the study of the classics and of a philological approach to texts, and were dismissive of the need for personal, moral cultivation. If, however, one looks more closely at their biographies and writings, differences appear. These may have been a matter of temperament, as Tansō writes, but it is also important to realise that they entered Sorai's school in different ways and at different ages, and that they had different social backgrounds. Shūnan and Shundai belonged to the warrior class; Nankaku belonged to the social layer of city-dwelling merchants and artisans (*chōnin* 町人).

Yamagata Shūnan, the youngest of the three, entered the school at the age of eighteen. He studied with Sorai for three years (1705–1707),[27] and then returned to Hagi, where he became reader-in waiting of the *daimyō* (Kyōhō 2; 1717). In 1719, he was involved in setting up the new domain school Meirinkan 明倫館. In Genbun 2 (1737), after the death of the first incumbent, Ogura Shōsai 小倉尚斎(1677–1737; *KGS* 830), he became director of the school. In 1748 he stepped down because of a chronic illness. In the twenty years between 1717 and 1737 he frequently visited Edo in the company of his lord, but the *gyōjō* makes no mention of visits to Sorai in this context. At the end of the *gyōjō*, when the chronological part is finished, the following is said about his relation to Sorai: "In his studies he exclusively followed master Sorai's teachings, and he made the Classics and literature 経術文章 the core [of his curriculum]. In prose, he made the Qin and the Han his point of reference,

---

[25] Tadamune was suggested by Shundai in a letter to Nankaku (*Shisen ni atauru sho* 與子遷書); see *Shishien kōkō* 紫芝園後稿 12:9a-10b (pp. 242–243): "You have received the command of our late Master and have compiled his remaining writings. The work is already being printed. This is truly something great. The only thing I especially regret is that you have not placed a preface by a noble man at the beginning of the [first] fascicle. ... You are close to Lord Iran 猗蘭 (= Tadamune). Because I suffer from a slight cold, I cannot now visit his lordship. That is why I say this to you." Cf. Hiraishi, *Kaidai*, p. 16.

[26] My general contention, for which I have no direct evidence, is that *Kanbun* texts were not a commercially viable product, and that a printer or bookshop had to be subsidized in order to undertake the printing of such texts. The obvious sources of money were the pupils of the private academies, or the authorities.

[27] The *Senkō* 先考 *Shūnan-sensei gyōjō* 行状 (*Shūnan-sensei bunshū* 10, separately paginated), p. 1b, says "at the age of nineteen" (Japanese style). Hiraishi, *Kaidai*, p. 5, says that Shūnan entered Sorai's school "in the beginning of the Hōei Era," so 1704–1705. Anyway, as a student he was senior to Shundai and Nankaku.

and in poetry, the Tang and the Ming."[28] Of course, Shūnan's son wrote the *gyōjō* in order to honour his father, not his father's teacher; still, the comment strikes one as utterly bland.

Both Shundai and Nankaku were older and had had a previous career. Shundai had studied Confucianism in Edo with Nakano Kiken 中野攝謙 (1667–1720; *KGS* 3136) and afterwards, during his 10-year banishment in Kyoto, with Itō Jinsai. Here he had also tried his hand at medicine. When he returned to Edo, in 1711, an old friend of his days in Kiken's school, Andō Tōya 安藤東野 (1783–1719; *KGS* 249), introduced him to Sorai. At the time, Shundai was thirty-one.

Nankaku had been a specialist in Japanese poetry and a member of Yanagisawa Yoshiyasu's *otogi-shū* 御伽衆 (personal entourage). It was Yoshiyasu's retirement and approaching death that made him turn to Chinese poetry and Sorai. Both Shundai and Nankaku eventually set themselves up as independent teachers in Edo.

As far as their thought and ideas were concerned, of the three, Shundai stood closest to Sorai.[29] The story is that, when he first met Sorai, he showed him his poetry, to which Sorai reacted with the words: "In the field of Chinese poetry and prose 詩文 (*shibun*), you have already established yourself. Apply yourself to the study of the Classics 経学 (*keigaku*)."[30]

Shundai's most important publications are *Keizai-roku* 経済録 (pref. 1729; not printed), and *Kōshi kego zōchū* 孔子家語増註 (printed 1736; 10 fasc.). A more popularizing book in *katakana*, *Seigaku mondō* 聖学問答 ("Questions and answers about the teaching of the Sages") was a great hit, to judge by the number of surviving copies. In it, we find statements like the following, that are pure Sorai: "In the Way of the Sages there definitely is no discussion of the good or bad at the bottom of a man's heart. The teachings of the Sages are skills that enter from the outside. In one's behaviour, one observes the Rites of the ancient kings. In dealing with affairs, one makes use of the Righteousness of the ancient kings. Someone who has the outward appearance of a gentleman is *deemed to be* a gentleman. One does not ask how that person's inner heart is."[31]

In the same *Seigaku mondō*, Shundai writes the following about his relationship with Sorai: "Through Sorai, we realised that the Way of the ancient kings should be sought in the Six Classics and that the way of Confucius was [identical with] the Way of the ancient kings. We also knew, that many words of Mencius are different from [those of] Confucius. Although I (= Shundai) followed Master Sorai and lis-

---

[28] See *Senkō Shūnan-sensei gyōjō* 行状 (fasc. 10, separately paginated), pp. 4b–5a. N.B. The preface of *Shūnan-sensei bunshū* is dated 1755 (Hōreki 5); the printer's colophon is dated Hōreki 10 (1760). The *Bunshū* contains three letters to Sorai, two of which Shūnan wrote on behalf of his father; see *op. cit.*, 10:5b–10a.

[29] On the other hand, no letters from Sorai to him are included in *Sorai-shū*, probably (Hiraishi's surmise) because Sorai and Shundai were estranged in Sorai's final years; see Hiraishi, *Kaidai*, p. 20.

[30] See Ichikawa, *Jugaku shi* vol. 5, p. 241; Bitō, *Kaidai*, NST 37, p. 491. The original *locus* is *Bunkai zakki* 文会雑記 1b.

[31] This passage from *Seigaku mondō* (2 fasc.; pr. 1736) is quoted in Inoue Tetsujirō, *Nihon Kogakuha no tetsugaku*, p. 691; see also the edition in *Sorai gakuha*, NST 37, p. 95.

tened to his discussions, initially I did not yet understand that he was right. When, however, I had immersed my heart in the Six Classics, had thought deeply and read widely in the ancient books, I probed the heart of the ancients and could elucidate [what I had read] earlier with [what I read] later, and left and right I met sources [of the Way].[32] After I had repeatedly studied [the Classics] for more than ten years, the web of doubts was torn for the first time. When you study the Way of the Sages, you should not only read such canonical books as the Six Classics, the *Analects*, and the *Xiaojing* 孝経 ("Classic of filial Piety"), but you should also widely read all books under heaven and understand even the books of the sundry teachers and the hundred schools. Otherwise, you will not be able to realise the subtle points of the Way of the Sages."[33]

On the other hand, Shundai's *Bunshū* contains a number of essays that are critical of Sorai, e.g. his *Sorai-sensei ibun go ni sho-su* 書徂徠先生遺文後 ("Written after [reading] Master Sorai's unpublished writings")[34]: "With his world-famous talents and his exceptional knowledge, Master Sorai discovered the ancient way and made the way of the ancient kings and the teachings of Confucius become famous after a thousand years. No merit is greater than this. However, as a man he had an unhealthy liking for odd things, and he delighted in the words of the modern scholars of ancient words and phrases. Therefore, the prose he wrote inevitably went beyond the norms. As I, Shundai, see it, in prose, synonyms like ... can in some contexts be used indifferently, but in others you have to select [which one] to use. The Master, as a rule, used them indifferently. For this reason, his usage was not correct, and this impaired the meaning [of his words]." There is more criticism elsewhere, but this must suffice to make the point.[35]

Hattori Nankaku specialised in the other leg of Sorai's teachings: Chinese poetry and prose.[36] Nankaku was born in Kyoto in 1683, in a merchant family with literary interests.[37] He left for Edo in 1696, apparently in the expectation of making a career with his literary talents.[38] A few years later, probably in Genroku 13 (1700),[39] he

---

[32] A reference to *Mengzi* 4B14. The text is 「取之左右逢其原」; Lau translates this as "he finds its source, wherever he turns." (*Mencius*, p. 130.)

[33] *Seigaku mondō* 1 (*Sorai gakuha*, NST 37, p. 65).

[34] *Shishien kōkō* 10:33a-34b (pp. 222–223).

[35] For more details, see Kojima, *Sorai-gaku*, pp. 194–201. These pages are exclusively concerned with Shundai's criticisms of Sorai. See also Lan, "Dazai Shundai to Sorai-gaku no sai-kōsei."

[36] For Nankaku, see Hino, *Nankaku denkō*, and Hino, "Kaidai: Hattori Nankaku no shōgai to shisō," *Sorai gakuha*, NST 37, pp. 515–531.

[37] His grandfather from his mother's side was Yamamoto Shunshō 山本春正 (1621–1682). According to Hino, *Nankaku denkō*, p. 34, Shunshō came from a family of lacquerers, but he also studied *waka* with Matsunaga Teitoku 松永貞徳 (1571–1653) and Kinoshita Chōshōshi 木下長嘯子 (1569–1649). He was spotted by Tokugawa Mitsukuni 徳川光圀 (1628–1700), who invited him to come to Edo. Ichikawa adds to this, that Shunshō formerly had gone to Edo at the invitation of Mito to edit the *Man'yōshū* (Ichikawa, *Jugaku shi* vol. 5, p. 258). In fact, he has a *Man'yōshū tokkai* 万葉集特解 (21 *kan*) to his name (ID 4065003), which is no longer extant.

[38] Hino, *Nankaku denkō*, p. 68

[39] Sources are conflicting in regard to the year: see Hino, *Nankaku denkō*, p. 65.

was employed by Yanagisawa Yoshiyasu for his skills as a *waka* poet and a painter and became a member of his *otogi-shū*. It is not known when exactly he became a student of Sorai's. Hino argues that it must have occurred sometime between the middle of Hōei 6 (1709) and Shōtoku 1 (1711), after Tsunayoshi had died, Yoshiyasu had retired, and Nankaku had to prepare for his own inevitable dismissal from the service of the Yanagisawa.[40]

When his patron died, in 1714, Nankaku opened his own school, teaching Chinese poetry and "ancient words and phrases."[41] He does not seem to have shared Sorai's enthusiasm for the study of spoken Chinese,[42] but otherwise he was true to Sorai's ideas about literature. In a letter to Hori Keizan, he wrote: "The way of study is based on imitation. Therefore, Mencius said: 'If you wear Yao's clothes, speak Yao's words, and act as Yao acted, then you *are* Yao.'[43] No one bothers, whether your heart and your virtue [are like Yao's]. In the way of study, it is the same ... Keep it up for a long time, and you will change into it; [acquired] customs will become like your original nature. Even though it came from the outside, it has become one with me. Therefore, Zisi 子思 spoke of the 'way of uniting inner and outer.'[44] Therefore, people who worry about imitating do not know the way of study."[45]

Amongst Sorai's disciples, Nankaku emerged as the central figure. This may have been the reason why he had frequent clashes with Shundai, even when, as senior students, they had to cooperate in such things as in the editing of *Bendō* and *Benmei*, which Shundai refused to proofread, or in organising a preface for their teachers *Bunshū*.[46] One of the clashes Hino discusses is the row about *Ken'enroku kō* 蘐園録稿, an anthology of poems of Sorai's disciples. It contained thirty-three of Nankaku's poems, and only seven by Shundai; Shundai fiercely disagreed with

---

[40] Hino, *Nankaku denkō*, pp. 106–107, 109–113. N.B. In his *kaidai* of *Sorai gakuha*, NST 37, Hino had put the dates much more precisely: 1701 – entry into the service of Yoshiyasu; 1712 – entry into Sorai's school (see NST 37, p. 516, 518), but in his *kaidai* of *Nankaku-sensei bunshū*, he dates the latter event to 1711 (Hōei 1; *op. cit.*, p. 5).

[41] Ichikawa, *Jugaku shi* vol. 5 p. 258. N.B. Hino puts the date of Nankaku's dismissal from the service of the Yanagisawa in the spring of 1718 (Kyōhō 3); see *Sorai gakuha*, NST 37, p. 520; *Nankaku-sensei bunshū, Kaidai*, p. 7. In Kyōhō 4 (1719) Asaka Tanpaku 安積澹泊 (1656–1737) invited him to come to Mito, as is proven by a letter from Nankaku to Tanpaku (*Bunshū shohen* 9). See Hino, *Nankaku-sensei bunshū, Kaidai*, p. 3, for an overview of the relations between Mito and Nankaku's family.

[42] See the discussion in Hino, *Nankaku denkō*, pp. 116–117.

[43] Quotation from *Mengzi* 6B2. Yao 尭 was one of the ancient Chinese kings.

[44] Quotation from *Zhongyong* 25. The original has 合外内, not 合内外, and Zisi is not talking about acquired habits, but about the virtues of Benevolence and Wisdom. Apparently, for Nankaku, that was neither here nor there.

[45] *Hori Keizan ni kotau* 答堀景山, quoted from Hino's *kaidai*, NST 37, p. 524. Cf. the article by Kojima in the present volume for the similar argument made by Sorai.

[46] Ichikawa, *Jugaku shi* vol. 5, p. 259; Hino, *Kaidai*, NST 37, p. 526. Cf. *supra*, note 25. He was jealous, concludes Hino, and also appalled at Nankaku's blithe obliviousness of the main task of scholarship: "bringing peace to the empire."

the selection criteria and, more in general, with Nankaku's ideas about poetry.[47] On the other hand, Nankaku *did* write an inscription for Shundai's grave.[48]

As we have seen, Nankaku organised the editing and printing of Sorai's *Bunshū*. In Hōreki 2 (1753), disturbed by the many pirated editions in circulation, he compiled a reasoned catalogue of Sorai's writings, *Butsu-fushi chojutsu shomoku ki* 物夫子著述書目記. There were many omissions, however, so Usami Shinsui 宇佐美濡水 (1701–1776) revised the list, adding another eighteen titles to Nankaku's thirty-six (*Butsu-fushi chojutsu shomoku hoki*).[49]

No biography (*gyōjō*) seems to have been composed after Nankaku's death, but at the end of his collected works, we find a *boshimei* 墓誌銘 ("grave inscription"). About Nankaku's relationship with Sorai, it says the following: "In regard to the interpretation of the Classics the Master stated [what he knew], but he did not engage in discussions. He said: 'I have received our onerous work 業 from old Sorai. What I teach nowadays, is what I have received formerly. I follow him conscientiously.'"[50]

4   Criticisms

Sorai was quite severely criticized. A good inventory and systematic discussion is given by Kojima in his *Sorai-gaku to han-Sorai* ("Sorai's School and his Opponents"). He lists no fewer than twenty-four *authors* from the second half of the Edo Period who wrote books critical of Sorai's ideas.[51] As Kojima shows, Sorai's opponents were highly critical not only of his ideas and methodology, but also of his person and character.[52] Sorai evidently was a controversial person, as we saw already in the quotations from Tansō's *Jurin-hyō*.

Interestingly, Sorai's major critics were located in the Kansai. Foremost among them were Goi Ranshū 五井蘭洲 (1697–1762; *KGS* 1909) and Nakai Chikuzan 中井竹山 (1730–1804), who were both employed at the Kaitokudō 懐徳堂, the "merchants' academy" in Osaka. Ranshū's *Hi Butsu hen* 非物篇 ("Refuting Sorai"; 6 fasc.) was a posthumous publication; it was edited (Meiwa 3, = 1766) and printed (Tenmei 4, = 1784) by his disciples Nakai Chikuzan and Chikuzan's younger brother, Nakai Riken 履軒 (1732–1817 or 1816). Chikuzan himself wrote a massive *Hi Chō* 非徴 ("Refuting [Rongo-]chō"; 8 fasc.), which he finished in Meiwa 4 (1767) and

---

[47] Hino, *Nankaku-sensei bunshū, Kaidai*, p. 7. See also Hino, *Kaidai*, NST 37, pp. 526–527. N.B. *Ken'enroku kō* (2 fasc.) was compiled by Usami Shinsui and published in Kyōhō 12 (1727).

[48] *Dazai-sensei bohi* 墓碑, in *Nankaku-sensei bunshū*, 4th set, 8:1a-3a (pp. 393–394).

[49] Based on Hino, *Nankaku-sensei bunshū, Kaidai*, p. 8. Nankaku's list in *Nankaku-sensei bunshū* 4th set, 6:3b-8a. It is interesting to notice that *Seidan* and *Taiheisaku* are missing. I have not been able to locate Shinsui's list. Contrary to Nankaku's list, it has no separate entry in *NKSM*.

[50] See *Nankaku-sensei bunshū*, 4th set, appendix, p. 2b.

[51] See Kojima, *Sorai-gaku*, pp. 201–203

[52] See Kojima, *Sorai-gaku*, pp. 201–219.

published in the same year as Ranshū's *Hi Butsu hen* appeared (Tenmei 4). Both works mainly contain criticisms of Sorai's *Rongo-chō*, but Chikuzan adds a first fascicle containing a general criticism of Sorai, while Ranshū has an appendix (fasc. 6, pp. 24a-40a), in which he takes issue with most (but not all) sections of *Bendō*.

The critique was most forcibly put by Nakai Chikuzan. In the general part of *Hi Chō*, he is primarily concerned with Sorai's attitude towards Itō Jinsai 伊藤仁斎 (1627–1705). The story is well known: the young Sorai read Jinsai's works, was impressed by them, and wrote Jinsai a letter. Jinsai, for whatever reason, did not respond to it, but after his death his heirs included the letter in their father's c.q. teacher's obituary collection *Kogaku-sensei ketsumei gyōjō* 古学先生碣銘行状 (1 fasc.; pr. 1707).[53] Sorai was not amused, and struck back with his *Ken'en zuihitsu* (5 fasc.; pr. 1714), which mostly consisted of attacks on Jinsai, and in which he espoused the orthodox Neo-Confucianism of the Song.[54] This book, and this move became, in their turn, the target of Chikuzan's attack. One of the things he says, near the beginning of *Hi Chō*, is:

> "At that time, Sorai was already fifty years old. His learning, too, had matured. When [Jinsai] gave his special ideas full reign, people were delighted; however, when he (= Sorai) defended his theses, the world seemed fed-up with them. On top of that, [Jinsai] had the talents of [his son] Tōgai,[55] who even surpassed his father, to add lustre to his own. Therefore, although [Sorai], once the book was printed, distributed his *[Ken'en] zuihitsu* to the four quarters, he found it impossible to turn around the attitude of the public. So, he could less and less suppress his anger. Methinks, he said to himself that it would be impossible to be victorious with a solid, subtle and polite narrative. In the end, he came to regard the shedding of his former learning [which was orthodox Neo-Confucianism of the Song] as of no more importance than discarding his tattered sandals. Straightaway, he came out with a plan to outdo Jinsai. At that time, Sorai was fifty-one years old. The ink of *[Ken'en] zuihitsu* had not yet dried, and he had already produced *Bendō*, with which he squashed *Dōji mon* 童子問. [Next,] he made *Benmei*, with which he squashed *Go-Mō jigi* 語孟字義; *Rongo-chō*, with which he squashed *[Rongo] kogi* 論語古義; and *[Dai]gaku-* and *[Chū] yō-kai*, with which he smothered [Jinsai's] *[Daigaku] teihon* 大学定本 and *[Chūyō] hakki* 中庸発揮. Where [Jinsai] had suppressed the Confucians of the Song and solely revered [Zi]si and Mencius, he slandered both [Zi]si and Mencius. Where [Jinsai] had opined that the *Great Learning* was not an ancient [text] of Confucius' school, he definitely regarded it as the rites for nourishing the elderly. The presentation became more and more special, and his theories, more and more original. He embellished them with the empty words "Rites and Music." In order to awaken [the public] he used the minor skills of literary composition. Thus, he did away with any real self-cultivation. He made it easy for people to lose themselves [in their activities], and difficult for them to regret [their deeds]. Thereupon, restless, nervous individuals, out of breath and sweaty from all their running around, changed their routines and turned to him. The hue and cry began from here. [Sorai] himself decided that his plan had been successful, and for the next thirteen years his standard remained planted in the Kantō."[56]

---

[53] Sorai's letter, *Itō-sensei ni yosuru sho*, signed Ogyū Mokei Sō'emon 茂卿宗右衛門, is to be found in Jinsai's *Gyōjō*, pp. 26a-27b.

[54] For details, see the *kaidai* by Takayama Daiki in this book.

[55] Itō Tōgai 東涯 (1670–1736). He succeeded his father as head of the family academy Kogidō 古義堂 and, with 281 titles to his name in NKSM, was a prolific author in his own right.

[56] *Hi Chō* 1:2a-b; *Kinsei kōki juka shū*, NST 47, pp. 45–46.

4.1 First Example

I will give one example of the arguments back and forth regarding the *Analects*, which was, after all, for both of them the key text of Confucianism. As my case, I have selected the following pronouncement of Confucius:

> "The Master said, 'If the people be led by laws, and uniformity sought to be given them by punishments, they will try to avoid the punishment, but have no sense of shame. If they be led by virtue, and uniformity sought to be given them by the rules of propriety, they will have the sense of shame, and moreover will become good.'"[57]

In Sorai's interpretation,[58] the "laws and punishments" are the ones established by the ancient kings. He does not spell it out, but the implication is that, therefore, they are intrinsically good and useful. If, however, you just apply the laws and punishments, the people will only try to evade the cruel penalties, and not feel shame. Hence, the next provision: "Lead them with Virtue." Here Sorai becomes original. "Virtue" he interprets as "*men of* virtue," who are used by the ruler to apply the Laws and Punishments. They give the people a good example to follow and thus, to change themselves. If uniformity is still not achieved, they have the Rites to accomplish that. "Later generations," Sorai claims, "did not know the meaning of the character *de* 德 ("virtue"). Incorrectly, they explain it as "an individual's personal virtue." "When someone would implement laws and punishments *without* possessing virtue, the people would not know where to put its hands and feet! How could it [even try to] avoid punishment?"

As his personal opinion, Sorai declares that there are two types of rulers: "Those who just implement the laws and punishments," and "those who implement virtue and rites." Men of the first category are intent on bringing order to the people quickly, in order to prevent them from doing wrong. Those of the second category "think much further." What they think, is not disclosed; Sorai merely remarks that this second quality is "highly regarded in the Way of the ancient kings."

The next point is the interpretation of the final four characters of section, "they will have shame and become good." The character at issue is *ge* 格. In the Old Commentaries it is glossed as *zheng* 正 ("correct," "to rectify"). Sorai, however, agrees with the gloss given by Zhu Xi (1130–1200): *zhi* 至 ("to arrive at, to get there"). To this, however, he adds the nuance of *gange* 感格, the *locus* of which compound is Zhu Xi's commentary on the last section of *The Mean*.[59] Zhu Xi introduces it in his paraphrase of the first four characters of the poem quoted there; he says: "They present [the offerings] and *their feelings reach* the boundary with the

---

[57] *Lunyu* 2.3: 「子曰、『道之以政、齊之以刑、民免而無恥。道之以德、齊之以禮、有恥且格。』」 The English translation is Legge's.

[58] See Matsudaira, *Rongo-chō shūran* 2:5b-6b.

[59] See *Zhongyong* 33. In the phrase 『詩』曰:奏假無言、時靡有爭, Zhu Xi glosses 奏 as 進 and 假 as 格, which explains how we arrive at the standard translation of this phrase in *Zhongyong*: "It is said in the Book of Poetry, 'In silence is [the offering] presented, and [the spirit] approached to; there is not the slightest contention.'" N.B. The poem quoted is *Shijing* 302.

gods 進而感格於神明之際; they maximize their sincerity and reverence; no words are spoken, and [yet those present] spontaneously are transformed and adapt."

It is strange to see Sorai agreeing with Zhu Xi, whom as a rule he loved to hate, but that is how he reached the interpretation he proposes: that *ge* does not just mean "they reach it," but that there is an emotional component to it ("their *feelings* reach..."). From here on, however, Sorai talks in riddles. He declares that *gan* and *ge* share the same pronunciation,[60] and that "therefore" it was often used, anciently, in the context of "august heaven, ghosts and spirits, and ancestral temples." For good measure, he quotes two more *loci*, this time from the *Shujing*, to prove his point, namely the phrase "the Miao arrived,"[61] and "... thus correcting my bad heart, ..." 格其非心.[62] One is inclined to think that in this last case "to rectify" would have done as well, but Sorai claims that in this case, too, *ge* has the sense of "being emotionally affected" 感動.

Having thus settled to his own satisfaction the interpretation of the word *ge* 格, Sorai has a go at *mian er wu chi* 免而無恥: "... they will try to avoid [punishment], but have no sense of shame". With help of four references to the *Analects*, he defines *mian* as "to avoid cruel punishment."[63] His conclusion is that "someone who leads with the laws and establishes order with help of punishments" will surely be able to see to it that the people avoids cruel punishment. In other words, not the people, but *the leaders of* the people have become the subject of the verb, while the first evidently is the case in the *Analects*.

In his criticism of this passage in *Rongo-chō*,[64] Nakai Chikuzan first tries to demolish Sorai's interpretation of "virtue" as "men of virtue." Citing three *loci*,[65] he concludes that "virtue" refers to "the virtue a person possesses," and not to the man who possesses it, just like "beauty" refers to "the beauty someone has received from nature / by birth" and not to the beautiful person. It is evident, Chikuzan continues, that in this section of the *Analects* "the laws and punishments" are contrasted with "virtue and rites." Sorai tries to negate this contrast by, first, glossing "virtue" as "men of virtue," and, second, by defining the "laws and punishments" as those of

---

[60] 蓋感格声音相通. This seems to be a ridiculous statement. The *fanjie* of the two characters are completely different.

[61] Reference to *Shujing: Da Yu mo* 21: 禹拜昌言曰:『俞。』班師振旅。帝乃誕敷文德, 舞干羽于兩階, 七旬有苗格. – "Yu did homage to the excellent words, and said, 'Yes.' (Thereupon) he led back his army, having drawn off the troops. The Di set about diffusing on a grand scale the virtuous influences of peace – with shields and feathers they danced between the two staircases (in his courtyard). In seventy days, the lord of Miao came (and made his submission)."

[62] Reference to *Shujing: Jiong ming* 冏命 1. The phrase is also quoted by Zhu Xi in his commentary on this section, specifically to illustrate "one theory" that holds that *ge* means "to rectify."

[63] The definition of "avoiding cruel punishments" derives from *Lunyu* 5.2. The other passages Sorai refers to are *Lunyu* 6.16, 6.19, and 8.3.

[64] See *Hi Chō* 1:41b-1:43a.

[65] *Shujing: Shun dian* 2: 舜讓于德, 弗嗣 – "Shun wished to decline in favour of some one more virtuous, and not to consent to be (Yao's) successor."; *Lunyu* 4.25: 子曰:『德不孤, 必有鄰。』』 – "The Master said, 'Virtue is not left to stand alone. He who practices it will have neighbours.'"; *Lunyu* 9.18: 子曰:『吾未見好德如好色者也。』』 – "The Master said, 'I have not seen one who loves virtue as he loves beauty.'"

the ancient kings, from which he concludes that those who implemented these "laws and punishments" as a matter of course possessed virtue.

Chikuzan cannot agree. A situation in which "laws and punishments" were those of the Ancient kings, and the men executing them were all men of virtue, obtained only during the three kingdoms of ancient China (Xia, Shang, and Zhou). In those days "avoiding punishment and not knowing shame" was not an issue; hence, the words of the *Analects* would not apply. Sorai's counter-argument ("try to rule *without* virtue, and the people would not know where to put its hand and feet") applies only to such periods of "cruel rule and licentious punishments" as the reign of the First Emperor of the Qin Dynasty (r. 221–209), or the Sui under Emperor Yang (569-604-617-618); it constitutes a completely different case. Thirdly, Sorai's statement, that "those who just implement the laws and punishments are intent on bringing order to the people quickly, in order to prevent them from doing wrong," is applicable "to government during brief interludes [without Rites], to the rule of the ordinary rulers of the Han and Tang.[66] In other words, Sorai's theories are mutually inconsistent.

In the second paragraph,[67] Chikuzan makes clear why he does not agree with Sorai's definition of *mian* as "to avoid cruel punishment." Chikuzan points out that this definition is much stronger than the definition given by Zhu Xi in his commentaries,[68] which rather tends towards an "outward adaptation to the circumstances": "They change their countenances [but not their hearts,] and do not dare to do bad things. ... Methinks, he never yet interpreted it in the sense of 'they [really had this intention.'" So, Sorai is wrong. He also goes against the meaning of the Classic, when he inserts his interpretation that "[the executors of] laws and punishments *make* the people avoid cruel punishment." As Chikuzan points out correctly, Sorai here has changed subject and object and, in this way, fails the explain the last words "know no shame."[69]

4.2   Second Example

In *Bendō* 18, Sorai discusses the concept of "heart" 心 (*xin*, J. *shin*). The casus is, "how does one control the heart?" Ranshū gives a partial quotation from *Bendō*: "The heart has no form. It is impossible to grasp it and control it.[70] Therefore the way of the early kings used rites to discipline the heart. Apart from rites, discussions of the way of controlling the heart are all far-fetched fabrications of personal

---

[66] *Hi Chō* 1:42b, lines 6–7: 是則権時之制、漢唐中主之治也. N.B. 「権時」 is explained, in a commentary on *Hou Han Shu* ("History of the Later Han Dynasty"), as "[the times when] they did not rely on the Rites," but on expediency 権; cf. Mor. VI: 15926–53.

[67] *Hi Chō* 1:43a.

[68] Chikuzan refers to Zhu Xi's commentary in *Sishu jizhu* and another, unidentified commentary.

[69] For unexplained reasons, Goi Ranshū does *not* discuss this section in his *Hi Butsu hen*. Of course, in his criticism of Sorai's interpretation of *Lunyu* 2.1 he has already said that Sorai's interpretation of "virtue" as "men of virtue" is wrong; see *Hi Butsu hen* 1:25a-25b.

[70] For a general discussion of "heart" in Neo-Confucian doctrine, see W.J. Boot, *Adoption and Adaptation*, Ch. III, pp. 146–156, 170–174.

wisdom. Why? The one that controls is the heart, but it is also the heart that is being controlled. Trying to use our hearts to control our hearts is like a crazed person personally trying to control his own craziness thereby. How could he possibly control it? For that reason, all of the discussions of later generations about controlling the heart [are based upon] misunderstandings of the way."[71]

Goi Ranshū's criticism in *Hi Butsu hen* (6:34a-b) is as follows: "To discipline the heart with the rites has of old been a technique to control the heart. However, the thing one does it with, is the heart. It is not the case that the rites themselves come and discipline my heart. Therefore, to discipline the heart with the rites is also a case of controlling the heart with the heart. It is like cutting a thing with a knife. The one who uses it is a man. It is not the case that the knife itself cuts a thing. Because he hates to speak of the heart, he has never yet exerted himself at the Way of controlling the heart; thus, he does not believe in it. That is all right. However, what he says about a crazy person controlling his own craziness, is not a good comparison. A crazy person who controls himself, is not considered as crazy. If he is crazy, then he does not control himself. He does not wish to control himself; that is also part of his madness."

These two examples must suffice to give an impression – not more – of the nature and the tone of the criticism generally levelled at Sorai. One of the interesting aspects of the discussion is that it is conducted through quotations from the Classics, rather than through reasoned argument. It also struck me, in the second example, that Ranshū accepted Sorai's definition of "the heart," although there were other definitions around. Minagawa Kien (we will come to him in a moment) defines it as "the place where thought and principles are located" (*shiryo jōri no aru tokoro* 思慮条理之所在).[72] Such a definition would have strengthened Ranshū's argument, by allowing him to claim that "the heart is strong enough to regulate itself."

4.3   Third Example

Another interesting opponent of Sorai, also from the Kansai, was the Kyoto scholar Minagawa Kien 皆川淇園 (1734–1807). Though he is not generally acknowledged as such, my reason for casting him for this role is the way in which Kien's *oeuvre* mirrors that of Sorai. He seems to have taken to heart Nakai Chikuzan's analysis of Sorai's writings after *Ken'en zuihitsu*, i.e., as attempts to best those by Itō Jinsai. Concretely, I think it is possible to pair off Kien's *Mongaku kyoyō* 問学挙要 ("The main points of study") with Sorai's *Gakusoku* 学則, his *Meichū* 名疇 ("Names and categories") with Sorai's *Bendō* and *Benmei*, and his *Kien tōyō* 淇園答要

---

[71] For this translation, I have followed Tucker; see his *Ogyū Sorai's Philosophical Masterworks*, p. 157. I have only substituted "heart" for "mind" as the translation of 心 (J. *shin*; Ch. *xin*). Cf. also Tucker's introduction in *Sources of Japanese Tradition* vol. I, 2 (2006), p. 193.

[72] Minagawa Kien, *Meichū* 6:1a.

("The main points of Kien's answers") with *Sorai-sensei tōmonsho* 答問書.[73] The first discusses the methodology of Confucian studies, comprising both the moral and the philological aspects. The second follows the dictionary format of *Xingli ziyi* 性理字義: major Confucian terms explained one by one. The third is a text written in *sōrōbun*. It consists of letters which, in the case of Kien, are addressed to an unnamed *daimyō*, while the letters in Sorai's *Tōmonsho* were ostensibly addressed to a couple of samurai. Of its three fascicles, the first treats the education of the samurai retainers (*what* they should study, and *how*); the second, the standard of samurai behaviour; and the third, model behaviour of a *daimyō*. *Mongaku kyoyō* and *Meichū* appeared in print during Kien's life. *Kien tōyō* only survives in some ten manuscripts.[74]

Kien did not engage in overt polemics with Sorai. This may partly have been due to his social position. As a schoolmaster, teaching Chinese to students interested in medicine or Chinese, he had little to gain from controversy and the accompanying notoriety. However, *showing* that he could outdo Sorai at his own game would increase his stature in the eyes of the *conoscenti* and be accepted at face-value by the ordinary bystanders. It may also be a character trait. After all, his brother Fujitani Nariakira 富士谷成章 (1738–1779), *did* engage in a spot of Sorai-bashing.[75]

Kien was certainly not attempting to emulate Sorai in the extravagance and eccentricity of his ideas. Kien's doctrinal position was orthodox to a fault. His originality lay in his methodology, in the way he arrived at his interpretations, not in the interpretations as such.

The first text at issue is *Mongaku kyoyō*. The writer of its preface, a student of Kien's private academy, asserts that "it discusses the main points of study and analyses the principles of literature incisively and fully," and that it represents Kien's "comprehensive method for systematizing the study of the Classics."[76] Secondary points on which the preface insists are that (1) Kien has taken his pedagogical method from Confucius, in that he "draws the bow but does not shoot," i.e., gives the clues, and then lets the students work it out for themselves.[77] (2) The goal that the dutiful student will eventually reach, is that he "will go back thousands of years and research the smallest [nuances of] words of the Sages and Wise Men."

At the outset of *Mongaku kyoyō*, Kien declares that "The 'Way of the Sages' begins with the cultivation of the self and ends with bringing peace to others. The

---

[73] See also the translation by Samuel Yamashita, and my review of the same.

[74] Parts of it are reproduced in Takimoto, *Nihon keizai taiten* vol. 51, pp. 406–416, and in Inoue, *Bushidō sōsho* vol. 2, pp. 233–243. For a discussion, see Boot (2006), "Minagawa Kien: *Kien tōyō* to *Meichū* no kankei ni tsuite." N.B. All quotations are based on the manuscript in the possession of Tokyo Toritsu Chūō Toshokan, no. 094508.

[75] Nariakira, who was a specialist in *Japanese* studies, wrote *Hi narubeshi* 非南留別志, which is a critique of Sorai's *Narubeshi*. It was published in 1795; the preface, by his son Fujitani Mitsue 御杖, is dated 1786.

[76] In the original: 「論学之要、晰文之理、切乎至乎。... 吾理経芸之大法」; see *Kinsei kōki juka shū*, NST 47, p. 359, p. 74. N.B. *Keigei* 経芸 in the sense of "studying or applying the Classics" is already attested in *Shiji*.

[77] The bow metaphor is taken from *Mengzi* 7A41.

essential purport of the Classics, multi-faceted though they may be, is to elucidate these two points." Two examples should show what he has in mind. The first example concerns virtues: with each virtue one should try to find out (*sijiu* 思求) the reason why this virtue should be practised, and what is bad about some actions, that they should not be practised. The second example he gives is the ambition of becoming a *junzi* 君子 ("gentleman"): one should try and find out why it would not do *not* to try to become one, and also, "whether the intention to become a gentleman is the same as, or different from the intention to become famous or to excel."[78]

In the final chapter, he returns to these moral concerns. The theme of this chapter is the identification of the scholar with the Sages. The formula Kien comes up with is "Thus my spirit and thoughts are also the spirit and thoughts of the ancients; they do not differ."[79] This postulates the existence of a common ground between the ancients and ourselves, that can explain how it is possible for us to identify with them, to understand them through the medium of the texts they created, and to pretend we are able to apply those to our present concerns.

The other four chapters of *Mongaku kyoyō* deal with philological methodology. In the second chapter, he discusses the three topics of "exactly distinguishing the meaning of characters," of "having a general idea of the historical setting in which the texts were composed," and of "knowing the ancient rhymes." Under "exactly distinguishing" Kien gives his definition of defining: "Scholars attach great importance to *mei-butsu* 名物. *Mei* are the individual characters (字 *ji*, = "words"); *butsu* are "the meanings of the individual words" (字義 *jigi*)."[80]

Clearly, already in *Mongaku kyoyō*, Kien is looking for ways to arrive at objective definitions of the meaning of words.[81] He is not satisfied with the usual, improvised glosses but is looking for an instrument that would enable him to standardize the operation. His pretension is that the Sages devised such instruments, and that one of these can be found in King Wen'd additions to the original *Yijing*[82]; these, he claims, are "all means with which to distinguish names and to open things" 並皆弁名開物之所以為作者也.

The chance is negligible, that Kien used the phrase *benmei kaibutsu*[83] without realising that *Benmei* was the title of one of Sorai's most important books, and that *butsu* ("thing") was a term Sorai used in the sense of the "realia" to which words refer.[84]

---

[78] *Kinsei kōki juka shū*, NST 47, p. 360; 76–77.

[79] *Kinsei kōki juka shū*, NST 47, p. 376; 121.

[80] The same idea is found in the postface of Kien's *Kyoji-kai* 虚字解 (1783). There, the compound 審名開物 is used, instead of *benmei kaibutsu*.

[81] *Kinsei kōki juka shū*, NST 47, pp. 362–363, pp. 83–84.

[82] *Kinsei kōki juka shū*, NST 47, p. 362, p. 83. It was commonly believed that King Wen had created the sixty-four hexagrams of the *Yijing*, together with the explanations of the hexagrams as a whole and of their individual lines.

[83] Or his student, who wrote the postface of *Kyoji-kai*, the phrase 審名開物 ("to clarify names and open up things"); cf. *supra*, n. 80.

[84] See e.g. *Gakusoku* 3: "The six classics describe physical realities. The Way exists in them in full" 夫六経物也、道具存焉. (Minear, "Ogyū Sorai's Instructions for Students, p. 20). See also Minear's discussion of "Physical Realities," *ibid.*, pp. 41–42, in reference to *Benmei*: "'Physical

The underlying argument, thus, becomes something like "both he (Sorai) and I (Kien) know that understanding a text depends on understanding the words of which it is composed. Hence, we have to gloss and explain words." To the next question, "How can we be sure that we give the correct interpretation?," their answers differed. Sorai's answer was "by getting into the spirit of the text."[85] Before long, the answer Kien arrived at became "by applying my objective method of 'opening up things'" – *kaibutsu* 開物.

The term *kaibutsu* stems from the Great Appendix of the *Yijing*. As Kien explains in *Kien tōyō*, "You ask with what aim the *Yijing* has been instituted? Well, mistaken theories abound, but the real purpose is as is stated in the Great Appendix, where it says: 'Well, what do the Changes do? The Changes open up things, perfect duties, and encompass the Way of the world; that is all there is to it.'"[86]

Kien's *Kaibutsugaku* is the result of insights that he reached fairly late in his life.[87] *Mongaku kyoyō*, published in An'ei 3 (1774) is still free of it. Ten years later, however, in Tenmei 4, the theory is expounded in the preface of Kien's *magnum opus*, *Meichū*, which was printed in 1788.[88] Kien presented this work as an exercise in "the rectification of names." In Kien's own words:

> "What is *meichū*? In this book it is my intention to correct the names (= give the correct definitions. WJB) of the concrete virtues 德物 Filial Piety, Brotherly Piety, Benevolence, and Duty; to clarify the way their meanings hang together 等類 by use of the method ... that [is expounded in] the Nine Categories; and to ensure that they will not suffer [any longer] under the perfunctory and unsystematic [definitions that have been their] ill [fate until now]. Therefore, I give [this book] the title 'Names and Categories.'"[89]

What follows is six solid fascicles of classical Chinese, arranged lexically, and as such comparable to *Benmei*. The book begins with Filial Piety and ends with xing 性

---

realities are he concrete terms of the instruction. ...' These physical realities are of two varieties. The first is events or actions 事, found in the rites and the music. The second category is elegant words 辞, found in the documents and the odes."

[85] More precisely: "Do not use mouth or ear, but consider the texts with heart and eye; ponder them and ponder again, and *as if by divine inspiration you will perceive their meaning* 思之又思、神其通之. The ancient literature, records, proprieties, and music are Chinese words, and we must try to listen to them with our eyes." (Quoted from Minear, "Ogyū Sorai's Instructions for Students," pp. 14–15.) Or: "I study the ancient words and study them, and finally I become one with them. Then my words, my tone, my spirit, and my intent all become similar to those found in the old literature. When words, tone, spirit, and intent all become similar to those of old, then there is no difference between the old on the one hand and what my eye sees and my mouth says on the other." (*op. cit.*, p. 18)

[86] *Kien tōyō* 1.11 (*Shūeki no koto* 周易之事).

[87] The best analysis of *kaibutsugaku* is Noguchi Takehiko, "Kaibutsu to seizō" (1993). See also Hamada, "Minagawa Kien ron" II (2002).

[88] Another text in which he explained his method was Ekigen 易原; this text was printed partly in Tenmei 6 (1786), and completely, i.e. including the second volume, in Kansei 5 (1793). Kien wrote quite a number of other texts regarding *kaibutsugaku*, but these were never published and have to be enjoyed as manuscripts.

[89] *Meichū*, Preface, 1b.

and ming 命; note, that the order is different from *Benmei*. The discussion of the terms is of a high standard, and one cannot but admire the way in which Kien juggles the Classics and other ancient texts in support of his arguments. The book was too long, however, too difficult, and too *mal à propos* to answer the needs of his patrons.[90] What was even more damning was, that the book showed that Kien himself could get by perfectly well without his *kaibutsugaku*. For 99% *Meichū* is ordinary commentary; it is only the first two lines of each section that are beholden to *kaibutsugaku*, and as a result are incomprehensible. The remainder makes perfect sense.

Perhaps because he felt a need to explain things to a more general public, Kien returned to the subject in his *Kien tōyō*. Here he writes:

> (*Kaibutsu* is) "To open and bring out the things that are hidden within the names (*na no uchi ni kakuretaru mono o hirakidasu*) ... 'Names' means 'characters' (*moji*). There exist approximately ten thousand of such names. ... These names derive from the [ten thousand] things. That is how 'things' have come to be present in human language. ... How, you ask, does one open language and names? Well, language and names all have their own 'voice-breath' 聲氣 (*seiki*), and this 'voice-breath' is formed from the things ... The 'voice-breath' comes into existence through a combination of the shape [of the organs of speech (= tongue, lips, throat)] and breath, in accordance with the thing for which one makes the sound. ... King Wen opened the things [hidden in] sixty-four names and fashioned their images 象 (*zō*) in the sixty-four hexagrams. ... If one does not apply this method of 'opening things,' one's disquisitions about such virtues as Benevolence, Duty, the Way, or Virtue will be purely personal conjectures."[91]

In this passage, Kien claims several things:

– **One,** that there is a unique "sound" for every "thing." This "sound" is inspired by the "thing" observed and is the result of a unique combination of *qi* ("vital breath") and *xing* ("shape"), i.e., the physical constellation of the organs of speech at the moment the word is spoken.
– **Two**, that his analytical method is expounded in the *Yijing*, and that the sixty-four hexagrams are the result of the application of this method by one of the ancient Sages, King Wen, who was the first to have engaged in *kaibutsu*.
– **Three,** that, as the example of King Wen's hexagrams shows, "opening a thing" would result, not in a definition in words, but in a graphic representation – in an "image." The definition would be given in another symbolic system than ordinary, discursive language.[92]
– **Four**, that only through the application of his method it would be possible to define the key terms of the Classics in such a way that these definitions would be objectively true and truly objective.

The basic idea of *Kaibutsugaku* is clear. It is, that "sounds" have an intrinsic meaning and that, therefore, the analysis of the *sound* of a word should allow us to

---

[90] An interesting article in this context is Miura Shūichi, "Bokumin to kami" (2007). It is an attempt to interpret one lemma of *Meichū* as actual advice to *daimyō*.

[91] *Kien tōyō* 1, 11: "Ekikyō no koto."

[92] Kien's own graphic representation, based on the hexagrams, is the *kyūchū* 九疇 ("Nine categories"). See Nakamura, *Minagawa Kien, Ōta Kinjō*, p. 45; Noguchi, "Kaibutsu to seizō," p. 4.

define it. Of course, the most interesting sounds are the pronunciations given by the Sages to the central terms of Confucianism, which existed as sounds long before they existed as characters. If we can reconstruct those sounds, we would know fully and objectively what the Sages meant with these words.

Thus, *Kien's kaibutsugaku* was a philological method. It promised to give incontrovertible definitions of single words – "incontrovertible" meaning in this case, that the definitions exactly coincided with what the Sages intended to express when they first voiced the concept. On a more mundane level, it could also be used to upstage Sorai's *kobunjigaku*. Kien, basing himself on the *sounds* of the words as they were *first pronounced* by the Sages, long before writing was invented, went back to a more ancient, and more basic level of language than Sorai had ever reached.

I hardly need to point out that Kien's idea was a non-starter. Bar a few onomatopoeic words, there is no relation between the sound and the meaning of words. Moreover, the reconstruction he attempted of the pronunciation of the terms in the days of the Sages was based on rhyme dictionaries, the oldest of which, *Yinjing* 韻鏡, dated back to the Tang dynasty. However, his criticism of Sorai was correct, in the sense that all glosses of ancient texts are to some extent arbitrary and based on personal intuitions. Sorai went further than most in this respect. Kien was not the only who was critical of this aspect of Sorai's work.

5   General Conclusion

As I have tried to show above, the reception of Sorai's thought in the second half of the Edo Period was philological in nature, rather than what we would nowadays call philosophical. Arguments hinged on the interpretation of words, and in order to interpret words, you had to juggle parallel passages elsewhere in the corpus. In this context, it was only logical that Sorai's *Rongo-chō* drew most of the ire. Everyone knew the *Lunyu*, and Sorai's interpretations went against not only the other commentaries, but also, sometimes, against plain common sense.

Another aspect that emerges from the materials introduced above is, that Sorai really managed to make people angry. When you deny the professional competence of your colleagues by querying their knowledge of Chinese, by slighting their favourite way of teaching (namely, lecturing), and by drastically reinterpreting the corpus, and, moreover, deny the importance of moral self-cultivation, you undermine the professional consensus of the *Kangakusha* 漢学者. Criticism inevitably became personal, as is shown in the introductory pages of Chikuzan's *Hi Chō*.

The defence Sorai received from his disciples was lukewarm. As the compilation of *Sorai-shū* indicates, they had other things on their minds, and there were limits to their loyalty. On the other hand, there also were positive results. Sorai's philological approach and his interpretations may have been criticised outside the circle of his own school, but they also inspired some scholars to try and do better. Kien is the most outrageous example of this trend that I know, but there were many scholars, Dazai Shundai first among them, who were inspired by Sorai to arrive at a better understanding of the ancient Chinese corpus, and to find a more objective method than Sorai to accomplish that.[93]

Bibliography

Bitō Masahide 尾藤正英. 1972. "Kaidai: Dazai Shundai no hito to shisō," NST 37. Tokyo: Iwanami Shoten.

Boot, W.J. 1983. *The Adoption and Adaptation of Neo-Confucianism in Japan: The Role of Fujiwara Seika and Hayashi Razan*, PhD dissertation, Leiden. (See the homepage of the Netherlands Association for Japanese Studies <ngjs.nl> – Specialist).

Boot, W.J. 1996. Review of Samuel Hideo Yamashita, *Master Sorai's Responsals: An Annotated Translation of Sorai-sensei Tōmonsho*, Hawai'i, 1994. *Journal of Japanese Studies* 22.2: 430–435.

Boot, W.J. 2006. "Minagawa Kien: *Kien tōyō* to *Meichū* no kankei ni tsuite," *Dai-29-kai tokushū. Kaigai kara mita Nihon bungaku no kenkyū: uchi to soto o nori-koete. Kokusai Nihon Bungaku Kenkyū Shūkai Kaigiroku*. Tokyo: Kokubungaku Shiryōkan Shuppan.

Boot, W.J. 2014. "Chinese Scholarship and Teaching in Eighteenth-Century Kyoto." In M. Hayek and A. Horiuchi, eds. *Listen, Copy, Read. Popular Learning in Early Modern Japan*. 226–250. Leiden: Brill.

Dazai Shundai 太宰春台. 1986. *Shundai-sensei Shishien kō* 紫芝園稿. Kinsei Juka Bunshū Shūsei vol. 6. Tokyo: Perikansha.

Hamada Shū 浜田秀. 2000, 2002. "Minagawa Kien ron I" 皆川淇園論. *Yamabe no michi* 44: 1–15; "Minagawa Kien ron II: 'Kyūchū' gainen o chūshin ni" 「九疇」概念を中心に. *Yamabe no michi* 46: 25–51.

Hino Tatsuo日野龍夫. 1972. "Kaidai: Hattori Nankaku no shōgai to shisō" 解題:服部南郭の生涯と思想. *Sorai gakuka*, NST 37. Tokyo: Iwanami Shoten.

Hino Tatsuo, ed. & introd. 1985. (*Kaidai*), *Nankaku-sensei bunshū* 南郭先生文集, Kinsei Juka Bunshū Shūsei vol. 7, Tokyo: Perikansha.

Hino Tatsuo. 1999. *Hattori Nankaku denkō* 伝攷, Tokyo: Perikansha.

Hiraishi Naoaki 平石直昭, ed. & introd. 1985. (*Kaidai*), *Sorai-shū, Sorai-shū ishū*. Kinsei Juka Bunshū Shūsei vol. 3. Tokyo: Perikansha.

Hirose Tansō 廣瀬淡窓. 1978. *Jurin-hyō* 儒林評. Seki Giichirō 関儀一郎, comp. Nihon Jurin Sōsho vol. 3. Rpt. Tokyo: Ōtori Shuppan.

Ichikawa Mototarō 市川本太郎. 1995. *Nihon Jugaku shi 5: Kinsei-hen, ge: Kogaku-ha, sono ta no gakuha*. Tokyo: Kyūko Shoin.

Inoue Tetsujirō井上哲次郎. 1906–1909. *Bushidō sōsho* 武士道叢書. 3 vols. Tokyo: Hakubunkan.

Inoue Tetsujirō. 1927. *Nihon Kogakuha no tetsugaku*. 25th pr. Tokyo: Fusanbō.

Iwahashi Junsei 岩橋遵成. 1934 *Sorai kenkyū*. Tokyo: Sekishoin.

Kojima Yasunori 小島康敬. 1994. *Sorai-gaku to han-Sorai* 徂徠学と反徂徠, Tokyo: Perikansha.

Lan Hung Yueh 藍弘岳. 2016. "Dazai Shundai to Sorai-gaku no sai-kōsei: 'Seijin no michi' to Nihon hihan o megutte" 太宰春台と徂徠学の再構成—「聖人の道」と日本批判をめぐって. *Shisō* 1112: 51–68.

---

[93] In his *kaidai* of *Kinsei kōki juka shū*, NST 47, Nakamura Yukihiko points out that Sorai's (and Jinsai's) philological methodology was **continued and rendered obsolete** 発展的解消 by the *Kochūgaku* and *Setchūgaku* scholars. On the other hand, political thought 経世論 became a widespread preoccupation; as an example, Nakamura mentions Hirose Tansō's *Ugen* 迂言 ("widely read by *daimyō*"), and indicates how it branched out into the *Kaibōron, Kaikokuron*, and *Jōiron* of the Bakumatsu Period (pp. 488–489).

Matsudaira Yorihiro 松平頼寛. *Rongo-chō shūran* 論語徴集覧, 20+1 fascicles. Preface dated Kan'en 3 (1750); printed Hōreki 10 (1760).

Minagawa Kien 皆川淇園. *Kien tōyō* 答要. (Only manuscript copies available; consult *NKSM*.)

Minagawa Kien. 1972. *Mongaku kyoyō* 問学挙要. In Nakamura Yukihiko 中村幸彦 and Okada Takehiko 岡田武彦, eds. *Kinsei kōki juka shū* 近世後期儒家集, NST 47. Tokyo: Iwanami Shoten.

Minagawa Kien, *Meichū* 名疇, pref. 1784, printed 1788.

Minear, Richard H. 1976. "Ogyū Sorai's Instructions for Students: A Translation and Commentary." *Harvard Journal of Asiatic Studies* 36: 5–81.

Miura Shūichi 三浦秀一. 2007. "Bokumin to kami: Minagawa Kien *Meichū* no tōjisha-ron to sono shisō kiban" 牧民と神—皆川淇園『名疇』の当事者論とその思想基盤. *Tasan-hak* 茶山学 11: 281–313.

Nakai Chikuzan 中井竹山. 1972. *Hi Chō* 非徴 (excerpt). In Nakamura Yukihiko and Okada Takehiko, eds. *Kinsei kōki juka shū* 近世後期儒家集, NST 47. Tokyo: Iwanami Shoten.

Nakamura Shunsaku 中村春作 et al. 1986. *Minagawa Kien, Ōta Kinjō* 太田錦城. Sōsho Nihon no Shisōka, vol. 26. Tokyo: Meitoku Shuppansha.

Noguchi Takehiko 野口武彦. 1990. "Kaibutsu to seizō: Minagawa Kien no 'kaibutsugaku' kaidoku no kokoromi"開物と声象—皆川淇園の「怪物学」解読のこころみ. *Edo bungaku* 1.2: 2–26. Reprinted in Noguchi Takehiko. 1993. *Edo shisōshi no chikei* 江戸思想史の地形, Tokyo: Perikansha.

Ogyū Sorai. 1973a. *Bendō*. In Yoshikawa Kōjirō 吉川幸次郎 et al., eds. *Ogyū Sorai*, NST 36. Tokyo: Iwanami Shoten.

Ogyū Sorai. 1973b. *Sorai-sensei tōmonsho* 徂徠先生答問書. In *Ogyū Sorai zenshū* vol. 1. Tokyo: Misuzu Shobō.

Ogyū Sorai. *Benmei* 弁明. NST 36.

Ogyū Sorai. *Gakusoku* 学則. NST 36.

Sugiura Masaomi 杉浦正. 1969. *Jugaku genryū* 儒学源流. In Takei Kazuo 武井一雄, ed. *Nihon kyōikushi shiryō* vol. 8. Kyoto: Rinsen Shoten.

Takimoto Seiichi 滝本誠一, comp. 1971. Nihon Keizai Taiten 日本経済大典. 54 vols. Rpt. Tokyo: Meiji Bunken.

Tucker, John A., trans. & introd. 2006. *Ogyū Sorai's Philosophical Masterworks. The* Bendō *and* Benmei. Honolulu: Association for Asian Studies/University of Hawai'i Press.

Wm. Theodore de Bary, Carol Gluck, Arthur E. Tiedemann, comp. 2006. *Sources of Japanese Tradition. Second edition, Volume two, Part 1*, New York: Columbia University Press.

Yamagata Shūnan 山形周南. 1760. *Shūnan-sensei bunshū* 周南先生文集. 10 fasc., 6 vols. (N.B. I quote from the copy in the possession of Naikaku Bunko, 206-052.)

Yamashita, Samuel Hideo. 1994. *Master Sorai's Responsals: An Annotated Translation of* Sorai sensei tōmonsho. Honolulu: University of Hawai'i Press.

Chapter 15
"Sorai's Teachings in East-Asia: The Formation of His Methodology of Studying the Classics and the Reception of His Works on the Classics"

Lᴀɴ Hung Yueh

1 Introduction

The "study of ancient words and phrases" (*kobunjigaku*) of Ogyū Sorai (1666–1728) is not merely a method for writing and reading literary treatises or prose and poetry in Classical Chinese. It is also important as a methodology that helped Sorai to interpret the primary corpus of "ancient words and phrases" (*kobunji*), which includes the Classics, i.e., the canonical texts of Confucianism. It gave Sorai his grasp on the "ancient language" and allowed him to create the classical scholarship he displayed in *Bendō* 弁道, *Benmei* 弁名, *Rongo-chō* 論語徴, etc. In this article, I shall, within the context of the history of Chinese studies in East Asia, present one possible solution to the question, how the study of ancient words and phrases as a method of interpreting texts in classical Chinese was re-applied by Sorai as a methodology for the study of the Classics, and how this enabled him to rejuvenate the study of these Classics.[1]

When we notice how the achievements of Dazai Shundai 太宰春台 (1680–1747) and Yamanoi Konron (Tei)山井崑崙・鼎(1681–1728), when introduced to Qing China and Chosŏn Korea, were appreciated by the scholars of the movement of Evidential Research (*Kaozhengxue*) in China and the Confucian scholars of Korea, we can safely conclude that in some respects Sorai's school came close to the evi-

---

[1]Previous studies of this problem include Hiraishi Naoaki, "Senchū, sengo Sorai-ron hihan" (1987), Sawai Keiichi, "'Hōhō' to shite no kobunjigaku" (1988), and Aihara Kōsaku, "Joji to kobunjigaku" (2004). Hiraishi, Sawai, and Aihara did not make the extra step towards an analysis of the relation between the study of ancient philology (*kobunjigaku*) as a methodology and Sorai's theory of poetry and prose. In this article, I intend to advance the analysis into this direction.

Lᴀɴ Hung Yueh (✉)
Faculty of Social Research and Cultural Studies, Hsinchu City, Taiwan

© Springer Nature Switzerland AG 2019   147
W. J. Bᴏᴏᴛ, Tᴀᴋᴀʏᴀᴍᴀ Daiki (eds.), *Tetsugaku Companion to Ogyū Sorai*,
Tetsugaku Companions to Japanese Philosophy 2,
https://doi.org/10.1007/978-3-030-15475-2_15

dential research of the Qing. I will, therefore, also pay attention to the achievements of Sorai's disciples and examine how the achievements of Sorai's school as a whole were received by the literati of Qing China and Chosŏn Korea. I will also compare Sorai's teachings with the thought of Dai Zhen 戴震 (1724–1777), who was easily the most important thinker of the middle Qing. On the basis of these investigations, I will clarify the characteristics and development of Sorai's teaching in East Asia.

2 The Formation of Sorai's Method for the Study of the Classics and the Study of the Classics by the Members of His School

2.1 The Theory of Literature of the School of Ancient Words and Phrases of the Ming and Ogyū Sorai's Method for the Study of the Classics

According to Sorai, the Six Classics were turned into books from the time of Confucius onwards, and the name did not imply that they were six sacred books. When he says that "the Six Classics are things," "the Six Classics" refer to the instruments with which, before Confucius, the Sages governed the country, and when he says that "one knows those 'things' through consulting the Six Classics,"[2] then he is referring to the Classics as the aforementioned corpus of texts. He states clearly that the *Lunyu* 論語 ("Analects") and *Liji* 礼記 ("Book of Rites") are commentaries (*den* 伝) and records (*ki* 記) that were added to the Six Classics later; they are the outcome of discussions between Confucius and his students about the "Way of the Former Kings," and were recorded by the students. Thus, Sorai situates them as books that explain the "meaning" of the Six Classics.[3]

On the other hand, in *Gakusoku* 学則 ("School rules") he declares that he is finding his "ancient words" 辞 in such "Masters" as *Guanzi* 管子, *Yanzi* 晏子, *Laozi* 老子, and *Liezi* 列子.[4] In the same vein, he states in the preface of *Benmei* that he finds his "names" 名 in books from before the Qin (221–206) and Han (202 B.C.–220 A.D.). In this way, the object that is to be interpreted through the methodology of "the study of ancient words and phrases" includes not only the Classical texts, i.e., the corpus of the Six Classics, *Lunyu*, and *Liji*, but also the Masters and Histories[5] that predate the Qin and Han. Therefore, the study of ancient words and phrases, in the sense of Sorai's method of interpreting the Classical texts, from the beginning

---

[2] Ogyū Sorai, *Benmei*: "Preface," *Ogyū Sorai*, NST vol. 36, p. 210, p. 41.

[3] See *Rongo-chō*: "Preface"; *Keishishi yōran*: "General Introduction"; *Ogyū Sorai*, NST vol. 36, *Bendō*, p. 200b, p. 12; cf. Tucker, *Sorai's Philosophical Masterworks*, p. 139.

[4] *Gakusoku* 2, *Ogyū Sorai*, NST vol. 36, p. 256b, p. 191.

[5] This division into genres goes back to the ancient Chinese division of texts in the "Four Warehouses" (*Siku* 四庫), i.e. the Classics 経, Masters 子, Histories 史, and Collections 集. (WJB)

was not restricted to the Classical texts but had the whole of the above "ancient words and phrases" as its object.

Sorai's method of interpreting the Classical texts within the context of these "ancient words and phrases" was a further development of the literary theory formulated by the school of ancient words and phrases of the Ming period. First, Wang Shizhen 王世貞 (1526–1590), who was *the* representative of this school, clearly regarded the Classical texts as "literature" and "history," and he expressed as his opinion that, from the point of view of style, the "Six Classics" and the old and recent texts that derived from them, were all varieties of descriptive prose that was related to the narrative style of historical texts.[6] In this way the school of ancient words and phrases played an important role in changing the perception of the Classical texts from sacralised "Classics," meant for the study of "The Way," into "historical prose" in which the "words" were cultivated and "affairs" 事 were recorded.

In China, in conjunction with the changing perception of the Classical texts that took place under the Ming, towards the end of the Ming a new type of scholarship arose that engaged in literary criticism of the ancient histories and Classical texts. This literary criticism did not stop at glossing individual characters; it also appraised from a specific point of view the rhetorical aspects of the phrasing and the "affairs" to which the texts referred.[7] This literary criticism of the Classical texts differed from the traditional commentaries on these texts; it was criticised by many as presumptuous, because it was preoccupied with things like grammar and because it read subjective thoughts into the Classical texts.[8] However, as one type of scholarly interpretation of the Classical texts, it did not necessarily conflict with the orthodox study of the Classics, whose method consisted of glossing the individual characters, and whose aim was the clarification of moral implications. As a matter of fact, some of the books in which the Classical texts are subjected to literary criticism use annotated editions of the Classical texts as their source and need the commentaries on the meaning of individual characters in the Classical texts as a precondition.[9] On the other hand, scholars of the Classics like Zhu Xi 朱熹 (1130–1200), too, attached importance to understanding the grammar of the Classical texts.[10]

In any event, the annotated editions of the Classical texts made during the Song were available, and by the end of the Ming a great many books in which the Classical texts were subjected to literary criticism had also been written. Apart from those, there was also an increase in the number of books that explored the truth or falsehood of the contents of the Classical texts; of books containing collated texts, intended to recover the original version of the sources; and of books reporting research of famous objects and institutions mentioned in the Classical texts; and, furthermore, of books about the "shape, sound, and meaning" of the "characters"

---

[6] See Wang Shizhen, *Yiyuan zhiyan* 芸苑卮言 1, p. 1111–1112.

[7] See Ho Mei-chen 侯美珍, "Ming-Qing shiren dui 'pingdian' de pipiao," pp. 230–243.

[8] See Ho Mei-chen, "Ming-Qing bagu qushi yu jingshu piaodian de xingqi," pp. 153–157.

[9] CHANG Su-ching 張素卿, "'Piaodian' de jieshi leixing," pp. 124–125.

[10] CHANG Su-ching, "'Piaodian' de jieshi leixing," pp. 94–98.

appearing in the Classical texts – in other words, phonological treatises, studies of characters, and glossaries.[11] Ogyū Sorai's study of ancient words and phrases as a method for interpreting Classical texts was established on the basis of this "knowledge from the Ming."

Next, let us look into the relation between the claims of the Ming school of ancient words and phrases in the field of literature, and of the *study* of ancient words and phrases as a method for interpreting Classical texts. According to letters collected in *Sorai-shū*, the process through which Sorai mastered the "ancient words and phrases" was as follows: first, by dint of reading only books dating from before the Western Han (25–220), just like Li and Wang had done, Sorai came to grasp the "words" 辞, "affairs" 事, and "rules" 法 of the old texts. Next, he began writing texts himself, applying the "words," "affairs," and "rules" of "ancient words and phrases," and in this way he trained himself. While doing that, he came to understand that the interpretations of the "meaning" of the old texts were fundamentally connected, and that it was not necessary to annotate each individual character. Differently, however, from Li and Wang, who had confined themselves to the "literary occupation" of writing and criticizing literary compositions, Sorai had the original idea to reinterpret their study of ancient words and phrases, centred on "words," as a "technique for interpreting the Classics" 経術.

The condition that made this possible was the change in the view of the Classics that I have outlined above. Sorai really thought that the "Six Classics" were "histories," just like the *Zuo zhuan* 左伝 and the *Shiji* 史記; that they were narrative texts that had been shaped according to the rules of rhetoric. Of course, they were difficult to understand; that was why one should first begin by studying ancient narrative texts like *Shiji* and *Zuo zhuan*, and then, on that basis, interpret the "Six Classics" as "historical," narrative texts.[12]

In this way, Sorai regarded the "Six Classics" as "history" and "prose." His interpretation of the "Six Classics" began from his recognition of the fact that the "Six Classics" and the "words" and "affairs" in the old texts dating from before the Qin and Han were mutually explanatory, and that there existed a continuity and relationship between them on the level of the "rules" of the "words." This insight he applied to the Classical texts. Basing himself on the literary theory of the Ming school of ancient words and phrases, he mastered a method for appraising ancient Chinese texts, which helped him to interpret even those "ancient words and phrases" that could not be fully grasped through individual glosses. He applied this to the interpretation of Classical texts and thus created the study of ancient words and phrases as a method for studying the Classics.

This study of ancient words and phrases as a method for studying the Classical texts does not end, however, when one has comprehended the "ancient words and phrases." The Classical texts and the other "ancient words and phrases" are different from the pseudo-ancient words and phrases of Li and Wang. In the ancient texts, there exists a whole world of "ancient language," which is shot through with values

---

[11] Lin Ching-chang 林慶彰, *Ming-dai jingxue yanjiu lunji*, pp. 70–134.

[12] Ogyū Sorai, *Sa Shi kaigyō in* 左史会業引, *Sorai-shū* 18:5b-6a; p. 185.

and standards and institutions that together are called "the Way of the Sages." The aim of "ancient words and phrases" as a method of classical scholarship is to interpret the "ancient words and phrases" of the Classical texts, and next, to understand the "ancient language" and the "Way of the Sages." One of the characteristics that distinguishes Sorai's methodology from the study of the Classics, more specifically, from the literary criticism of the Classical texts as it was practised at the end of the Ming, is precisely that it does not regard the Classical texts as mere literary and historical works. It does not merely give a subjective, literary appreciation of these texts, but that it makes a positive effort to extract from the Classical texts a "Way of the Sages" ("Rites" and "Righteousness") in the form of norms and institutions. In short, Sorai's methodology builds on a method of literary criticism that sees the Classical texts as a corpus of "ancient words and phrases" (instances of ancient, classical Chinese), but then aims to elucidate the "Way of the Sages" that is contained in the "ancient words" and "ancient meanings."

It would take too long to explain this in detail, but clearly, when he read the "ancient words and phrases," Sorai was attentive to the possibility that there existed a double "rhetoric." It was precisely through this approach that, having read the "ancient words and phrases" (i.e., "ancient Chinese"), he discovered that in the linguistic world of the ancient worthies (the ancient language in the broad sense) there was a "rhetoric" being practised that was based on the "lawlike pronouncements of the ancient kings" (the ancient language in the narrow sense). This discovery made it possible for him to enter the linguistic world in which the "Way of the Sages" was practised, and even, to reconstruct this "Way of the Sages." Those works of his that are related to the study of the Classics (*Bendō, Benmei, Rongo-chō*, and the *Liji*-related *Chūyō-kai* and *Daigaku-kai*), are the crystallization of his thought; they result from his understanding of the "Way of the Sages" through the application of this method. The method of annotating that we see in these commentaries on Classical texts is based on the method of literary criticism, and shows that Sorai has absorbed, in a critical way, the results of the traditional commentaries. It is Sorai's version of the study of ancient words and phrases, which he constructed with the aim of elucidating and explaining the "Way of the Sages."

2.2 The Classical Studies of Sorai's School: Dazai Shundai, Yamanoi Konron, Nemoto Sonshi

After Sorai's death, a great many books about the Classics appeared that were based on Sorai's study of the Classical corpus. Within the field of the East-Asian cultural sphere, the most important contributions were made by Dazai Shundai, Yamanoi Konron, and Nemoto Sonshi (Bui) 根本遜志・武夷 (1699–1764). This does not mean that they studied the Classical texts with the same methodology of ancient words and phrases as Sorai, but they were, like him, dissatisfied with the orthodox Neo-Confucian studies of the Classics and set great store by the annotations of the Classical texts from *before* the Song.

First, among Dazai Shundai's contributions to the study of the Classics we find such writings as *Rongo kunko* 論語古訓 ("Ancient glosses of the Analects"), *Rongo kokun gaiden* 論語古訓外伝 ("External tradition of the ancient glosses of the Analects"), and *Shi Sho koden* 詩書古伝 ("Ancient commentaries on the *Book of Songs* and the *Book of Documents*"). Apart from these, he had also re-cut and printed *Kobun Kōkyō* 古文孝経 ("Ancient Text of the Classic of Filial Piety"), i.e., the *Kobun Kōkyō* from the tradition of Mr. Kong 孔氏伝, and he published an explanation of this Classic in Japanese, entitled *Kobun Kōkyō kokujikai* 国字解, and a reprint of his abridged explanation of its preface (*Jūkoku Kobun Kōkyō jo ryakkai* 重刻古文孝経序略解). Finally, he published an annotated edition of *Kongzi jiayu*, entitled *Kōshi Kego zōchū* 孔子家語増註 ("Confucius' House Conversations with augmented commentary"). Clearly, *Xiaojing* and *Kongzi jiayu* were important scholarly interests for him. Compared to Sorai, Shundai relied more heavily on Kong Anguo 孔安国 (dates unknown; Eastern Han Dynasty), and also on the interpretations and discussions of the Classical texts by other Confucians of the Han. He stated, for instance, that "Glosses began with the *Erya* 爾雅,[13] and we must follow the theories of the Confucians of the Han; some of their glosses cannot really be relied on, but seven or eight out of ten are theories handed down in the school of Confucius."[14] This is why Shundai's understanding of the "Way of the Sages" deviates from Sorai's.[15]

Next, the aim of Sorai's own scholarship had not been to return to the old commentaries of the Han. His aim was to reconstruct the Way of the Sages while criticizing orthodox Neo-Confucianism, so he encouraged others to sort out and read the old commentaries from before the Song. In fact, Sorai's students Yamanoi Konron and Nemoto Sonshi spent 3 years in the Ashikaga School, cataloguing and collating its old books.[16] Due to Yamanoi's efforts, *Shichi-Kei Mōshi kōbun* 七経孟子考文 ("Collated text of the Seven Classics and Mencius") was finished in 1726. Thereafter, Sorai's younger brother Ogyū Hokkei 北渓, with the cooperation of Sorai's students Ishikawa Daihan (Korekiyo) 石川大凡・之清 (dates unknown), Miura Chikkei (Yoshikata) 三浦竹渓・義質 (1689–1756), Kimura Baiken (Akira) 木村梅軒・晟 (1701–1752), Usami Shinsui 宇佐美灊水 (1701–1776) and others collated and supplemented this text, and in 1731 published *Shichi-Kei Mōshi kōbun hoi* 補遺 ("Supplement to the collated text of the Seven Classics and Mencius"). Yamanoi Konron chiefly collated the texts of the Seven Classics (*Yijing, Shujing, Shijing, Liji, Chunqiu, Lunyu, Xiaojing*) and *Mengzi* that were kept in the Ashikaga School in the form of old manuscript copies and of printed books from the Song and Ming.[17] Around 1750, Nemoto Bui published a *Rongo Shūkai giso* 論語集解義疏

---

[13] One of the Thirteen Classics. It is a kind of dictionary (3 fasc.; nineteen sections), dating from the end of the third or the beginning of the second century BC. The author is not known. (WJB)

[14] Dazai Shundai, *Seigaku mondō, Sorai gakuha*, NST 37, p. 131.

[15] Lan Hung Yueh, "Dazai Shundai to Sorai-gaku no sai-kōsei," *Shisō* 1112 (2016).

[16] Takahashi Satoshi 高橋智, "Keichō-kan *Rongo Shūkai* no kenkyū," *Shidō Bunko ronshū* 30 (1996), p. 112.

[17] Sueki Yasuhiko 末木恭彦, *Sorai to Konron*, pp. 159–162.

("Explanation of the Collected Commentaries of the Analects"). This shows how much importance Sorai's students attached to the ancient commentaries from before the Song. They rediscovered the old versions of the Classical texts that remained in Japan, and they also exerted themselves at the collation of these texts. In some respects, the advances they made in the collation of Classical texts came close to the evidential research of the Qing.

3 The Reception and Criticism of the Classical Studies of Sorai's School in Qing China

3.1 The Import and Reception of the Writings of Sorai's School

Wang Peng (Zhuli) 汪鵬 · 竹里, who visited Japan seven times, played an important role in the cultural exchange between Qing China and Tokugawa Japan. He brought back to China many of the ancient Chinese books that had disappeared in China and had been re-discovered in Japan.[18] The above-mentioned *Kobun Kōkyō*, *Shichi-Kei Mōshi kōbun hoi*, and *Rongo shūkai giso* were brought back by him. Apart from these, he also imported into China Sorai's *Rongo-chō*, *Rongo-chō shūran* 集覧, which includes *Rongo-chō*, and Dazai Shundai's *Rongo kokun* and *Rongo kokun gaiden*.[19] According to Fujitsuka Chikashi, *Rongo-chō*, *Daigaku-kai*, *Chūyō-kai*, and Shundai's *Shi Sho koden*, but also *Hi Sorai-gaku*[20] 非徂徠学 ("Rejecting Sorai's Teachings"), which is critical of Sorai, are already listed in a document of Bunka 6 (1809), entitled "Chinese ships export a number of Japanese printed books."[21] Apart from these, also *Benmei*, *Bendō*, and *Sorai-shū* were brought to China.[22] Of these writings, all related to Sorai's school, best known among the Confucian scholars of the Qing were *Shichi-Kei Mōshi kōbun hoi*, *Rongo shūkai giso*, *Kobun kōkyō*, and the typical Sorai-book *Rongo-chō*.

First, *Shichi-Kei Mōshi kōbun hoi* was included in such collections as *Siku quanshu* 四庫全書 ("All Books of the Four Warehouses") and Bao Tingbo's 鮑廷博 (1728–1814) *Zhibuzuzhai congshu* 知不足斎叢書 ("Collectaneum of the Knowledge-Is-Insufficient Studio"). It was highly appreciated by the evidential research movement of the Qing. After he had read this work, Lu Wenchao 盧文弨 (1717–1796) sighed that "even in such a small country, out in the sea, there are people who read books!"[23] Ruan Yuan 阮元 (1764–1849), too, wrote appreciatively

---

[18] Matsura Akira 松浦章, *Edo-jidai Tōsen ni yoru Nit-Chū bunka kōryū*, pp. 204–207.

[19] Fujitsuka Chikashi 藤塚鄰, *Rongo sōsetsu*, p. 295.

[20] Written by Kani Yōsai 蟹養斎 (1705–1778; *KGS* 1372), and printed in 1765.

[21] Fujitsuka Chikashi, *Rongo sōsetsu*, p. 296.

[22] Fujitsuka Chikashi, *Rongo sōsetsu*, p. 313.

[23] Lu Wenchao 盧文弨, "Zhou Yi zhushu jizheng tici," *Guoxue jiben congshu* vol. 7, p. 88.

of this book because of its value in the collation of Classical texts.[24] Others, too, like Wang Mingsheng 王鳴盛 (1722–1797), cited it when collating Classical texts.[25]

Wang also published *Rongo shūkai giso*. It was this last book that, together with *Shichi-Kei Mōshi kōbun hoi*, stimulated the development of collation-based research under the Qing.[26] When, however, Wang used the original Ashikaga text 足利本 to collate *Lunyu yishu* 論語義疏 by Huang Kan 皇侃 (488–545), he re-arranged the contents after the pattern of the commentaries and sub-commentaries printed under the Ming, and changed the title to *Lunyu Jijie yishu* 論語集解義疏. That is why *Rongo Shūkai giso* was sometimes distrusted by the Critical Philologists of the Qing.[27] Because of these connections the great Sinologist of modern Japan, Kano Naoki 狩野直喜 (1868–1947), noticed the value and the importance of *Shichi-Kei Mōshi kōbun hoi* within the history of Chinese studies in East Asia, and wrote his article "Yamanoi Tei to *Shichi-Kei Mōshi kōbun hoi*."[28] It seems likely that this article is to some extent responsible for the tendency of later Japanese researchers to interpret Sorai's teachings from the viewpoint of the critical philologists of the Qing.

Next – because *Kobun Kōkyō*, compiled and collated by Dazai Shundai, was also included in *Zhibuzuzhai congshu* and *Sishu Quanshu*, under the title *Guwen Xiaojing Kong-shi zhuan* 古文孝経孔氏伝 ("The Ancient Text of the Classic of Filial Piety, with commentary by Mr Kong"), it was widely read. The authenticity of this text, too, became the subject of debate from the middle of the Qing onwards. The theories that held that the book was a forgery can be divided into the following four types: (1) The assertion that *Xiaojing gu Kongshi yibian* 孝経古孔氏一篇, which is listed in the *Yiwen-zhi* 藝文志 ("Treatise on Bibliography") of the *Han Shu* 漢書, was a forgery, attributed by its anonymous author to Kong Anguo.[29] (2) The theory that *Guwen Xiaojing Kong-shi zhuan* was a forgery by Wang Su 王肅 (fl. 265).[30] (3) The theory that the text was forged or reworked under the Sui by Liu Xuan 劉炫 (546–613).[31] (4) The theory that it is a forgery made by the Japanese scholar Dazai Shundai.[32]

---

[24] Ruan Yuan, "Ke *Qijing Mengzi kaowen bing buyi* xu," *Guoxue jiben congshu* vol. 7, p. 37.

[25] Gu Yongxin 顧永新, "*Qijing Mengzi kaowen buyi* kaoshu," *Beijing Daxue xuebao: Zhexue Shehui Kexue ban* 39, 1 (2002), pp. 84–91.

[26] Takahashi Satoshi, "Keichō-kan *Rongo Shūkai* no kenkyū," p. 110.

[27] For *Rongo giso* and the critical philology of the Qing, see Daibō Masanobu 大坊真伸, "Nemoto Bui no *Rongo giso* honkoku ni mirareru kaihen ni tsuite," *Daitō Bunka Daigaku Kangakkaishi* 46 (2006), and "*Rongo giso* to Shinchō Kōshōgaku: *Shisho kōi* 四書考異 o chūshin ni," *Jinbun kagaku* 13 (2008).

[28] Kano Naoki 狩野直喜, "Yamanoi Tei to *Shichi-Kei Mōshi kōbun hoi*," *Shina-gaku bunsō* (Kōbundō, 1928).

[29] Zhao Shaozu 趙紹祖, "*Guwen Xiaojing Kong-shi zhuan*," *Xueshu biji congkan* vol. 7, p. 99.

[30] Ding Yan 丁宴, "Riben *Guwen Xiaojing Kong-shi zhuan* bian wei," *Xiaojing wenxian jicheng* vol. 12, pp. 17–21.

[31] Lu Wenchao, "Xinke *Guwen Xiaojing Kong-shi zhuan* xu," *Guoxue jiben congshu* vol. 2, pp. 21–23.

[32] Sun Zhizu 孫志祖, "*Xiaojing Kong-shi zhuan*," *Qing-dai xueshu biji congkan* vol. 27, p. 173.

Why was this work, which was suspected of being a forgery, included in the *Siku Quanshu*? According to the editors of *Siku Quanshu*, they had included it because "those who loved antiquity were loath to let it go."[33] The fact that he was sometimes put down as a composer of forgeries shows that the scholars of the Qing held Dazai Shundai in lower esteem than Yamanoi Konron.

The next question is, how the scholars of the Qing understood Sorai's *Rongo-chō*. This problem has already been discussed in detail by Fujitsuka Chikashi.[34] He discusses how *Rongo-chō* is cited in such books as *Jingjushuo* 経句説 ("Explanation of clauses in the Classics") by Wu Ying 吳英 (dates unknown), *Wuqijing bu* 吾妻鏡補 ("Additions to the *Mirror of the East*") by Weng Guangping 翁廣平 (1760–1842), *Jingxue zhiyi* 経学質疑 ("Questions about the Study of the Classics") by Di Ziji 狄子奇 (dates unknown), *Lunyu zhengyi* ("The Correct Interpretation to the Analects") by Liu Baonan 劉宝楠 (b. 1791), and *Chunzaidang suibi* 春在堂隨筆 ("Commonplace Book of the Hall where Spring is Present") by Yu Yue 俞樾 (1821–1906). Fujitsuka also points out that the parts of *Rongo-chō* that are quoted in Liu Baonan's *Lunyu zhengyi* 論語正義 ("The correct meaning of the Analects") actually were added by his son Liu Gongmian 劉恭冕 (1824–1883), and that the copies of *Rongo-chō* that Liu Gongmian and Yu Yue saw, all were printed books that Dai Wang 戴望 (1837–1873) had bought in a bookshop in Hangzhou in Dongzhi 5 (1866). Fujitsuka also establishes that Qian Yong 錢泳 (1759–1844) rearranged *Bendō* and *Benmei*, added his own preface and a *Ribenguo Culai-xiansheng xiaozhuan*日本国祖來先生小伝 ("Short Biography of Master Sorai of the country of Japan"), which was based on *Sentetsu sōdan* 先哲叢談 ("Collected Stories of Former Wise Men"), and published it under the title *Haiwai xinshu* 海外新書 ("A New Book from Overseas").[35]

Best known among the scholars mentioned above, who had read *Rongo-chō*, is Liu Baonan with his *Lunyu zhengyi*. However, he only quoted two passages. In *Chunzaidang suibi* seventeen passages are quoted, but its author does not comment on them.[36] The one who went furthest in quoting *Rongo-chō* in his own works, and in criticizing it, was Wu Ying in his *Jingjushuo*. He quotes *Rongo-chō* eleven times in this work.[37] When we read these quotations, we see that there are only two places where he quotes *Rongo-chō* approvingly.[38] Moreover, as was to be expected, he is unable to understand Sorai's theory of the "Way of the Sages" and criticizes Sorai's ideas about Mencius.[39] In this way, the works of Sorai's school that were imported

[33] Ji Yun 紀昀 *et al.*, "*Guwen Xiaojing Kong-shi zhuan* tiyao," *Yingyin Wenyuange Siku Quanshu 5: Jing zongyi lei* vol. 182, p. 2.

[34] Fujitsuka Chikashi, *Rongo sōsetsu*, pp. 291–361.

[35] Qian Yong, comp., *Haiwai xinshu*(Zheng Zhao鄭照, ed., 1836; copy in the possession of Keiō Gijuku Daigaku).

[36] Chiang Hsun-yi 蔣薰誼, "*Lunyuzheng* yu *Jingjushuo* de sixiang bijiao," p. 3.

[37] Chiang Hsun-yi, "*Lunyuzheng* yu *Jingjushuo* de sixiang bijiao," p. 6.

[38] These are 「居蔡山節藻梲」 (*Jingjushuo* 24; *Lunyu* 5.18) and 「如用之、則吾従先進」 (*Jingjushuo* 25; *Lunyu* 11.1).

[39] See 「而不與焉」 (*Jingjushuo* 18; *Lunyu* 8.18).

into China in the middle of the Qing, were taken notice of, to some extent, by Chinese scholars and remained known. One cannot, however, maintain that Sorai's theories were really taken seriously.

By the end of the Qing, scholars appeared who had lived in Japan for a long time, like Huang Zunxian 黄遵憲 (1848–1905), Tang Caichang 唐才常 (1867–1900), and Zhang Taiyan 章太炎 (1869–1936). How did *they* look at the writings and the doctrines of Sorai's school? First, in his *Riben guozhi* 日本国志 ("Gazetteer of Japan"), Huang Zunxian concisely but accurately introduces Sorai's pedigree, the methodology of ancient words and phrases, the essence of his Confucian thought, i.e., that he wanted to be rid of the orthodox Neo-Confucianism of the Song, and the most important of his writings.[40] At the end of the Qing, this is perhaps the best-organized treatment of Sorai by any Chinese.

On the other hand, Tang Caichang, basing himself on a discussion in *Bankoku shiki* 万国史記 ("Historical Record of Ten thousand Countries"),[41] claimed that Ogyū Sorai's arguments, too, had been of importance in the opening of Japan.[42] In another piece of writing, Tang claims that "The message of equal rights 平権 of Confucius and Mencius was made explicit by Butsu Mokei (= Ogyū Sorai)."[43] It is an intriguing question, why Tang considered Ogyū Sorai's thought from such a point of view, but I cannot explore it here any further.

Sorai was mainly seen as a scholar of the Classics, a Sinologist.[44] Zhang Taiyan's argument can be called representative of the theories about Sorai that saw him from this point of view. As I have said already, in his opinion, Sorai's and his disciple Shundai's study of the Classics consisted of "glosses and evidential research, and once in a while they say something worthwhile," but if you compared them with Chinese scholars like Dai Zhen and Duan Yucai 段玉裁 (1735–1815), the *crème de la crème* of evidential research, then the scholarly level of Japanese Confucians like Sorai was low. In the end, because of the difference in language, they were not be able, either, to understand the phonology from before the Zhou and Qin.[45]

Zhang Taiyan's idea of Sorai is one of the stereotypes one often encounters when Chinese consider Sinology as practised in Japan. This viewpoint is inspired by a feeling of superiority of China versus barbarians, and by the pride of being a successor of the evidential research of the Qing; it is completely one-sided. As I will explain below, the phonological study of characters had already developed in Tokugawa Japan, and Sorai's school was also involved in it. Moreover, Sorai's methodology may have had a common origin with the evidential research of the Qing Period, yet, its nature was different. The methodology of ancient words and

---

[40] Huang Zunxian, "Xueshuzhi" 学術志 1, *Riben guozhi* 32, *Huang Zunxian quanshu* vol. 2, p. 1403.

[41] *Bankoku shiki* (5 vols) was written Okamoto Kansuke 岡本監輔 (1839–1904) and published in 1879. (WJB)

[42] Tang Caichang, "Geguo zhengjiao gongli zonglun," *Tang Caichang ji* 1, p. 24.

[43] Tang Caichang, "Riben Kuanyong yilai daishishu," *Tang Caichang ji*, p. 214.

[44] Yu Yue, "Ji Ribenguo renyu," *Xueshu biji congkan* vol. 9, pp. 227–228.

[45] Zhang Taiyan, *Taiyan wenlu chupian*, *Zhang Taiyan quanji* vol. 4, App., fasc. 2, p. 321.

phrases should not be judged from the viewpoint of the evidential research of the Qing. There were differences between these two methodologies; in the following section we will reflect on this problem, through a comparison with Dai Zhen.

3.2   A Comparison of Sorai and Dai Zhen

Within the scope of the present article, it is impossible to give a detailed account of Dai Zhen's classical studies, but when we combine the researches of Kondō Mitsuo, Yoshida Jun, and Kinoshita Tetsuya,[46] the following points emerge on which he was different from Sorai. First, Dai Zhen's idea, that through the study of the Classical texts one tried to grasp the "principles of action 理義 of the Wise Men and Sages" (also: "the will 心志 of the ancient Sages and Wise Men") may resemble Sorai's ideas, but there is a difference. The "Way of the Sages" that Sorai seeks may equally be an expression dependent on the "will" of the Sages, but Sorai does not assume that behind the "Way of the Sages" or the "will" of the Sages there exist universal "principles of action." We could also phrase it as follows: differently from the Sages in Sorai's thought, the Sages of whom Dai Zhen is thinking are not so terribly distant from ordinary men. This relates to the difference in their understanding of Mencius' thought, and to the relative importance they attach to Mencius. As appears clearly from the fact that the object of research in Dai Zhen's most important work, *Mengzi ziyi shuzheng* 孟子字義疏証 ("Evidential commentary on the meaning of characters in Mencius"), is Mencius' thought, Dai Zhen, for all his criticism of the School of Principle 理学, in the end professes the kind of Confucianism that honours Mencius and belongs to the Mencian tradition. On the contrary, in the Confucian thought of Sorai and his school, Mencius is precisely the culprit who caused scholars of later generations to misunderstand the "Way of the Sages." When you look at it from Sorai's point of view, Dai Zhen's so-called "new teaching of principles of action" 新義理学 still remained a Confucianism of Mencian derivation.

Apart from books on arithmetic,[47] Dai Zhen also wrote about astronomy and geography,[48] but in Sorai's school one does not encounter any writings about such topics. Even though Sorai had some knowledge of calendar-making, he did not leave any writings dealing with that topic.[49] In his way of thinking, heaven was

---

[46] Kondō Mitsuo 近藤光男, *Shin-chō kōshōgaku no kenkyū*; Yoshida Jun 吉田純, *Shin-chō kōshōgaku no gunzō*; Kinoshita Tetsuya 木下鉄矢, *Shin-dai gakujutsu to gengogaku: Ko'ongaku no shisō to keifu*.

[47] For Dai Zhen's works, see *Dai Zhen quanshu* 戴震全書. His works about arithmetic are *Cesuan* 策算, *Suanxue chugao sizhong* 算学初稿四種, *Jiuzhang suanshu dinge butu* 九章算術訂訛補図, and *Wujing suanshu kaozheng* 五経算術考証.

[48] Dai Zhen's works in these fields are *Yuan xiang* 原象, *Xu tianwenlüe* 続天文略, *Shuidiji chugao* 水地記初稿, and *Shuijing kaoci* 水経考次.

[49] In his second reply to Suishindō 復水神童第二書, Sorai says of calendar-making and mathematics that "he has not yet studied them," but he does make some critical remarks about contemporary mathematics (*Sorai-shū* 24:16a-17b; pp. 260–261). N.B. Suishindō is Mizuashi Hakusen 水足博泉 (1707–1732; *KGS* 4269).

"a living being," so astronomers would never be able to grasp the movements of nature in a completely correct way.[50] To elaborate somewhat more on this point – it has been pointed out that "Just like modern science and modern thought, Dai Zhen's method respected mathematical certainty but, however innovative he may have been, … in the end he did not have in himself scepticism in the modern sense – not even the slightest notion of doubt towards dogma."[51] On the other hand, Ogyū Sorai's view of nature as a living being could be understood as a certain kind of scepticism. It is not my intention, however, to claim here that Sorai's thought was more modern than that of Dai Zhen. Rather, I think that in their thought and methodology both Dai Zhen and Sorai returned to the scholarship of ancient China, and in this way fulfilled a role in helping the *literati* of Japan and China to break away from the *Yijing*-inspired, numerological view of nature – from the numerological model of explaining nature that was also an inherent part of the orthodox Neo-Confucianism of the Song.[52]

We also see differences in the field of phonology, which Dai Zhen regarded as important. As mentioned above, Sorai, too, had noticed the importance of the sounds (phonemes) in the interpretation of the Classical texts; he even wrote a book entitled *Ingai* 韻粲 ("An outline of sounds"). According to Sorai, when he began the study of "ancient words and phrases," he also applied himself to the "study of sounds." Through applying this knowledge to the "old texts," he came to understand profound points in the interpretation of the Classical texts.[53] He remarks that not only in the Six Classics, the *Lunyu*, and the *Erya*, but also in books about linguistics dating from the Han, such as Kong Anguo's commentaries on the Classical texts, *Shuowen jiezi* 説文解字 ("Explaining texts and analysing characters") by Xu Shen 許慎 (58?-147?), and *Shi ming* 釈名 ("Explaining the names") by Liu Xi 劉熙 (dates unknown), already methods to explain the meaning of characters with help of sounds were used.[54] And in *Rongo-chō*, Sorai does in fact give explanations in which he makes use of his phonological knowledge. In this way, "the study of sounds" had become part and parcel of the methodology of ancient words and phrases.

Therefore, just like Dai Zhen, Sorai, too, most certainly regarded such books from ancient China as the *Erya*, which contains glosses of characters, as important. After all, it was through the use of such sources that he had discovered the method of interpreting the Classical texts. Between the two, however, there was the following important difference: Sorai still relied on the system of sounds of *Yinjing*, even though he knew that *Yinjing* 韻鏡 ("Mirror of rhymes"), which was corrected and printed by Zhang Linzhi 張麟之 (dates unknown) of the Southern Song, did *not*

---

[50] Ogyū Sorai, *Ken'en zuihitsu*, p. 152; the second reply to Suishindō, etc.

[51] Kawahara Hideki 川原秀城, "Tai Shin to seiyō sangaku," *Seigaku tōzen to Higashi Ajia*, p. 218.

[52] Kawahara Hideki, "Seiō gakujutsu no tōzen to Chūgoku, Chōsen, Nihon," *Seigaku tōzen*, p. 83–101.

[53] Ogyū Sorai, *Ingai*, *Ogyū Sorai zenshū* vol. 2, p. 669.

[54] See Ogyū Sorai, *Ingai*, *Ogyū Sorai zenshū* vol. 2, p. 673.

represent the "old sounds" and that occasionally its method could *not* be trusted. He also tried to understand the system of "ancient sounds" that lay behind the characters through the *Kan'on* and *Go'on* pronunciations that had been transmitted in Japan.[55] The only thing he has to show for it, however, is *Jibo Wa-doku Kan Go seidaku zu* 字母和読漢呉清濁図 ("Chart of phonetic characters, Japanese readings, Kan- and Go-on, not-vocalised and vocalised"); he never expanded this into a systematic, phonological study of characters.

Dazai Shundai had different ideas from Sorai. He pointed out that it was problematic to understand *Yinjing* only through the *fanjie* method 反切法,[56] and through the categories of *Kan'on* and *Go'on*, in which the sounds had become adapted to the phonology of Japanese. Instead, Shundai insisted that *Yinjing* should be studied with help to "Chinese sounds (華音・唐音)."[57] Shundai will not only have had a better knowledge of Chinese phonology than Sorai, he also integrated this knowledge into the formation of his own scholarship in a more practical way than Sorai.[58] For instance, when he corrected and published *Kobun Kōkyō*, he added the Chinese sounds to the phrase 「仲尼閒居、曾子侍坐」 ("Confucius sat relaxed, Zengzi sat next to him in attendance"), saying that "the character 閒 (*jiān, xián, jiàn*) rhymes with 閑 (*xián*), and the character 坐 is composed of *c[ái]* 才 and *[w]ò* 臥.[59] Following Shundai's way of thinking and appreciating the importance that in his master's scholarship was attached to Chinese phonology, Shundai's student Bun'yū 文雄 (1700–1763) decided to take the pronunciation of Hangzhou as the standard pronunciation of Chinese, and wrote many studies of the pronunciation of Chinese characters, the first of which was *Makō inkyō* 磨光韻鏡 ("Mirror of rhymes, polished to brightness"). He had a strong and profound influence on the study of the pronunciation of Chinese characters of later generations.[60]

In Tokugawa Japan, the study of the pronunciation of characters developed on the basis of rhyme mirrors. This is not the place to go into detail, but scholars from outside Sorai's school such as Motoori Norinaga 本居宣長 (1730–1801), too, studied

[55] Ogyū Sorai, *Ingai*, p. 675, and the appendices "Go-in shichi-in sōtsū zu" 五音七音相通図 and "Jibo Wa-doku Kan-Go seidaku zu" 字母和読漢呉清濁図.

[56] A traditional Chinese way of indicating the pronunciation of characters, by giving two other characters, the first of which has the same initial phoneme as the character that is to be explained, and the second, the same middle and final phonemes as the character to be explained; this second character also indicates the tone.

[57] Dazai Shundai, "Makō kōkyō jo 磨光光鏡序" (*Shundai-sensei Shishien kō* 5:14b-16b; p. 147–148): "He who wishes to bring order to the rhyme mirrors, first must study the Chinese sounds. When one has studied the Chinese sounds and practised them, only then one can clearly understand the four tones and distinguish the seven sounds. Inside and outside open up and come together, and one can distinguish all of the hundred different pronunciations." (5:16a)

[58] Of Sorai's references to, and presentations of Chinese sounds, it has been said that "Put in an extreme way, he was aiming at an effect of abstruse learning." (Yuzawa Tadayuki 湯沢質幸, "Kinsei jugaku ni okeru Tō-on," *Kokugo ronkyū* vol. 8, p. 368.

[59] Dazai Shundai, *Kōkyō* (printed Kyōhō 17 / 1732; copy in the possession of Naikaku Bunko), p. 1a.

[60] Yuzawa Tadayuki, "Bun'yū ni okeru *Inkyō* to Tō-on," *Tsukuba Gakuin Daigaku kiyō* 5 (2010); id., *Edo-ki Kanji-on kenkyū ni okeru Tō-on juyō*, pp. 141–162.

the pronunciation of characters on the basis of the rhyme mirrors, and developed the study of Japanese phonology, which centred on the "chart of fifty sounds."[61] Of course, the Japanese pronunciation of characters came into existence through a process of abstracting and selecting from the Chinese sounds that were imported together with written *Kanbun*. As the study of the pronunciation of characters developed in Tokugawa Japan, it was also applied in order to comprehend the "Way of the Sages" by interpreting the sounds of the Classical texts, but it was not systematized in a way comparable to the evidential research of the Qing Period, and no precise phonology of ancient Chinese ever developed. Instead, it played a certain role in the elucidation of the sounds of ancient Japanese. In that sense, it is connected, though indirectly, with the discovery of a uniquely Japanese "Way" and with the formation of modern Japanese nationalism.

Dai Zhen, on the other hand, did not rely on the *Yinjing*, for *Yinjing* had been lost in China early on and was re-imported only at the end of the Qing. He based himself on the phonological studies of Gu Yanwu 顧炎武 (1613–1682) and others, who had been active at the end of the Ming and in the early Qing. He liberated himself from the traditional way of studying the pronunciation of characters, which had been influenced by the "image-number learning."[62] Moreover, relying on the systematic arrangement of sounds in four categories[63] that had probably been rediscovered because of the contact with Manchu, and through his study of a rhyme book entitled *Huangyin* 廣韻 ("Broad rhymes"), he developed his own systematic phonology of the sounds of the characters, which he summarised in his *Shengleibiao* 声類表 ("Table of sounds [arranged] by category").[64] Dai Zhen still tried to comprehend "The Way" through considering the "old sounds" of the Classical texts that he had reconstructed in this way, but Duan Yucai and others based themselves on the insights brought by Dai Zhen's researches and went on to develop the field of study of ancient phonology and the Classical texts.

Sorai was unable to conduct research into the pronunciation of characters that would lead to results as precise and systematic as Dai Zhen's, and the results of his research into phonology do not seem to have had an appreciable influence on

---

[61] Yuzawa Tadayuki, *Edo-ki Kanji'on kenkyū ni okeru Tō-on juyō*, pp. 247–265; Tei Kankō 釘貫亨, "Nihongogakushi ni okeru 'on'in' no mondai," pp. 222–225. N.B. This chart, the *Gojūon-zu* 五十音図, gives the syllabic signs (two sets of them, *hiragana* and *katakana*, which are completely parallel) that are used for writing Japanese, in an order that was inspired by the syllabic system of Sanskrit. Though known as the "chart of fifty sounds," the actual number is, or rather, was forty-eight. (WJB)

[62] The *Xiangshu xue* 象数学 was one of the two approaches to the study of the *Yijing* that had articulated themselves by the late Tang. It was "visually interpretive – concentrated on cosmology – and focused on using the malleable iconography of the *Yijing* to explicate the inanimate workings of nature." The *Xiangshu xue* must be contrasted with the *Yili xue* 義理学 ("meaning-principle learning"), which "was derived from a literal interpretation of the *Yijing* text and exhibited a moralistic understanding of it in its application to the world." (Wyatt, *The Recluse of Loyang*, p. 4. Wyatt in turn refers to Smith, "Sung Literati Thought and the *I Ching*," pp. 217–218.) (WJB)

[63] The Chinese term is *dengyun* 等韻. It is a schematic arrangement of the thirty-six initial consonants 字母 combined with the (rhyming) vowels 字音 in four categories, called *deng*. (WJB)

[64] Kinoshita Tetsuya 木下鉄矢, *Shin-dai gakujutsu to gengogaku*, chapters 4 and 5.

researchers of later generations.[65] In Sorai's scholarship the emphasis did not lie on the accuracy and the scholarly quality of his interpretation of the Classical texts. As many studies have shown, it lay with his study of ancient words and phrases, conceived as a method to comprehend the differences between the past and the present, "the here and the there," which was an inspiration for Dutch Studies and National Studies, and even for the study of Japanese literature in the Early Modern Period.

In the end, Sorai's importance lay in the revolutionary character of his discourse about the "Way of the Sages" that he had deduced through his study of ancient words and phrases, and in the influence on the history of thought that it turned out to have. Yet, when we think of the way in which he inspired the methodology of Dutch Studies,[66] and of the importance his student Dazai Shundai and others attached to the commentaries of the Han and the study of the pronunciation of Chinese characters, we still could claim that Sorai's position in the history of Japanese thought does in fact resemble that of Dai Zhen.

Both the evidential research of the Qing and Sorai's researches can be regarded as a further development of the classical studies of the Ming Period, but in his own, personal method of studying the Classics Sorai attached more importance to the rhetoric of classical Chinese than to an accurate study of the sounds or the glosses, or the collation of texts. When, however, we turn our attention to the achievements of a Dazai Shundai or a Yamanoi Konron, we see that Sorai's school, too, in some respects came close to the evidential research of the Qing Dynasty.

Next, let us examine the reception of the classical studies of Sorai's school in the Chosŏn Kingdom.

4 The Import and Reception of Writings of Sorai's School in the Chosŏn Kingdom

Japanese Confucianism was mainly introduced to Korea through the Korea envoys. Relatively early, the Korean *literati* noted the Confucianism of the Hayashi, and of Yamazaki Ansai 山崎闇斎 (1618–1682), Kaibara Ekiken 貝原益軒 (1630–1714), and Itō Jinsai 伊藤仁斎 (1627–1705), but not, as yet, the writings of Sorai's school.[67] The first book that introduced the scholarship of Sorai's school probably was *Hwagukchi* 和国志 (1764)[68] by Wŏn Chunggŏ 元重挙 (1719–1790), one of the envoys of the embassy of 1764. Amongst the books he quotes is an *Ogyū Sorai bunshū*, which apparently he had read.[69] He also had written conversations with

---

[65] Yuzawa Tadayuki, "Kinsei ingaku ni okeru Go'on Kan'on no bunrui to inkyō."

[66] Satō Shōsuke 佐藤昌介, *Yōgakushi kenkyū josetsu* Ch. 2; Sugimoto Tsutomu 杉本つとむ, "Sorai to sono gengo kenkyū."

[67] Ha Ubong 河宇鳳, *Chōsen Jitsugakusha no mita Kinsei Nihon*, pp. 83–86, 153–156.

[68] For the presumable year of writing, I follow the reconstruction in Ha Ubong, *Chōsen Ōchō jidai no sekaikan to Nihon ninshiki*, p. 220.

[69] Ha Ubong, *Chōsen Ōchō jidai no sekaikan to Nihon ninshiki*, p. 221.

literati of Sorai's school, so he had some knowledge of Sorai's teachings.[70] In *Itan ŭi sŏl* 異端之説 ("Heterodox theories"; *Hwagukchi* 2), he shows his understanding of the characteristics of Sorai's scholarship such as his study of ancient words and phrases and his criticism of Mencius and of the Neo-Confucianism of the Song.[71] On the other hand, he praises Sorai as an "outstanding, great and special talent"; he mentions with appreciation that Sorai "teaches his students to use rhyme books with Chinese sounds"; and he also praises Dazai Shundai as being superior to Sorai in "argumentation."[72] The next is Yi Tŏngmu 李德懋 (1741–1793) who, in the first fascicle of his *Ch'ŏngnyŏng kukchi* 蜻蛉国志 (1778), entitled *Inmulp'yŏn* 人物篇 ("People"), discusses the fact that Sorai was influenced by Li and Wang and criticized the School of Principle, and also mentions the study of spoken Chinese and Dazai Shundai; he praises Sorai as a "great scholar from abroad."[73] Yi likely based himself on the descriptions in *Hwagukchi*.

The one who really immersed himself in the classical studies and the thought of Sorai's school was Chŏng Yagyong 丁若鏞 (1762–1836). In his *Ilbonnon* 日本論 ("About Japan"), Chŏng Yagyong argues on the evidence of the scholarship of Itō Jinsai, Ogyū Sorai, and Dazai Shundai that there is no need any longer to be anxious about aggression from Japan, for Sorai's interpretation of the Classics is "a brilliant piece of writing."[74] He had most certainly read the commentaries on the classical texts by Sorai and Shundai, and he quotes from them abundantly in his main work, *Non'ŏ kokŭm chu* 論語古今注 ("Old and new annotations of the Analects").[75] The only text, however, that he really used was *Rongo kokun gaiden* 論語古訓外伝 ("External tradition of the ancient glosses of the Analects").[76]

Much research has already been done on the relation between the classical studies of Sorai's school and that of Chŏng Yagyong. First, according to Ha Ubong, in most of his quotations of Sorai's and Shundai's theories about the Classics Chŏng Yagyong disagrees with them. Sorai's theories he severely criticized, but he had a relatively good opinion of those of Shundai and quotes them as proof of his own theories.[77] According to Ha, like Sorai and Shundai, Chŏng Yagyong showed an inclination for "ancient studies" and the "study of practical politics," free from Zhu Xi's teachings, but he was not as radical as our two Japanese.[78] Especially in his theory of human nature, Chŏng Yagyong may have criticized the theory of human nature of the School of Principle, but he also criticized the "Three Types of Nature

---

[70] Lan Hung Yueh, "Sorai-gakuha bunshi to Chōsen Tsūshinshi."

[71] Wŏn Chunggŏ, *Hwagukchi*, p. 325.

[72] Wŏn Chunggŏ, *Hwagukchi*, p. 326, 362, 361.

[73] Yi Tŏngmu, *Ch'ŏngnyŏng kukchi*, *Ch'ŏngjanggwan chŏnsŏ* 青莊館全書, p. 161, 162.

[74] Chŏng Yagyong, *Ilbonnon* 1, *Yŏyutang chŏnjip* vol. 12, p. 332.

[75] Sorai's opinions are quoted fifty times, and Shundai's, 148 times; see Ha Ubong, *Chōsen Jitsugakusha no mita Kinsei Nihon*, p. 273.

[76] Ha Ubong, *Chōsen Jitsugakusha no mita Kinsei Nihon*, p. 275.

[77] Ha Ubong, *Chōsen Jitsugakusha no mita Kinsei Nihon*, p. 276、277.

[78] Ha Ubong, *Chōsen Jitsugakusha no mita Kinsei Nihon*, pp. 278–291.

Theory"[79] of which Shundai approved. Instead, he developed a theory of human nature that held that "the ten thousand people are all equal," which he based on Confucius' words "in their natures, they are close," and he criticized Sorai's and Shundai's view that "the people" are lacking in intelligence.[80]

Basing himself on the Ha Ubong's arguments, Chang Kun-Chiang makes more or less the same points, but then draws attention to the differences between Sorai and Shundai on the one hand, and Chŏng Yagyong on the other in regard to Mencius and the old commentaries. In short, compared to the philosophical standpoint of Sorai and Shundai, who were fundamentally critical of Mencius, Chŏng Yagyong evidently venerated Mencius, and he did not put much trust in the old commentaries.[81]

Tsai Chen-feng, too, points out that in early modern East Asia there was a trend in the study of the Four Books that was critical of Zhu Xi, but that, within this context, Chŏng Yagyong's scholarship was different from that of Itō Jinsai or of Ogyū Sorai. Where Jinsai was convinced that only the Three Books (*Lunyu, Mengzi, Zhongyong*) mattered, and Sorai, that the Six Classics and *Lunyu* were authoritative, Chŏng may have criticized Zhu Xi's study of the Four Books, but he still remained a kind of Four Books scholar.[82] Tsai also states that, in his study of the Four Books, Chŏng Yagyong has dissociated himself from the worldview of "principle and material force" of the orthodox School of Principle, and that he interprets the Four Books through the relationship he posits between the discourse on Human Nature and the rites, music, penal laws and administrative institutions of the kingly one. For this reason, Tsai argues, Chŏng gave a different interpretation of "the investigation of things and the extension of knowledge" of *Daxue*, which was the theoretical foundation of the study of the Four Books.[83]

A contrario, Yi Kiwŏn emphasizes the continuity between Chŏng Yagyong's interpretation of *Lunyu* and the interpretations of Sorai and Shundai. According to Yi, Chŏng Yagyong, getting a hint from Shundai's interpretation of *itan* 異端 ("heterodox") as *tatan* 多端 ("many-sidedness"), came up with the idea that "'Heterodoxy' means that one does not continue the 'clues' [left by] the Former Kings," and criticized Korean Zhu Xi Learning as heterodox.[84] Yi also discusses the influence Chŏng

---

[79] This theory, called 性三品説, holds that there are three types of human nature: smart, ordinary, and dumb 上知, 中人, 下愚. Supposedly, it goes back all the way to Confucius; see Mor. IV: 10478-47-8 for a short discussion and references. (WJB)

[80] Ha Ubong, *Chōsen Jitsugakusha no mita Kinsei Nihon*, pp. 291–302. The reference is to *Lunyu* 17.2–3: "The Master said: '*By nature, men are nearly alike*; by practice, they get to be wide apart.'" And: "The Master said: 'There are only the *wise of the highest class*, and *the stupid of the lowest class*, who cannot be changed.'" (WJB)

[81] Chang Kun-Chiang 張崑將, "Ding Ruoyong yu Taizai Chuntai dui *Lunyu* de jieshi bijiao,' *Dongya shiyuzhong de Chashan-xue*, pp. 43–94.

[82] Tsai Chen-feng 蔡振豊, "Ding Ruoyong de Sishu xue," *Dongya shiyuzhong de Chashan-xue*, pp. 156–163.

[83] Tsai Chen-feng, "Ting Ruoyong de Sishu xue," *Dongya shiyuzhong de Chashan-xue*, pp. 163–176.

[84] Ri Kigen 李基原, *Sorai-gaku to Chōsen jugaku*, pp. 243–246. The quotation is from Chŏng's *Non'ŏ kogŭm chu*, the commentary to *Lunyu* 2.

Yagyong underwent from the Sorai School's method of interpreting the Classics through the use of "ancient words," and examines the differences between Chŏng on the one hand, and Sorai and Shundai on the other, in their theories of Human Nature and Heaven.[85]

Summarising these earlier studies, I conclude that, just like the members of Sorai's school, Chŏng Yagyong criticized the interpretation of the Classics as given by the School of Principle, i.e., by the orthodox Neo-Confucianism of the Song; that his interpretation of the theory of Human Nature is different from theirs; and that his Confucianism implied the veneration of Mencius and the study of the Four Books. In this article, I will not disagree with these conclusions, but I do believe that it is necessary to study these problems more deeply, keeping in mind the philosophical differences with Shundai and Sorai.

Above, I examined the differences between Sorai's method of classical studies and the method followed by the movement of evidential research of the Qing Dynasty, but Chŏng Yagyong, too, was quite aware of this movement. For instance, in his *Mae-ssi sŏp'yŏng* 梅氏書平 ("An evaluation of Mr Mei's *Book of Documents*"), Chŏng develops his own argument through quotations from the works of such great scholars of the evidential research movement as Mao Jiling 毛奇齡 (1623–1716), Yan Ruoju 閻若璩 (1636–1704), and Zhu Yizun 朱彝尊 (1629–1709). He also refers to Dazai Shundai's *Kobun Kōkyō Kō-shi den* 古文孝経孔氏伝, which is included in the aforementioned *Zhibuzuzhai congshu*, and criticizes it for being a forgery.[86]

Another scholar was Sŏng Haeŭng 成海応 (1760–1839), who claimed that *Kobun Kōkyō Kō-shi den* and *Rongo giso* were Japanese forgeries.[87] Another scholar, Kim Wandang 金阮堂 (1786–1856), who was very active in the import of Qing culture into Korea, had read *Shichi-Kei Mōshi kōbun* – through the writings of Ruan Yuan.[88] Kim Maesun 金邁淳 (1776–1840) pointed out that discussions in Dazai Shundai's *Rongo kokun gaiden* resembled the argument in Ruan Yuan's *Xingming guxun* 性命古訓 ("Ancient glosses on nature and fate"), and explored their different attitudes towards Mencius.[89] Even more important was that the Qing scholar Mei Zengliang 梅曾亮 (1786–1865) read Kim Maesun's treatise, agreed with his criticism, and censured Sorai and Shundai as "evident followers of heterodoxy" for their criticism of Mencius.[90]

Thus, it was not only the envoys to Japan who brought back materials of Sorai's School, the envoys to Beijing, too, brought with them books in which scholars of the evidential research movement of the Qing Dynasty had written down their views on

[85] Ri Kigen, *Sorai-gaku to Chōsen jugaku*, pp., 246–267.

[86] *Chŏng Yagyong, Mae-ssi sŏp'yŏng, Yŏyutang chŏnjip* vol. 13, p. 61.

[87] Sŏng Haeŭng, "Chae Ilbon-dok hu," *Yŏngyŏngjae chŏnjip* vol. 21, p. 2; *id.*, "Waebon Hwang Kan Non'ŏ ŭiso hu," *Yŏngyŏngjae chŏnjip*, p. 433.

[88] Fujitsuka Chikashi, *Shin-chō bunka tōden no kenkyū*, pp. 107–108.

[89] Kim Maesun, *T'aisan-jip* fasc. 3, Hanguk Yŏkdae Munjip Ch'onggan vol. 17, p. 250, 251.

[90] Mei Zengliang, "T'aisan-shi lun Riben xunzhuanshu hou. Gengzi," *Baijianshanfang shiwenji* vol. 6, p. 128, 129.

Sorai's school. On the other hand, the discussions of Sorai's school by Korean *literati* were read in Qing China. In this sense, in the Chinese world of the nineteenth-century, the classical studies of Sorai's school may have been reviewed critically, but they were becoming common knowledge. Compared to other criticasters of orthodox Neo-Confucianism, however, its philosophical system, constructed as it was as a criticism even of Mencius, was quite unusual. For that reason, although some of the interpretations of the Classic by members of Sorai's school were known through quotations and became the object of discussions, its influence in intellectual circles outside of Japan may not have been so strong, after all.

Bibliography

Aihara Kōsaku 相原耕作. 2004. "Joji to kobunjigaku: Ogyū Sorai seiji-ron josetsu" 助字と古文辞学—荻生徂徠政治論序説. *Tōkyō Toritsu Daigaku Hōgakkai zasshi* 44: 2.

Boot, W.J. 2000. "The death of a shogun: deification in early modern Japan." In John Breen and Mark Teeuwen, eds. *Shinto in History, Ways of the Kami*. 144–166. Richmond: Curzon Press.

Chang Kun-Chiang 張崑將. 2006. "Ding Ruoyong yu Taizai Chuntai dui *Lunyu* de jieshi bijiao" 丁若鏞与太宰春台対『論語』的解釈比較. *Dongya shiyuzhong de Chashan-xue yu Chaoxian ruxue* 東亜視域中的茶山学与朝鮮儒学. Huang Junjie 黄俊傑, ed. Taiwan Daxue Chuban Zhongxin.43–94.

CHANG Su-ching 張素卿. 2005. "'Piaodian' de jieshi leixing: cong duzhe biaomo dujing dao jingshu piaodian de zemian kaocha" 「評点」的解釈類型:従読者標抹読経到経書評点的側面考察. *Dongya chuanshi Han-ji wenxian yijie fangfa chutan* 東亜伝世漢籍文献訳解方法初探. Taiwan Daxue Chuban Zhongxin.

Chiang Hsun-yi 蔣薫誼. "*Lunyu-zheng* yu *Jingjushuo* de sixiang bijiao: jian lun Qing ru dui Ogyū Sorai de bipan" 『論語徵』與『経句説』的思想比較—兼論清儒對荻生徂徠的批判. Outline of MA thesis.

Chŏng Yagyong 丁若鏞. 2012. *Ilbonnon* 日本論. In *Munjip* 文集, *Kyokam, p'yochŏm chŏngbon Yŏyutang chŏnjip* 校勘.標点定本与猶堂全書 vol. 2. Tasan Haksul Munhwa Chaetan.

Chŏng Yagyong. 2012. *Mae-ssi sŏp'yŏng* 梅氏書平. *Kyokam, p'yochŏm chŏngbon Yŏyutang chŏnjip* vol. 13. Tasan Haksul Munhwa Chaetan.

Dai Zhen 戴震. 1994–1997. *Dai Zhen quanshu* 戴震全書. Zhang Dainian 張岱年, ed. 6 vols. Huangshan Shushe.

Daibō Masanobu 大坊真伸. 2006. "Nemoto Bui no *Rongo giso* honkoku ni mirareru kaihen ni tsuite" 根本武夷の『論語義疏』翻刻に見られる改編について. *Daitō Bunka Daigaku Kangakkaishi* 45.

Daibō Masanobu. 2008. *Rongo giso* to Shinchō kōshōgaku: Shisho kōi o chūshin ni" 『論語義疏』と清朝考証学—『四書考異』を中心に. *Jinbun kagaku* 13.

Dazai Shundai太宰春台. 1732. *Kōkyō* 孝経 (printed Kyōhō 17; copy in the possession of Naikaku Bunko).

Dazai Shundai. 1972. *Seigaku mondō* 聖学問答. In Yoshikawa Kōjirō et al., eds. *Sorai gakuha*, NST 37. Tokyo: Iwanami Shoten.

Dazai Shundai. 1986. *Shundai-sensei Shishien kō* 春台先生紫芝園稿. Kojima Yasunori, ed. & Intr. Kinsei Juka Bunshū Shūsei vol. 6. Tokyo: Perikansha.

Ding Yan 丁宴. 2011. "Riben *Guwen Xiaojing Kong-shi zhuan* bian wei" 日本『古文孝経孔伝』弁偽. *Xiaojing zhengwen* 孝経徵文. In Wu Ping 呉平 et al., eds. *Xiaojing wenxian jicheng* 孝経文献集成 vol. 12. Guangling Shushe.

Fujitsuka Chikashi 藤塚鄰. 1949. *Rongo sōsetsu* 論語総説. Tokyo: Kōbundō.

Fujitsuka Chikashi. 1975. Shin-chō bunka tōden no kenkyū: Kakei, Dōkō gakudan to Ri-chō no Kim Wandang 清朝文化東伝の研究:嘉慶・道光学壇と李朝の金阮堂. Tokyo: Kokusho Kankōkai.

Gu Yongxin 顧永新. 2002. "*Qijing Mengzi kaowen buyi* kaoshu" 『七経孟子考文補遺』考述. *Beijing Daxue xuebao: Zhexue Shehui Kexue ban* 39.1: 84–91.

Ha Ubong 河宇鳳. 2001. *Chōsen Jitsugakusha no mita Kinsei Nihon* 朝鮮実学者の見た近世日本. Inoue Atsushi 井上厚史, trans. Tokyo: Perikansha.

Ha Ubong. 2008. *Chōsen Ōchō jidai no sekaikan to Nihon ninshiki* 朝鮮王朝時代の世界観と日本認識. Kim Yanggi 金両基 and Obata Michihiro 小幡倫裕, trans. Tokyo: Akashi Shoten.

Hiraishi Naoaki 平石直昭. 1987. "Senchū, sengo Sorai-ron hihan: shoki Maruyama, Yoshikawa ryō-gakusetsu no kentō o chūshin ni" 戦中・戦後徂徠論批判—初期丸山・吉川両学説の検討を中心に. *Shakaikagaku kenkyū* 39: 1.

Ho Mei-chen 侯美珍. 2004. "Ming-Qing shiren dui 'pingdian' de pipiao" 明清士人対「評点」的批評. *Zongguo wenzhe yanjiu tongxun* 中国文哲研究通訊 14: 3.

Ho Mei-chen. 2009. "Ming-Qing bagu qushi yu jingshu piaodian de xingqi" 明清八股取士与経書評点的興起. *Jingxue yanjiu qikan* 経学研究期刊 7: 9.

Huang Zunxian 黄遵憲. 2005. "Xueshuzhi" 学術志1. *Riben guozhi* 日本国志 32. *Huang Zunxian quanshu* vol. 2. Zhonghua Shuju.

Ji Yun 紀昀 et al. 1983. "*Guwen Xiaojing Kong-shi zhuan* tiyao" 『古文孝経孔氏伝』提要. *Yingyin Wenyuange Siku Quanshu 5: Jing zongyi lei* 景印文淵閣四庫全書5: 経総義類 vol. 182. Taiwan Shangwu Yinshuguan.

Kano Naoki 狩野直喜.1926. "Yamanoi Tei to *Shichi-Kei Mōshi kōbun hoi*" 山井鼎と『七経孟子考文補遺』. *Shina-gaku bunsō* 支那学文叢. Kōbundō.

Kawahara Hideki 川原秀城. 2015. "Tai Shin to seiyō sangaku" 戴震と西洋暦算学. In Kawahara Hideki, ed. *Seigaku tōzen to Higashi Ajia* 西学東漸と東アジア. Tokyo: Iwanami Shoten.

Kawahara Hideki. 2015. "Seiō gakujutsu no tōzen to Chūgoku, Chōsen, Nihon" 西欧学術の東漸と中国・朝鮮・日本. In Kawahara, ed. *Seigaku tōzen to Higashi Ajia*. 83–101.

Kim Maesun 金邁淳. 1999. *T'aisan-jip*台山集3. Hanguk Yŏkdae Munjip Ch'onggan 韓国歴代文集叢刊vol. 17. Kyŏngmun Ch'ulbansa.

Kinoshita Tetsuya 木下鉄矢. 2016. *Shin-dai gakujutsu to gengogaku: Ko'ongaku no shisō to keifu* 清代学術と言語学—古音学の思想と系譜. Tokyo: Bensei Shuppansha.

Kondō Mitsuo 近藤光男. 1987. *Shin-chō kōshōgaku no kenkyū* 清朝考証学の研究. Kenbun Shuppansha.

Lan Hung Yueh 藍弘岳. 2014. "Sorai-gakuha bunshi to Chōsen Tsūshinshi: 'Kobunjigaku' no tenkai o megutte" 徂徠学派文士と朝鮮通信使—「古文辞学」の展開をめぐって. *Nihon Kanbungaku kenkyū* 9.

Lan Hung Yueh. 2016. "Dazai Shundai to Sorai-gaku no sai-kōsei: 'Seijin no michi' to Nihon hihan o megutte" 太宰春台と徂徠学の再構成—「聖人の道」と日本批判をめぐって. *Shisō* 1112.

Lin Ching-chang 林慶彰. 1994. *Ming-dai jingxue yanjiu lunji* 明代経学研究論集. Wen Shi Zhe Chubanshe.

Lu Wenchao 盧文弨. 1937. "Zhou Yi zhushu jizheng tici" 周易注疏輯正題辞. *Baojingdang wenji* 抱経堂文集 1. Guoxue Jiben Congshu 国学基本叢書 vol. 7. Shangwu Yinshuguan.

Lu Wenchao. 1937. "Xinke *Guwen Xiaojing Kong-shi zhuan* xu" 新刻『古文孝経孔氏伝』序. *Baojingdang wenji* 1. Guoxue Jiben Congshu 国学基本叢書 vol. 2. Shangwu Yinshuguan.

Matsura Akira 松浦章. 2007. *Edo-jidai Tōsen ni yoru Nit-Chū bunka kōryū* 江戸時代唐船による日中文化交流. Kyoto: Shibunkaku.

Mei Zengliang 梅曽亮. 2012. "T'aisan-shi lun Riben xunzhuanshu hou. Gengzi" 台山氏論日本訓伝書後 庚子. *Baijianshanfang shiwenji* 柏梘山房詩文集 vol. 6. Shanghai Guji Chubanshe.

Ogyū Sorai 荻生徂徠. 1974. *Ingai* 韻糜. *Ogyū Sorai zenshū* vol. 2. Tokyo: Misuzu Shobō.

Ogyū Sorai. 1976. *Ken'en zuihitsu* 藘園随筆. *Ogyū Sorai zenshū* vol. 17. Tokyo: Misuzu Shobō.

Ogyū Sorai. 1985. *Sorai-shū* 徂徠集. Hiraishi Naoaki 平石直昭, ed. & intr. Kinsei Juka Bunshū Shūsei vol. 3. Tokyo: Perikansha.

Qian Yong 銭泳, comp. 1836. *Haiwai xinshu* 海外新書. Zheng Zhao 鄭照, ed.

Ri Kigen (Yi Kiwŏn) 李基原. 2011. *Sorai-gaku to Chōsen jugaku: Shundai kara Tei Jakuyō made* 徂徠学と朝鮮儒学—春台から丁若鏞まで. Tokyo: Perikansha.

Ruan Yuan 阮元. "Ke Qijing Mengzi kaowen bing buyi xu" 刻七経孟子考文竝補遺序. *Yanjingshi ji* 擘経室集. Guoxue Jiben Congshu 国学基本叢書 vol. 7.

Satō Shōsuke 佐藤昌介. 1964. *Yōgakushi kenkyū josetsu: Yōgaku to hōken kenryoku* 洋学史研究序説—洋学と封建権力. Tokyo: Iwanami Shoten.

Sawai Keiichi 澤井啓一. 1988. "'Hōhō' to shite no kobunjigaku" <方法>としての古文辞学. *Shisō* 766.

Smith, Jr., Kidder. 1990. "Sung Literati Thought and the *I Ching*." In Smith, Jr., Kidder et al., eds. *Sung Dynastic Uses of the* I Ching. Princeton: Princeton University Press.

Sonehara Satoshi 曽根原理. 2008. *Shinkun Ieyasu no tanjō: Tōshōgū to gongen-sama* 神君家康の誕生—東照宮と権現様. Tokyo: Yoshikawa Kōbunkan.

Sŏng Haeŭng 成海応. 1982. "Chae Ilbon-dok hu" 題日本牘後. *Yŏngyŏngjae chŏnjip* 研経斎全集, Appendix 2, vol 21. Omunsa.

Sŏng Haeŭng. "Waebon Hwang Kan *Non'ŏ ŭiso* hu" 倭本皇侃論語義疏後. *Yŏngyŏngjae chŏnjip* Appendix 1.

Sueki Yasuhiko 末木恭彦. 2016. *Sorai to Konron* 徂徠と崑崙. Yokohama: Shunpūsha.

Sugimoto Tsutomu 杉本つとむ. 1975. "Sorai to sono gengo kenkyū: Rangogaku to no kanren o shu to shite" 徂徠とその言語研究—蘭語学との関連を主として. *Kokubungaku kenkyū* 56.

Sun Zhizu 孫志祖. 2005. "*Xiaojing Kong-shi zhuan*" 孝経孔氏伝. *Dushu cuolu xubian* 読書脞録続編. Qing-dai Xueshu Biji Congkan 清代学術筆記叢刊 vol. 27. Xueyuan Chubanshe.

Takahashi Satoshi 高橋智. 1996. "Keichō-kan *Rongo Shūkai* no kenkyū" 慶長刊論語集解の研究. *Shidō Bunko ronshū* 30.

Tang Caichang 唐才常. 2011. "Geguo zhengjiao gongli zonglun" 各国政教公理総論. *Tang Caichang ji* 1. Yuelu Shushe.

Tang Caichang. 2011. "Riben Kuanyong yilai dashishu" 日本寛永以來大事述. *Tang Caichang ji*.

Tei Kankō 釘貫亨. 1997. "Nihongo gakushi ni okeru 'on'in' no mondai" 日本語学史における「音韻」の問題. *Nagoya Daigaku Bungakubu kenkyū ronshū: Bungaku* 43.

Tsai Chen-feng 蔡振豊. 2006. "Ding Ruoyong de Sishu xue" 丁若鏞的四書学. *Dongya shiyu-zhong de Chashan-xue yu Chaoxian ruxue* 東亜視域中的茶山学与朝鮮儒学, Huang Junjie 黄俊傑, ed. Taiwan Daxue Chuban Zhongxin. 156–163.

Tucker, John A., trans. & introd. 2006. *Ogyū Sorai's Philosophical Masterworks. The Bendō and Benmei.* Honolulu: Association for Asian Studies/University of Hawai'i Press.

Wang Shizhen 王世貞. 1983. *Yiyuan zhiyan* 芸苑卮言 In Xu Lidai Shihua 続歴代詩話 vol. 2. Yiwen Yinshuguan.

Wŏn Chunggŏ 元重挙. 1990. *Hwagukchi* 和国志. In *Sŏbyŏk haewe suwi ilbon* 栖碧海外蒐位佚本 30. Yi Usŏng 李佑成, ed. Seoul: Asea Munhwasa.

Wyatt, Don J. 1996. *The Recluse of Loyang. Shao Yung and the Moral Evolution of Early Sung Thought.* Honolulu: University of Hawai'i Press.

Yi Tŏngmu 李德懋. 2000. *Ch'ŏngnyŏng kukchi* 蜻蛉国志. In *Ch'ŏngjanggwan chŏnsŏ* 青荘館全書 64. P'yochŏm Yŏng'in Hanguk Munjip Ch'onggan 標点影印韓国文集叢刊 vol. 259. Seoul: Kyŏng'in Munhwasa.

Yoshida Jun 吉田純. 2006. *Shin-chō kōshōgaku no gunzō* 清朝考証学の群像. Tokyo: Sōbunsha.

Yoshikawa Kōjirō 吉川幸次郎 et al. eds. 1972. *Sorai gakuha*. NST 37. Tokyo: Iwanami Shoten.

Yoshikawa Kōjirō et al. eds. 1973. *Ogyū Sorai*. NST vol. 36. Tokyo: Iwanami Shoten.

Yu Yue 俞樾. 1995. "Ji Ribenguo renyu" 記日本国人語. *Chaxiangshi congchao* 茶香室叢鈔. In Xueshu Biji Congkan 学術筆記叢刊 vol. 9. Zhonghua Shuju.

Yuzawa Tadayuki 湯沢質幸. 1996. *Edo-ki Kanji-on kenkyū ni okeru Tō-on juyō* 江戸期漢字音研究における唐音受容. Tokyo: Benseisha.

Yuzawa Tadayuki. 2000. "Kinsei jugaku ni okeru Tō-on: Ogyū Sorai o chūshin ni" 近世儒学における唐音—荻生徂徠を中心として. In Satō Kiyoji 佐藤喜代治, ed. *Kokugo ronkyū* 国語論究 vol. 8: *Kokugoshi no shinshiten* 国語史の新視点. Tokyo: Meiji Shoin.

Yuzawa Tadayuki. 2006. "Kinsei ingaku ni okeru Go'on Kan'on no bunrui to inkyō: Sorai to Bun'yū" 近世韻学における呉音漢音の分類と韻鏡—徂徠と文雄. *Tsukuba Daigaku chiiki kenkyū* 27.

Yuzawa Tadayuki. 2010. "Bun'yū ni okeru *Inkyō* to Tō-on" 文雄における韻鏡と唐音. *Tsukuba Gakuin Daigaku kiyō* 5.

Zhang Taiyan 章太炎. 1985. *Taiyan wenlu chupian* 太炎文録初編. *Zhang Taiyan quanji* vol. 4, App., fasc. 2. Shanghai Renmin Chubanshe.

Zhao Shaozu 趙紹祖. 1997. "*Guwen Xiaojing Kong-shi zhuan*" 古文孝経孔氏伝. *Dushu ouji* 読書偶記. Xueshu Biji Congkan 学術筆記叢刊 vol. 7. Zhonghua Shuju.

Chapter 16
The Study of Sorai's Thought in Modern Japan

TAKAYAMA Daiki

1 Introduction

Ogyū Sorai is one of the scholars of early modern Japan who had the greatest impact on later generations. His scholarship brought changes not only to Confucianism, but also to many other fields such as literature, medicine, and the arts, e.g. painting. Not only the men who belonged to his school, but also many who belonged to schools that were antagonistic to his, tell that the advent of Sorai's teachings was an important turning point in the history of scholarship. When one studies the history of thought of early modern Japan, it is, therefore, impossible to evade the problem how to position Ogyū Sorai. This situation turns tracing the history of the study of Sorai's thought into the near equivalent of tracing the history of the study of Japan's early modern thought as a whole. In this article, therefore, I will give a bird's-eye view of the currents in the study of the history of Japan's early modern thought since the war; within that context I will then comment on the trends in the study of Sorai.

The scholars who studied Sorai's thought have published their results in a variety of regions and in a variety of languages. Because it will be difficult to treat them all within the few pages at my disposal, in this article I will treat only those studies that were written in Japanese. At first sight, this may not appear to be a logical selection criterion, but on the other hand, for readers who are not specialists in Japanese studies it might be useful to know the context in which the history of thought of early modern Japan has been researched within Japan itself.

TAKAYAMA Daiki (✉)
Graduate School of Arts and Sciences, The University of Tokyo,
Meguro-ku, Tokyo, Japan

© Springer Nature Switzerland AG 2019
W. J. BOOT, TAKAYAMA Daiki (eds.), *Tetsugaku Companion to Ogyū Sorai*,
Tetsugaku Companions to Japanese Philosophy 2,
https://doi.org/10.1007/978-3-030-15475-2_16

2   The Theories of "Modernization" and of "Japanization"

When we systematise the history of research on early modern Japanese thought, we often distinguish between the theories of "modernization" and of "Japanization."[1] The first theory locates the thought of the Edo Period (1600–1868) on the ladder leading to modern thought, while the second understands early modern Japanese thought as the process of the Japanese modification of Neo-Confucianism, i.e., in the first place, of the teachings of Zhu Xi (1130–1200).

Representative of the modernization approach is Maruyama Masao's *Nihon seiji shisōshi kenkyū*.[2] The scheme outlined in this book is that "the way of thinking of the school of Zhu Xi" began to disintegrate in the second half of the seventeenth century, and that in its stead Ogyū Sorai appeared, whose thought contained the sprouts of "modern consciousness." In Sorai's thought Maruyama discovered such "modern" elements as the separation of *public*, i.e., "things political," from *private*, i.e., "the internal life," and the "autonomous subject" who "consciously creates" order; these he highly valued.

As Maruyama himself confessed in later years (notably in the author's preface to the English translation of his book), the assumption of *Nihon seiji shisōshi kenkyū*, that Zhu Xi's teachings were the ideology that was the foundation of the social order of the Edo Period was problematic. As Bitō Masahide made clear in his *Nihon hōken shisōshi kenkyū* ("Study of the intellectual history of Japan's feudal thought"; 1961) and Watanabe Hiroshi in his *Kinsei Nihon shakai to Sō-gaku* ("The society of Early Modern Japan and orthodox Neo-Confucianism"; 1985), Zhu Xi's teachings (orthodox Neo-Confucianism) had not penetrated deeply into the society of the early Edo Period.

In response to this criticism of Maruyama's earlier argument, a search was undertaken for other ideologies that might have supported the social and political order and that thus could take the place of Zhu Xi's teachings. Candidates that suggested themselves were the early modern ideology of Japan as a "Divine Country," which hinges on Ieyasu's deification (Sonehara Satoshi),[3] military studies (Maeda Tsutomu),[4] or the thought of the "*Taiheiki yomi*" (Wakao Masaki).[5] Sorai's thought

---

[1] The representative example is Hiraishi Naoki, "Senchū, sengo Sorai-ron hihan," 1987.

[2] The original Japanese title is *Nihon seiji shisōshi kenkyū* (1952). The book was translated into English by Hane Mikiso and published under the title *Studies in the Intellectual History of Tokugawa Japan* (1974).

[3] After his death, the first shogun of the Tokugawa dynasty, Tokugawa Ieyasu (1542–1616), was enshrined in Nikkō and deified as Tōshōgū-daigongen 東照宮大権現, according to a mixed Buddhist and Shinto ritus. The reference is to Sonehara Satoshi, *Shinkun Ieyasu no tanjō: Tōshōgū to gongen-sama*, 2008. In English, see Boot, W.J., "The death of a shogun: deification in early modern Japan," 2000. (WJB)

[4] Reference to Maeda Tsutomu, *Kinsei Nihon jugaku to heigaku*, 1996.

[5] Reference to Wakao Masaki, "*Taiheiki-yomi*" no jidai: Kinsei seiji shisōshi no kōsō, 1999. N.B. *Taiheiki-yomi* are persons who spoke to an audience consisting mostly of samurai about episodes of the *Taihei-ki* 太平記 ("Record of Great Peace"), which treats the fighting in Japan from ca 1330 till ca 1390, i.e. the time of Emperor Go-Daigo (1288–1318–1339–1339) and of the Southern and

was interpreted anew in connection with these ideologies, which were considered as supportive of the social and political order; Maeda discerned influence of "military studies" in Sorai's teachings, and Wakao, of the *Taiheiki-yomi*.

There are, however, some doubts about all arguments that go into this direction. The point is that studies that look for ideologies that are supportive of the social and political order are based on the premise that in any political system there necessarily exists a moral teaching that systematically explains the "legitimacy" of the regime. One reason, however, why in the present case the discussion about a state ideology has not yet reached a conclusion, may very well be that within the political system of the Edo Period such a moral teaching did not exist.[6] There is not a trace of evidence that the Tokugawa government or the houses of the feudal lords (*daimyō*) ever attempted to establish any of the candidates for such an ideology as an orthodox teaching, or tried to promulgate its teachings among the people. This means that we will have to reconsider the notion as such, that a political system necessarily secures the submissiveness of the people through one or other systematic theory.

Some scholars are of the opinion that Maruyama's *Nihon seiji shisōshi kenkyū* contains some points that should be taken into account when interpreting Sorai's thought, even though there are problems with his understanding of history or, more specifically, of the position Zhu Xi's teachings occupied during the Edo Period. Hiraishi Naoaki is one of those who take this standpoint; he clearly states that his aim is to develop further the arguments made by Maruyama.[7] Thus, Hiraishi continues *Maruyama's theory* of the "autonomous subject," who creates order, and pays attention to the nature of the "cognitive subject" in Sorai's teachings. In Sorai's thought, he has discovered the image of a "subject" who objectifies the "framework of language and institutions" that determines his own, individual cognition, and who artificially constructs a "framework" for perceiving the world. For many readers, terms like "the liberation from the magical consciousness" or "the founding of modernity" in Hiraishi's articles will have an old-fashioned feel about them. The sharp observations, however, of the way in which language and institutions determine man's consciousness are an important characteristic of Sorai's teachings, and the elucidation of their philosophical background is a major research theme.

The opposite of the "modernization" theory is the "Japanization" theory. As representative of this latter theory I will cite research by Bitō Masahide.[8] Bitō is of the opinion that, rather than the moral improvement of each individual, Sorai regarded as important the peace and quiet of society as a whole - the concept of "bringing peace to the realm." Thus, in Sorai's thought "is reflected the way of thinking of the

---

Northern Court. These talks were not just explications of the text, but typically also treated its implications and the lessons to be drawn, especially in the military field. (WJB)

[6] This important problem was raised by Watanabe Hiroshi in his "'Go-ikō' to shōchō: Tokugawa seiji taisei no issokumen," *Higashi-Ajia no ōken to shisō*, 1997. Together with the ambiguity of "system-supporting moral teaching" or "ideology" as an analytical concept, this is a problem that needs to be considered anew.

[7] See Hiraishi Naoaki, "Sorai-gaku no sai-kōsei," *Shisō* 766 (1998).

[8] Bitō Masahide, "Kokkashugi to shite no sokei to shite no Sorai," 1974.

Japanese, that gives precedence to the organization over the individual, and that tries to conceptualize the correct way of living of the individual exclusively according to his role within the organization."[9]

The most interesting aspect of Bitō's approach is that he interpreted the scholarship of the Edo Period within the context of his own, original understanding of the social stratification of the Edo Period as being based on a division of labour - in his words, the "system of tasks" 役の体系 (yaku no taikei). Although among present-day Japanese historians Bitō's "system of tasks" is regarded as of secondary importance, his insight the people of the Edo Period lived within such status groups and that this conditioned their way of thinking, is richly suggestive. In order to understand the ideas that we encounter in Sorai's discussions of human talent and of the governmental system, which all assume some sort of a division of labour, we really must have another look at Bitō's theories and integrate them with insights gained by modern Japanese historical research on status groups.

3   The History of Thought of East-Asia and Postmodernism

Since the end of the eighties, there have been numerous attempts to broaden our horizon to "East-Asia" and to try to understand the thought of early modern Japan within that context. The concept of a history of thought that is based, not on single countries, but on "East-Asia" as a single unit is already discernible in arguments Shimada Kenji made in the nineteen-sixties, so the idea is not really new.[10]

Shimada proposed to organise the history of thought of all the regions of East-Asia within one scheme of "turning outward" versus "turning inward." Since the eighties, however, "East-Asian" history of thought has focussed on the fact that Japanese society and the societies of all other areas of "East-Asia" differed from each other in many respects, and that thought developed within separate frameworks. Scholars stopped combining the Confucianism of the various regions into one scheme or one single narrative, and began to split up and compare the different kinds of Confucianism of the various regions of "East-Asia." The special issue of Shisō,[11] entitled "Confucianism and Asian Society," is a memorial to this current of research.

Up till the present, there have been numerous studies from the standpoint of "East-Asian history of thought." Important contributions are the studies by Kataoka Ryū and Lan Hung Yueh. Kataoka posits that in the seventeenth century relativistic ideas were spreading within the East-Asian scholarly world, and that Sorai's teachings were an attempt to "sublate" such trends of thought - to rephrase them on a higher plane.[12] Lan has carefully researched the influence that the Ming literary

---

[9] Bitō, op. cit., p. 56.

[10] Shimada Kenji, Shushi-gaku to Yōmei-gaku, 1967.

[11] Shisō 792 (1990).

[12] Kataoka Ryū, "Jūnana-seiki no gakujutsu shichō to Ogyū Sorai," Chūgoku 16 (2001).

movement of Li Panlong and Wang Shizhen exerted on Sorai, and he has analysed the position that Sorai's teachings occupy within the literary history and the history of Confucianism in East-Asia.[13]

Although studies of the type "History of East-Asian thought" have brought forth outstanding results, one gets the impression that the last several years the studies that follow this approach have come up against a wall. When they explain, area by area, the varieties of thought, most studies seek the cause of these variations in differences in social structure that have already become generally accepted (e.g. that differently from China and Korea, Japan did not have an examination system). They have not succeeded in opening up new prospects. We have to reconsider the present climate in which something is treated as innovative research when it calls itself "East-Asian ...," and we have to think carefully how we can break out of the present impasse.

When we enter the nineteen-nineties, we see that, on the one hand, attempts are made to establish a viewpoint from which "modernization" and "Japanization" will fuse into one, while on the other hand critics like Koyasu Nobukuni and others, who are influenced by postmodern thought, condemn all studies that regard as self-evident the values of "modernity" and the framework of "Japan."

Studies of the postmodern type were of great importance in that they stirred interest in the methodology of the study of the history of thought. Koyasu's research broke free from the narrative of "modernity" and "Japan"; his aim was to explain the "epoch-making character" that Sorai's teachings had had within the "intellectual space" of eighteenth-century Japan. As regards the reactions, however, of scholars of the period concerned to Sorai's teachings, Koyasu only treats a small number of examples.[14] Although he was good at pointing out the problematic points in the research on Sorai of the Meiji Period and later, he was unable to present a clear understanding of the "intellectual space" of the Edo Period. Kojima Yasunori and Takahashi Hiromi had already undertaken research, not only of Sorai, but also of the Confucians, literati, and Buddhist priests who clustered around Sorai's school.[15] Through their researches, nowadays even nameless scholars of the Edo Period have entered our field of vision, so the "epoch-making character" of Sorai's teachings should have become more than clear.

In the scholarly world of Japan, postmodern studies of the history of thought of early modern Japan are presently in decline. The reason is that these studies are at the mercy of all the concepts taken over from contemporary French thought; at first sight, they seem to be profoundly meaningful, but not infrequently their contents turn out to have little substance.

---

[13] Lan Hung Yueh, "Tokugawa zenki ni okeru Min-dai kobunji-ha no juyō to Ogyū Sorai no 'kobun-jigaku'," *Nihon Kangaku kenkyū* 3 (2008); id., "Sorai-gakuha bunshi to Chōsen tsūshinshi," *Nihon Kangaku kenkyū* 9 (2014).

[14] Koyasu Nobukuni, *'Jiken' to shite no Sorai-gaku*, 1990.

[15] These studies are collected in Kojima Yasunori, *Sorai-gaku to han-Sorai*, 1987, 1994; Takahashi Hiromi, *Edo no baroque: Sorai-gaku shūhen*, 1991.

4 The Theories of "Mode of Thought" and "Concepts of Social Order"

The direction research has taken since the year 2000 often is summarized in the words "hyper-specialization." Even in the nineteen-nineties, when there was a strong interest in methodology, research based on a careful examination of the sources was making progress in the wake of Hiraishi Naoaki's magisterial *Ogyū Sorai nenpu kō* ("Study of Ogyū Sorai's chronological biography"). Moreover, because mutual contacts between researchers from different backgrounds intensified, knowledge of so-called "positivistic" studies of the history of thought came to be generally shared. In the two-thousands, scholars were looking for new sources concerning points of discussion that had come up in the methodological debate of the preceding period (media, the mind-body problem, language, the Other) and research developed in which these sources were carefully read and interpreted. As meticulous studies of different, individual themes have increased, I think we can correctly qualify the research of the last years as "hyper-specialisation."

When, however, one takes a bird's-eye view of the last ten to fifteen years, a trend appears that is different from what went on before. This is, that studies that approach thought from its relation with the actual governmental system and with specific literary techniques have increased.

I will take the studies of Sorai's theory of language as an example. Sorai developed an interesting argument about language, in the course of which he criticised the custom of reading Chinese as if it were Japanese, and advocated reading Chinese as Chinese. In the nineteen-nineties, Sorai's theory of language was frequently discussed in the context of the postmodern theory of "discourse," and of the problem of the formation of the nation state. In articles contributed to '*Kundoku' ron: Higashi-Ajia Kanbun sekai to Nihongo* ("On *kundoku*: The East-Asian world of Classical Chinese and the language of Japan")[16] the current of the nineteen-nineties still continued, but at the same time there also was a strong tendency to value Sorai's theories as assertions about the reading of sources and the techniques of study that even nowadays could be highly stimulating.

Apart from these, there is a study by Maeda Tsutomu that focusses on Sorai's argument that "lecturing" (*kōshaku* 講釈) should be abolished and "group reading" (*kaidoku* 会読, i.e., a way of teaching that resembles seminars) should be encouraged. This is, in other words, a study of the history of thought that hinges on problems of the educational system.[17]

Parallel to such developments, a consciousness spread that pre-modern East-Asian scholarship was not an approach of the various problems of human society that was just lagging behind modern Western thought, but that it was a *different* approach. For instance, '*Hōken*,' '*gunken*': *Higashi-Ajia shakai taiseiron no shinsō* ("A re-appreciation of 'feudal states' and 'administrative prefectures': the deep

---

[16] Edited by Nakamura Shunsaku et al., 2008.

[17] Maeda Tsutomu, *Edo no dokushokai*, 2012.

layer of East-Asian social system theory")[18] resulted from collaborative research, in which scholars tried to re-evaluate the concepts "feudal" and "prefectural," also used by Sorai, as concepts to analyse the political system. I will, therefore, use the approaches called "mode of thought" and "concepts of social order" in order to think through the research currents that have become noticeable since 2000.[19]

The "mode of thought" approach goes back to ideas of the young Maruyama. He argued that the thought of the Edo Period might not have shed its "feudal restrictions," but that "change had gone ahead, inconspicuously but steadily, deeply underneath the superficial discourse on politics, within the *mode of thought* as such."[20] He aimed to extract the *form* of a philosopher's thought and the *framework of his consciousness* from his concrete discourse on politics. (This he called "mode of thought.") This approach was taken over also by scholars who were negative towards his idea of "feudal restrictions."

Because the "mode of thought" approach reduces the thought it has as its object to a high dimension of abstraction, many trappings of the actual thought are removed. When, however, you are studying a thinker who was active in multiple fields, it is an effective method. For instance, Sorai initially studied the archaising literature of Li Panlong and Wang Shizhen of the Ming and propagated "the study of ancient words and phrases." Later on, he constructed his own, original system of learning. Confronted with such transitions, research of the "mode of thought" approach will interpret this as "Sorai applied the 'mode of thought' that he had obtained and developed in the field of literature to the interpretation of the Classics and the theory of government." In this way, it will clarify the "form" of thinking that was common to Sorai's endeavours in the fields of literature and thought, and to his "mode of being" as a "conscious subject." Sawai Keiichi and Aihara Kōsaku wrote excellent studies, that make full use of the advantages of this "mode of thought" approach in their research into the interrelations between Sorai's literary and linguistic theory, his interpretation of the Classics, and his theory of government.[21] More recent examples of research of this same "mode of thought" approach are two articles by Bandō Yōsuke, in which he focusses on the form of thinking that is common to *both* master artisans and artists *and* to Sorai's thought.[22]

On the other hand, the approach I call "concepts of social order" or "concepts of political systems" does not focus on the framework of consciousness of the thinker,

---

[18] Edited by Zhang Xiang and Sonoda Hidehiro, 2006.

[19] The opposition between the theories of "mode of thought" and "conceptualisation of the social order," was explained to me by Kōno Yūri (Tokyo Metropolitan University). I am deeply grateful to him. The appellation "conceptualisation of the social order" is based on the following studies: Karube Tadashi, "Modanizumu to chitsujo kōsō" (1999); Nakada Yoshikazu, "Kinsei Nihon bushi to 'gakkō no sei' no chitsujo kōsō ni tsuite" (2006). See also Kōno Yūri, *Gi-shi no seijigaku* (2017), introductory chapter.

[20] Maruyama Masao, *Nihon seiji shisōshi kenkyū* (rpt, 1983), p. 14.

[21] See such articles as Sawai Keiichi, "18-seiki Nihon ni okeru 'ninshiki-ron' no tankyū" (1994); Aihara Kōsaku, "Kobunjigaku to Sorai-gaku no seiji shisō" (2006).

[22] Bandō Yōsuke, "Gijutsu no shisō to shite no Sorai-gaku" (2010); id., "Ogyū Sorai to geidō shisō," (2016).

but on the kind of social order he concretely attempts to create. This approach assumes that also in the discourse on policy and political systems, which the "mode of thought" approach treats as "superficial," there exist philosophical possibilities that are worth looking into. (It distinguishes itself from political or social history in that it also analyses "concepts" that were not realized.) Studies of this type search for problems with which people of former times were confronted, and they interpret their "thought" as attempts to solve those problems. Therefore, such researchers are interested not so much in tracing the development and changes of thought in one or other period, but in discovering multiple "concepts," in the sense of "convincing solutions." Watanabe Hiroshi's discourse on Sorai and the present author's research have such a point of departure.[23]

I will explain this point with help of the argument Sorai made about "being bound to the soil." In this argument, Sorai maintains that the mobility of the people should be restricted through a system of census registers and the issuance of travel documents. (This is a "concept" that was not adopted by the Tokugawa regime.) If one approaches this argument from the standpoint of "mode of thought," one will perceive a "subject" hiding behind the proposed policy of binding the people to the soil, and that this "subject" "artificially creates" an order that is opposed to a "natural" development called social mobility. Next, one will probably develop an argument to the effect that, "superficially," Sorai's proposal is reactionary, but that within the "subject's" nature there are points that should be positively evaluated.

The "concepts of social order" approach, on the other hand, will begin by listening to Sorai's claim that stabilizing human relations through binding people to the soil is necessary for the peace and quiet of the empire.[24] In the cities with their unstable human relationships, people no longer take in interest in each other. As a result, only a few still remember that they should support the weak and not abandon them. When we consider the instability caused by globalization and the resistance that it triggers, followers of the approach of "concepts of social order" could well interpret arguments such as this one by Sorai as illuminating.

There are very few examples of arguments made by thinkers of the Edo Period that could be applied nowadays just as they are. However, the problems with which they were wrestling and the problems with which modern man is confronted do at least show a partial overlap. The approach of "concepts of social order" allows us to regard those arguments as precious resources of thought, instead of turning them into abstract formula's in the dimension of "mode of thought."

My impression is that from the two-thousands onwards the balance in study of the history of early modern Japanese thought has shifted from ideas inspired by the

---

[23] See Watanabe Hiroshi, *Nihon seiji shisōshi: 17 - 19 seiki* (2010); Takayama Daiki, *Kinsei Nihon no "reigaku" to "shūji"* (2016).

[24] Watanabe interprets the argument that people should be attached to the soil as one instance of "conceptualisations of coexistence." Examples of studies that analyse the argument that people should be attached to the soil without reducing it to "mode of thought" are Watanabe Hiroshi, "Jugakushi no idō no ichi-kaishaku" (1997); id., *Nihon seiji shisōshi: 17 - 19 seiki* (2010); Tajiri Yūichirō, *Ogyū Sorai* (2008); Takayama Daiki, *Kinsei Nihon no "reigaku" to "shūji"* (2016).

"mode of thought" approach to ideas consonant with the approach of "concepts of social order." Interestingly, this shift reminds one of the way in which Sorai and his teachings appeared on the scene in the Edo Period. In his teachings, Sorai broke away from the problem area of the subject, with such concepts as "the heart" and "human nature," and turned the focus on the problems of the governmental system. Sorai did not try to find out what nature of "the heart" of the great men of antiquity (the "Sages") had been like, but he poured his energy into elucidating the intentions with which they designed the concrete details of their system.

Opinions will differ on the question, whether these variations of pseudo-Sorai's are useful, just like there have been both praise and blame for Sorai's own teachings. If one wants to avoid, however, that "the second time round it will be a farce," it is necessary at the very least that those who occupy themselves with the study of the history of early modern Japanese thought soberly position themselves *vis-à-vis* Sorai's teachings and their later developments, including the criticisms that have been directed at them.

N.B This article is a substantially enlarged and revised version of Takayama Daiki, "21-seiki no Sorai-gaku," *Shisō* 1112 (2016).

Bibliography

Aihara Kōsaku 相原耕作. 2006. "Kobunjigaku to Sorai-gaku no seiji shisō: Ogyū Sorai *Bendō*, *Benmei* ni soku-shite" 古文辞学と徂徠学の政治思想―荻生徂徠『弁道』『弁名』に即して. *Hōgakkai zasshi* 46: 2.

Bandō Yōsuke 板東洋介. 2010. "Gijutsu no shisō to shite no Sorai-gaku" 技術の思想としての徂徠学. *Rinrigakju kiyō* 18.

Bandō Yōsuke. 2016. "Ogyū Sorai to geidō shisō" 荻生徂徠と芸道思想. *Shisō* 1112.

Bitō Masahide 尾藤正英. 1961. *Nihon hōken shisōshi kenkyū* 日本封建思想史研究. Tokyo: Aoki Shoten.

Bitō Masahide. 1974. "Kokkashugi to shite no sokei to shite no Sorai" 国家主義としての祖型としての徂徠. In Bitō Masahide, ed. *Ogyū Sorai*. Nihon no Meicho 16. Tokyo: Chūō Kōronsha.

Hiraishi Naoki 平石直昭. 1987. "Senchū, sengo Sorai-ron hihan" 戦中・戦後徂徠論批判. *Shakaikagaku kenkyū* 社会科学研究 39: 1.

Hiraishi Naoaki. 1998. "Sorai-gaku no sai-kōsei" 徂徠学の再構成. *Shisō* 766.

Karube Tadashi 苅部直. 1999. "Modanizumu to chitsujo kōsō: Nakai Masakazu (1900–1952) o meguru shō-kō" モダニズムと秩序構想―中井正一をめぐる小考. In Inoue Tatsuo 井上達夫 *et al.*, eds. *Hō no rinkai II: Chitsujo-zō no tenkan* 法の臨界II 秩序像の転換. Tokyo: Tōkyō Daigaku Shuppankai.

*Re-published under a different title in Karube Tadashi. 2013. *Chitsujo no yume: seiji shisō ronshū* 秩序の夢―政治思想論集. Tokyo: Chikuma Shobō.

Kataoka Ryū 片岡龍. 2001. "Jūnana-seiki no gakujutsu shichō to Ogyū Sorai" 十七世紀の学術思潮と荻生徂徠. *Chūgoku: Shakai to Bunka* 16: 143–178.

Kojima Yasunori 小島康敬. 1987. *Sorai-gaku to han-Sorai* 徂徠学と反徂徠.Tokyo: Perikansha. 1st edn. 1994. Rev. & enl. edn.

Kōno Yūri 河野有理. 2017. *Gi-shi no seijigaku: shin Nihon seiji shisōshi kenkyū* 偽史の政治学―新日本政治思想史. Tokyo: Hakusuisha.

Koyasu Nobukuni 子安宣邦. 1990. *'Jiken' to shite no Sorai-gaku* 「事件」としての徂徠学. Tokyo: Seidosha.

Lan Hung Yueh 藍弘岳. 2008. "Tokugawa-zenki ni okeru Min-dai kobunjiha no juyō to Ogyū Sorai no 'Kobunjigaku': Ri, Ō kankei chosaku no shōrai to Ogyū Sorai no shubunron no tenkai" 徳川前期における明代古文辞派の受容と荻生徂徠の「古文辞学」―李・王関係著作の将来と荻生徂徠の詩文論の展開. *Nihon Kangaku kenkyū* 3.

Lan Hung Yueh. 2014. "Sorai-gakuha bunshi to Chōsen tsūshinsi: 'Kobunjigaku' no tenka o megutte" 徂徠学派文士と朝鮮通信使: 「古文辞学」の展開をめぐって. *Nihon Kangaku kenkyū* 9.

Maeda Tsutomu 前田勉. 1996. *Kinsei Nihon jugaku to heigaku* 近世日本儒学と兵学. Tokyo: Perikansha.

Maeda Tsutomu. 2012. *Edo no dokushokai* 江戸の読書会. Tokyo: Heibonsha.

Maruyama Masao 丸山眞男. 1952. *Nihon seiji shisōshi kenkyū* 日本政治思想史研究, Tokyo: Tōkyō Daigaku Shuppankai.

*Translation: Hane Mikiso. 1974. *Studies in the Intellectual History of Tokugawa Japan*, Tokyo: Tokyo University Press.

Nakamura Shunsaku 中村春作 et al., eds. 2008. *"Kundoku" ron: Higashi-Ajia Kanbun sekai to Nihongo* 「訓読」論―東アジア漢文世界と日本語, Tokyo: Bensei Shuppan.

Nakada Yoshikazu 中田喜万. 2006. "Kinsei Nihon bushi to 'gakkō no sei' no chitsujo kōsō ni tsuite" 近世日本武士と「学校の政」の秩序構想について. *Chūgoku: Shakai to bunka* 21.

Sawai Keiichi 澤井啓一. 1994. "18-seiki Nihon ni okeru 'ninshiki-ron' no tankyū: Sorai, Norinaga no gengo chitsujo-kan" 十八世紀日本における〈認識論〉の探求―徂徠・宣長の言語秩序観. In Momokawa Takahito 百川敬仁 et al., eds. 1994. *Edo bunka no hen'yō: 18-seiki Nihon no keiken* 江戸文化の変容―十八世紀日本の経験. Tokyo: Heibonsha.

Shimada Kenji 島田虔次. 1967. *Shushi-gaku to Yōmei-gaku* 朱子学と陽明学. Tokyo: Iwanami Shoten.

Tajiri Yūichirō 田尻祐一郎. 2008. *Ogyū Sorai* 荻生徂徠. Sōsho Nihon no Shisō vol. 15. Tokyo: Meitoku Shuppansha.

Takahashi Hiromi 高橋博巳. 1991. *Edo no baroque: Sorai-gaku shūhen* 江戸のバロック―徂徠学周辺. Tokyo: Perikansha.

Takayama Daiki 高山大毅. 2016. *Kinsei Nihon no "reigaku" to "shūji": Ogyū Sorai igo no "setsujin" no seido kōsō* 近世日本の「礼楽」と「修辞」―荻生徂徠以後の「接人」の制度構想. Tokyo: Tōkyō Daigaku Shuppankai.

Takayama Daiki. 2016. *"21-seiki no Sorai-gaku"* 二一世紀の徂徠学. *Shisō* 1112: 8–14.

Wakao Masaki 若尾政希. 1999. *"Taiheiki-yomi" no jidai: Kinsei seiji shisōshi no kōsō* 「太平記読み」の時代―近世政治思想史の構想. Heibonsha Sensho 192. Tokyo: Heibonsha.

Watanabe Hiroshi 渡辺浩. 1985. *Kinsei Nihon shakai to Sō-gaku* 近世日本社会と宋学. Tokyo: Tōkyō Daigaku Shuppankai.

Watanabe Hiroshi. 1997a. *Higashi-Ajia no ōken to shisō* 東アジアの王権と思想. Tokyo: Tōkyō Daigaku Shuppankai.

Watanabe Hiroshi. 1997b. "Jugakushi no idō no ichi-kaishaku: 'Shushi-gaku' ikō no Chūgoku to Nihon" 儒学史の異同の一解釈―「朱子学」以降の中国と日本. In *Higashi-Ajia no ōken to shiso*, 70–114.

Watanabe Hiroshi. 2010. *Nihon seiji shisōshi: 17 - 19 seiki* 日本政治思想史―十七~十九世紀. Tokyo: Tōkyō Daigaku Shuppankai.

Zhang Xiang 張翔, Sonoda Hidehiro 園田英弘, eds. 2006. *"Hōken", "Gunken" saikō: Higashi-Ajia shakai taiseiron no shinsō* 「封建」・「郡県」再考―東アジア社会体制論の深層. Kyoto: Shibunkaku.

Index

© Springer Nature Switzerland AG 2019
W. J. Boot, Takayama Daiki (eds.), *Tetsugaku Companion to Ogyū Sorai*,
Tetsugaku Companions to Japanese Philosophy 2,
https://doi.org/10.1007/978-3-030-15475-2

Printed by Printforce, the Netherlands